The AGI Generation

Preparing Today's Students to Build Tomorrow's Intelligent World

BY

SUSIE HALA

INTELLIGLOSS PRESS

AF714714

Legal Disclaimer

Educational Purpose Disclaimer

"This publication is part of the IntelliGloss AI Education Series, a structured curriculum support system for AI literacy in grades 6–12."

The information presented in this publication is provided for educational and informational purposes only. This book is intended to support educators, administrators, parents, and learners in understanding the concepts, opportunities, and challenges associated with artificial intelligence in education. It is not intended to serve as legal, technical, policy, cybersecurity, or professional advice.

Readers should consult qualified professionals, institutional guidelines, and local regulations before implementing any educational programs, technologies, or policies described in this book.

Technology and Accuracy Disclaimer
Artificial intelligence is a rapidly evolving field. While every effort has been made to ensure the accuracy and reliability of the information presented at the time of publication, technologies, policies, research findings, and best practices may change over time. The author and publisher make no guarantees that all information will remain current or applicable in future technological environments.

Readers are encouraged to verify tools, platforms, and recommendations independently before using them in educational settings.

Implementation Responsibility
Schools, educators, and institutions are solely responsible for determining how and whether to implement artificial intelligence tools, strategies, or classroom activities discussed in this book. Educational environments vary widely, and policies regarding technology use, student privacy, and curriculum development differ by district, state, and country.

The author and publisher assume no responsibility for outcomes resulting from the implementation of ideas, examples, or frameworks described in this book.

Student Safety and Data Privacy
Artificial intelligence tools may involve the collection or processing of data. Educators and institutions are responsible for ensuring that any technology used complies with applicable student privacy laws, data protection regulations, and school policies, including but not limited to FERPA, COPPA, GDPR, or other relevant regulations depending on jurisdiction.

The author and publisher are not responsible for the privacy practices, security policies, or data handling procedures of third-party platforms or software mentioned in this book.

Third-Party Tools and References
This book may reference third-party technologies, organizations, research studies, or platforms for illustrative and educational purposes. Such references do not constitute endorsements or guarantees regarding the performance, reliability, safety, or suitability of those tools for educational use.

Educators and institutions should conduct their own evaluations and risk assessments before adopting any technology.

No Professional Liability
The author and publisher shall not be held liable for any direct, indirect, incidental, or consequential damages resulting from the use or misuse of the information contained in this book. This includes but is not limited to decisions related to curriculum design, technology adoption, classroom instruction, institutional policies, or educational outcomes.

Educational Interpretation
The concepts and examples provided in this book are intended to support discussion and learning. They should not be interpreted as official standards, mandatory guidelines, or universally applicable policies for artificial intelligence education.

Schools and educators are encouraged to adapt the ideas presented here according to their local policies, cultural context, educational standards, and student needs.

Author's Intent
The goal of this book is to promote responsible AI literacy, thoughtful discussion, and ethical awareness as schools prepare students for a world increasingly shaped by intelligent technologies.

The author encourages readers to approach artificial intelligence education with curiosity, caution, and a commitment to responsible learning.

Title: The AGI Generation Preparing Today's Students to Build Tomorrow's Intelligent World

ISBN : 978-1-972925-28-7

Copyright © 2026 by Susie Hala
All rights reserved.

No part of this publication may be reproduced, stored in a retrieval system, transmitted, or distributed in any form or by any means—electronic, mechanical, photocopying, recording, or otherwise—without the prior written permission of the author, except in the case of brief quotations used in reviews, educational discussions, or scholarly references.

Published by
IntelliGloss Press
United States of America

This book is intended for educational and informational purposes. Artificial intelligence technologies and policies evolve rapidly, and the author makes no guarantee regarding the completeness, accuracy, or continued applicability of the information presented. Educators, schools, and institutions are responsible for evaluating and implementing technologies in accordance with their own policies, legal requirements, and educational standards.

Unauthorized reproduction of this work may result in legal action.

Dedication This book is dedicated to the next generation of learners— the students who will grow up in a world shaped by intelligent technology, and who deserve to understand it with clarity, confidence, and purpose.

To the educators who show up every day with dedication and heart, guiding students through a rapidly changing world— your role has never been more important.

To the parents and families who support learning at home, encouraging curiosity, responsibility, and growth— you are the foundation of every child's success.

And to my granddaughters, whose curiosity, imagination, and future inspire me to do this work— this book is for you. May you not only learn how to use technology, but understand it, question it, and shape it for the good of all.

About the Author

Susie Hala Founder of the IntelliGloss AI Education Series

Susie Hala is an author, educator, and curriculum developer dedicated to advancing responsible AI literacy in schools. She is the creator of the IntelliGloss AI Education Series — a comprehensive 60-book curriculum that progresses from Artificial Narrow Intelligence (ANI) through Artificial General Intelligence (AGI) to Artificial Superintelligence (ASI).

Drawing from her experience with early rule-based systems at AT&T and the development of modern AI-integrated platforms, Susie translates complex concepts into clear, classroom-ready materials. Her work emphasizes not just how AI works, but how it will reshape human potential, relationships, and society.

Her mission is to help students and educators approach the age of AGI with understanding, critical thinking, and deep human values.

Preface

Two Students. Two Paths. One Future.

Imagine two students graduating in the coming years. Both know how to use powerful AI tools. One uses them to complete tasks quickly. The other understands how these systems work, their capabilities, their limitations, and what it means when AI moves from narrow tools to general intelligence.

The second student is better prepared to thrive, lead, and make wise decisions as AGI becomes part of everyday life.

This book is written for that second student.

As we enter the age of Artificial General Intelligence, understanding not just *how* to use AI, but *what it means for humanity*, becomes essential. This is the journey we begin in Module 2.

A Note from the Author

AI Is a Tool — AGI Will Challenge What It Means to Be Human

Artificial Intelligence is a powerful assistant, but it does not make decisions — people do.

As we move from narrow AI to general intelligence, this truth becomes even more important. AGI systems may one day match or exceed human ability across many tasks, yet they will still lack human judgment, empathy, values, and moral responsibility.

This book explores both the exciting possibilities and the serious responsibilities that come with AGI. Students will learn to approach these powerful technologies with curiosity, caution, and a strong commitment to human-centered values.

Bringing Clarity to Artificial Intelligence

One of the greatest challenges in learning about AGI is the confusion around key terms. This book provides clear definitions to build a strong foundation.

Key Concepts

- **Chatbot**: A conversational interface that responds to user prompts.
- **Generative AI**: Systems that create new content based on patterns learned from data.

- **Agentic AI**: Systems that can plan, make decisions, and carry out multi-step tasks toward goals.
- **Autonomy**: The degree to which an AI system can operate independently.
- **Hallucination**: When an AI produces plausible but incorrect or fabricated information.

The AI Use Continuum Assistive Use → Augmented Use → Agentic Use

Understanding these distinctions becomes especially important as we explore the transition from narrow AI to AGI.

The IntelliGloss Instructional Approach

This book continues the IntelliGloss AI Education Series with the same classroom-ready structure you know from Module 1:

- AI Family section
- 31 chapters with clear learning objectives
- Summary, Reflection, Worksheet, Quiz, and Answer Key for each chapter
- Glossary and teacher support materials

Module 2 raises the level of discussion to prepare students for the profound changes AGI will bring.

Why AGI Education Matters Now

We are no longer just preparing students for a world with smarter tools. We are preparing them for a world where artificial general intelligence may reshape education, work, creativity, relationships, and what it means to be human.

This book helps students understand these changes with clarity, think critically about them, and uphold human values as technology advances.

Human Values Family

The Human Values Family represents the guiding principles — ethics, responsibility, trust, and human well-being — that must remain at the center of AGI development and use.

Even as AI becomes more capable, humans must remain the decision makers. These values ensure that AGI serves humanity rather than diminishes it. Students will explore how to apply these principles as we move into a new era of intelligence.

This version is **clean, professional, slightly more advanced** than Module 1, and ready to use. It maintains consistency with your series while feeling distinct for the AGI level.

Executive Summary

IntelliGloss AI Education Series

Teaching How Artificial Intelligence Actually Works

Artificial intelligence is already shaping how students learn, write, research, and make decisions. Yet in many classrooms, students are being introduced to AI tools without understanding how these systems actually function.

This creates a critical gap.

Students may become efficient users of technology, but without foundational knowledge, they are not equipped to think critically, evaluate outputs, or use AI responsibly. As AI continues to expand across every industry, this gap will only grow more significant.

The **IntelliGloss AI Education Series** was created to address this challenge.

The Problem

Most current approaches to AI in education focus on tool usage rather than system understanding. As a result:

- Students rely on AI without understanding its limitations
- Educators lack structured frameworks for teaching AI concepts
- Key terms such as generative AI, agentic AI, and autonomy are often introduced without clear definitions
- Responsibility and ethical use are not consistently emphasized

Without clarity, artificial intelligence becomes difficult to teach, difficult to learn, and difficult to manage in a school environment.

The Solution

The IntelliGloss AI Education Series provides a structured, classroom-ready approach to artificial intelligence literacy for grades 6–12.

Rather than focusing on individual tools, this series teaches students how AI works as a complete system—from foundational components to real-world applications.

Students learn to move beyond surface-level interaction and develop true understanding.

The IntelliGloss Framework

The series introduces AI through a clear and connected structure, including:

- Foundational building blocks such as data, algorithms, tokens, and models
- System-level understanding through categories such as intelligence level, behavior, and control
- Real-world context through applications, limitations, and responsible use
- Human-centered learning through ethics, responsibility, trust, and student safety

This structured approach transforms artificial intelligence from a confusing concept into an understandable system.

Instructional Design

Each book in the series is designed for practical classroom use and includes:

- Structured chapters aligned with instructional pacing
- Clear, student-friendly explanations
- Reflection sections to reinforce understanding
- Worksheets, quizzes, and answer keys
- Teacher implementation support

No prior technical background is required for educators or students.

Guiding Principle

A central message of the IntelliGloss series is:

Artificial Intelligence is a tool—not a decision maker.

Students learn that while AI can support thinking and provide information, all decisions, actions, and responsibilities remain with humans. This principle reinforces critical thinking, accountability, and responsible technology use.

Why It Matters

AI literacy is no longer optional. It is a foundational skill.

Students who understand how AI works will be better prepared to:

- Think critically about information
- Adapt to emerging technologies
- Use AI responsibly and ethically
- Succeed in an increasingly AI-driven world

Our Goal

The IntelliGloss AI Education Series is designed to help schools move beyond simply using artificial intelligence tools and toward a deeper understanding of how these systems actually work.

By providing clear structure, defined concepts, and real-world context, this series equips students and educators with the knowledge needed to think critically, evaluate information, and use AI responsibly.

The goal is not just to introduce technology—but to build understanding, confidence, and accountability in an AI-driven world.

This is not just about learning to use AI—it is about preparing students to understand it, question it, and lead with it.

Clarity leads to confidence.
Understanding leads to responsible use.

Mission Statement

The mission of the IntelliGloss AI Education Series is to make artificial intelligence clear, structured, and accessible for every student and educator.

In a world where AI is rapidly transforming how information is created, used, and understood, this series is designed to move beyond surface-level interaction and provide a deeper understanding of how intelligent systems actually work.

Through clear explanations, organized frameworks, and real-world context, IntelliGloss equips learners with the ability to think critically, evaluate information, and engage with technology responsibly.

This mission is grounded in a simple belief:
students should not only learn how to use artificial intelligence—they should understand it.

By building both technical awareness and human-centered understanding, the IntelliGloss AI Education Series prepares students to navigate, question, and shape a future increasingly influenced by intelligent technologies.

The goal is not just to keep up with artificial intelligence—but to understand it, guide it, and use it responsibly.

Vision Statement

The vision of the IntelliGloss AI Education Series is to create a future where artificial intelligence is clearly understood, responsibly used, and thoughtfully integrated into education and everyday life.

In this future, students are not passive users of technology, but informed thinkers who understand how intelligent systems work, recognize their limitations, and apply them with purpose and responsibility.

Educators are equipped with clear frameworks and structured resources that make artificial intelligence accessible, teachable, and meaningful across all subjects—not just in technical fields.

Schools become environments where technology is not simply adopted, but understood—where students are encouraged to question, evaluate, and engage with AI in ways that support learning, creativity, and ethical awareness.

As artificial intelligence continues to evolve, this vision supports a generation that is prepared not only to adapt to change, but to lead it with knowledge, confidence, and integrity.

The future of artificial intelligence will not be defined by technology alone—but by the understanding and responsibility of those who use it.

AI Family Section Understanding the Building Blocks of Artificial General Intelligence

Welcome to the AI Family Section!

Just like every family has different members who work together, artificial intelligence is made up of many "families" of components that work as a team. In this section, we will meet the most important AI Families — from the smallest building blocks to the large systems that power intelligent machines.

Understanding these families will help you see AI not as magic, but as a structured system built by humans. This knowledge is essential as we explore Artificial General Intelligence (AGI) and how it may change our world.

Why This Matters When you understand how AI is built, you become a smarter user, a better thinker, and a more responsible citizen in the age of AGI. You will also start to see how cybersecurity, ethics, and human values connect to these technical foundations.

Connecting AI Understanding to Cybersecurity Awareness

Definition

Understanding artificial intelligence is the first step toward understanding cybersecurity. While cybersecurity focuses on protecting systems, data, and users, artificial intelligence explains how those systems are built, how they function, and where they may be vulnerable.

The Connection

Every AI system is made up of components such as data, algorithms, models, and infrastructure. These same components are also the targets of cybersecurity threats.

When students understand:

How data is collected and stored

How algorithms make decisions

How AI models process information

How systems operate across frontend and backend layers

They begin to recognize where risks can exist and how systems can be misused.

Why This Matters

In today's digital world, students are not just users of technology—they are participants in complex systems powered by artificial intelligence.

Without understanding how these systems work:

Technology becomes something they trust without question

Risks become harder to recognize

Decisions are made without awareness of consequences

With understanding:

Students become more aware of how their data is used

They recognize how systems can be manipulated

They make more informed and responsible choices

Building Digital Readiness

Digital readiness is not only about using tools. It is about understanding the systems behind those tools.

By learning how AI works, students develop:

- Awareness of digital environments
- Confidence in navigating technology
- A foundation for future learning, including cybersecurity

Conclusion

Cybersecurity begins with understanding.

Before students can protect systems, they must first understand how those systems are built and how they operate. This is why learning artificial intelligence is not only about innovation—it is also about responsibility.

The Foundation of Artificial Intelligence

Definition

The foundation of Artificial Intelligence (AI) refers to the core building blocks that allow AI systems to function. These building blocks work together to help machines learn from information, recognize patterns, and make decisions. AI is not magic—it is a system built on structured components that operate behind the scenes.

Understanding the Foundation in Simple Terms

Artificial Intelligence can be compared to a house. Before a house is complete, it must be built on a strong foundation. This foundation includes concrete, wiring, plumbing, and support structures that are not always visible but are essential for the house to function properly.

In the same way, AI systems rely on foundational components that are not visible to users but are necessary for AI tools to work. When people use AI applications such as chatbots or design tools, they are interacting with the surface. The true power of AI comes from what is underneath.

Key Components of the AI Foundation

1. Data (The Information)

Data is the starting point of all AI systems. It includes text, images, numbers, audio, and other forms of information. AI systems learn by analyzing patterns within this data.

2. Algorithms (The Instructions)

Algorithms are step-by-step instructions that tell the AI system how to process data. They guide how the system learns, identifies patterns, and produces results.

3. Models (The Trained System)

A model is created when data and algorithms are combined through a training process. The model acts as the "brain" of the AI system, allowing it to make predictions and generate responses.

4. Computing Power (The Engine)

AI systems require powerful computers to process large amounts of data. This includes specialized hardware such as processors and graphics processing units (GPUs) that allow AI to function efficiently.

5. Infrastructure (The Environment)

Infrastructure refers to the systems that support AI operations, including servers, storage, networks, and energy systems. Data centers are a key part of this infrastructure, providing the physical space where AI systems operate.

How These Components Work Together

AI systems function by combining all foundational components into a single process. Data is collected and analyzed using algorithms. This process creates a model that can recognize patterns and make decisions. The entire system is powered by computing machines and supported by infrastructure.

Why Understanding the Foundation Matters

Many people use AI tools without understanding how they work. This can lead to confusion, misuse, or over-reliance on technology. By understanding the foundation of AI, students and educators can:

Develop critical thinking skills

Use AI tools more responsibly

Recognize the limitations of AI systems

Build a deeper understanding of modern technology

Real-World Example

When a student asks a chatbot a question, the response does not come from "thinking" like a human. Instead, the AI system uses a trained model that has learned patterns from large amounts of data. It follows algorithms to predict the most appropriate answer, using powerful computers and infrastructure to deliver the response quickly.

This process is also influenced by how the question is asked. The words, structure, and clarity of a question—often referred to as a *prompt*—can affect the quality of the response. Learning how to communicate effectively with AI systems is an important skill known as prompt engineering. For further understanding, students and educators may explore *What to Say When You Talk to Yourself: A Guide to Prompt Engineering* by Susie Hala, which explains how carefully structured prompts can guide AI responses more effectively.

Conclusion

The foundation of Artificial Intelligence is built on data, algorithms, models, computing power, and infrastructure. These components work together to create systems that can learn, predict, and assist humans. Understanding this foundation helps students move beyond simply using AI tools and toward truly understanding how artificial intelligence works.

The Foundational Families of Artificial Intelligence

Introduction

Artificial intelligence is often described as a powerful technology, but in reality, it is not a single system. It is a combination of multiple components working together to create intelligent behavior.

To better understand how artificial intelligence works, it is helpful to break it down into organized groups. In the IntelliGloss framework, these groups are called **Foundational Families of Artificial Intelligence**.

Each family represents a key part of how AI systems are built and operate. Some families focus on how information is created and stored. Others focus on how machines learn, make decisions, process language, or perform tasks. Additional families represent the physical hardware, energy systems, and global infrastructure that make artificial intelligence possible.

When these families work together, they form a complete AI system.

This approach allows students and educators to move beyond simply using artificial intelligence tools and begin to understand what is happening behind the scenes. Instead of viewing AI as a mystery, learners can see it as a structured system made up of clearly defined components.

The diagram on the next page provides a visual overview of these families and how they connect to form the foundation of artificial intelligence.

By learning each family step by step, students develop a deeper understanding of how AI systems process information, learn from data, and interact with the world.

Understanding the Foundational Families of Artificial Intelligence is the first step toward true AI literacy.

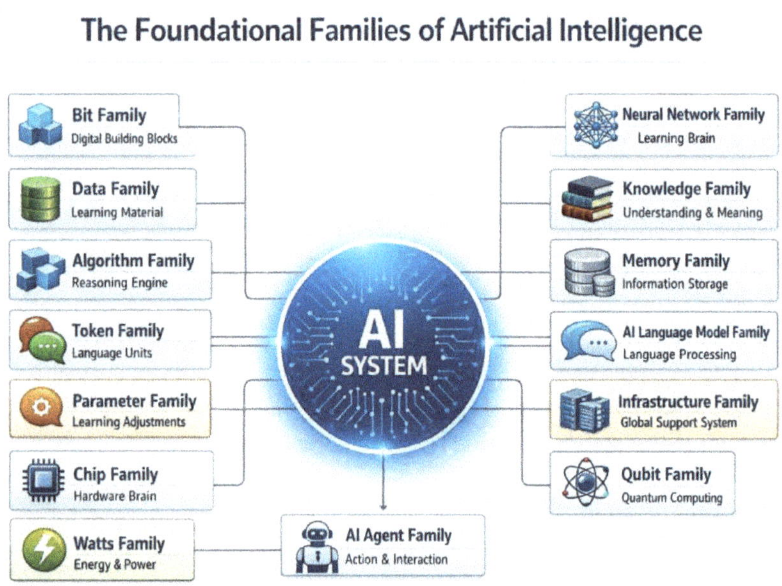

The Foundational Families of Artificial Intelligence

Family	Role	Description
Bit Family	Digital Building Blocks	The smallest unit of digital information (0 or 1). All computing systems begin with bits.
Algorithm Family	Reasoning Engine	Step-by-step instructions that tell computers how to solve problems and process information.
Token Family	Language Units	Pieces of text used by AI models to understand and generate human language.

Family	Role	Description
Parameter Family	Learning Adjustment System	Adjustable numerical values inside AI models that allow them to learn patterns from data.
Data Family	Learning Material	The information AI studies in order to learn patterns, relationships, and knowledge.
Logic Family	Decision Rules	The reasoning structures that allow AI systems to make decisions and evaluate conditions.
Memory Family	Information Storage	Systems that store and retrieve information so AI models can access past knowledge and context.
Knowledge Family	Understanding & Meaning	Structured information that allows AI to represent facts, relationships, and concepts.
Neural Network Family	Learning Brain	Interconnected layers of artificial neurons that enable AI systems to recognize patterns, learn from data, and make predictions.
AI Model Family	Intelligence Engine	The trained system that uses data, parameters, and neural networks to perform tasks such as prediction, classification, and generation.
AI Translator Architecture Family	Language Conversion System	Systems that transform input into output, enabling AI to convert text, speech, or images into meaningful responses.
AI Agent Family	Action and Task Execution System	AI systems designed to perceive information, make decisions, and carry out tasks autonomously or semi-autonomously.
Chip Family	Hardware Brain	Physical processors (GPUs, TPUs, CPUs, NPUs) that perform AI computations.
Watts Family	Energy Power	The electrical power required to run AI hardware and data centers.
AI Energy Family	Energy Source System	The total energy consumed over time to operate AI systems, including training and real-time usage.
Infrastructure Family	Global Support System	Data centers, internet networks, cloud systems, and global infrastructure that allow AI to operate and scale.
Ingredient Family	System Composition	The essential components that come together to create an AI system, including data, algorithms, models, hardware, and energy.
Qubit Family	Quantum Information Units	Quantum bits that can represent multiple states simultaneously, forming the foundation of quantum computing.

The Bit Family

Introduction

The Bit Family represents the starting point of all digital technology. Every computer system, application, and artificial intelligence model is built from bits—the smallest unit of information in computing.

A bit can hold one of two values: 0 or 1. While this may seem simple, these two values form the foundation of everything digital. When bits are combined and organized, they create larger units of data that allow computers to store text, display images, play videos, and run complex systems.

From a single bit to massive data systems, all digital information follows this same structure. This is how computers are able to represent and process the world in a form they can understand.

In artificial intelligence, bits are essential because they store the data that models learn from, process the calculations that drive decision-making, and support the systems that generate responses.

Understanding the Bit Family helps students see how simple binary signals grow into powerful technologies. It reveals that behind every advanced AI system is a foundation built from the most basic building blocks of information.

Bit Family — Visual Understanding of Data Size

How Much Data Can Each Unit Hold? (Simple Examples)

Unit	Size	Photos (Approx.)	Video (Approx. Hours)
Bit	1 bit	N/A	N/A
Byte	8 bits	1 character	N/A
Kilobyte (KB)	~1,000 bytes	Part of a paragraph	N/A
Megabyte (MB)	~1,000 KB	~1 photo	~1 minute of video
Gigabyte (GB)	~1,000 MB	~250 photos	~1–2 hours of video
Terabyte (TB)	~1,000 GB	~250,000 photos	~1,000–2,000 hours of video
Petabyte (PB)	~1,000 TB	~250 million photos	~1–2 million hours of video
Exabyte (EB)	~1,000 PB	~250 billion photos	~1–2 billion hours of video
Zettabyte (ZB)	~1,000 EB	~250 trillion photos	~1–2 trillion hours of video
Yottabyte (YB)	~1,000 ZB	~250 quadrillion photos	~1–2 quadrillion hours of video

---

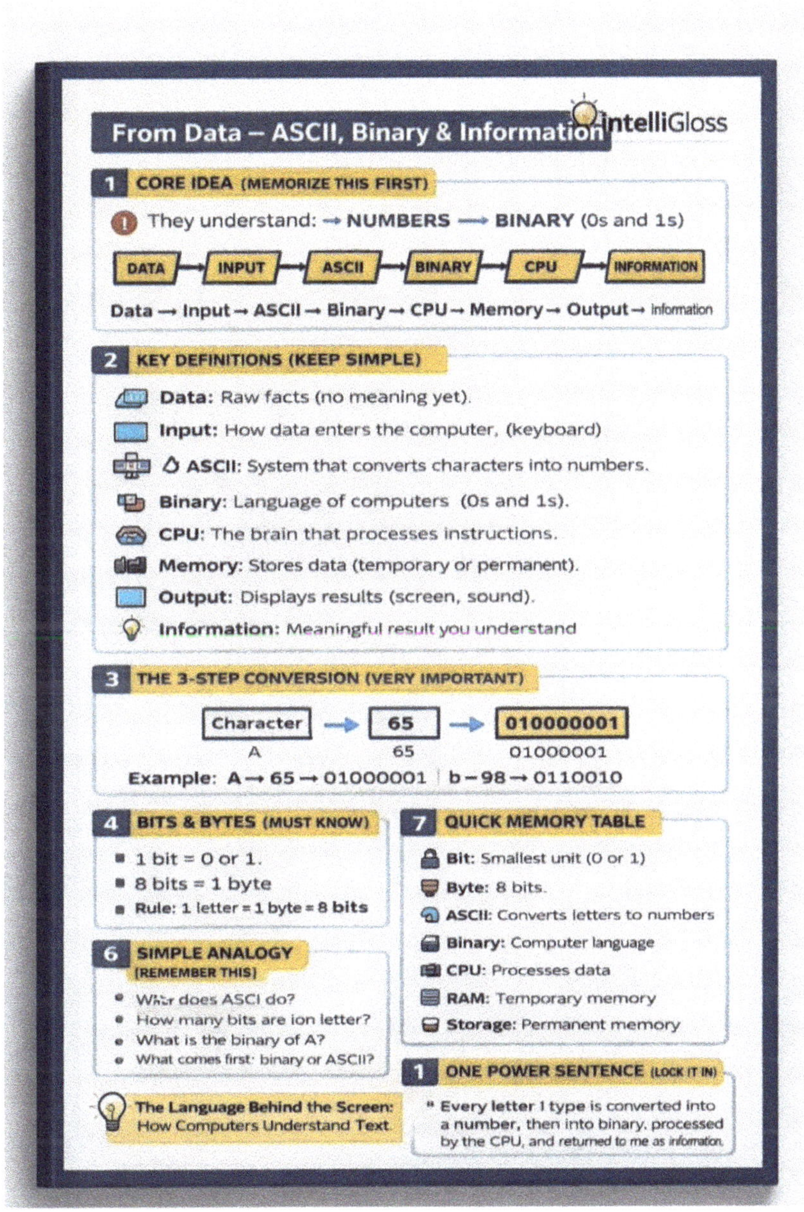

The Algorithm Family

Definition and Overview

The **Algorithm Family** represents the *thinking engine* of artificial intelligence — the set of mathematical instructions that guide how AI analyzes data, learns patterns, and makes decisions.

An **algorithm** is a sequence of steps designed to solve a problem or complete a task. In AI, algorithms tell the system *how to learn*, *how to predict*, and *how to improve* with every iteration.

In simple terms:

The Algorithm Family is the *logic of intelligence* — the invisible code that transforms data into decisions and predictions into progress.

How Algorithms Power AI

Every AI system — from simple chatbots to large-scale deep learning models — relies on algorithms as its foundation.
They determine how the model:

- Processes and cleans data,
- Identifies relationships between variables,
- Learns from feedback, and
- Improves over time.

Without algorithms, even the most powerful dataset or neural network would remain static and lifeless.

In essence, **algorithms are the teachers** that train AI how to think.

Why the Algorithm Family Matters

Algorithms are what separate automation from intelligence.
They allow machines to **reason**, **adapt**, and **learn** — not just follow commands.
For prompt engineers, understanding algorithmic behavior helps explain *why* AI sometimes misunderstands a question, repeats patterns, or changes tone after feedback.

Every AI response you receive follows an underlying process — a pattern recognition journey from input to output.

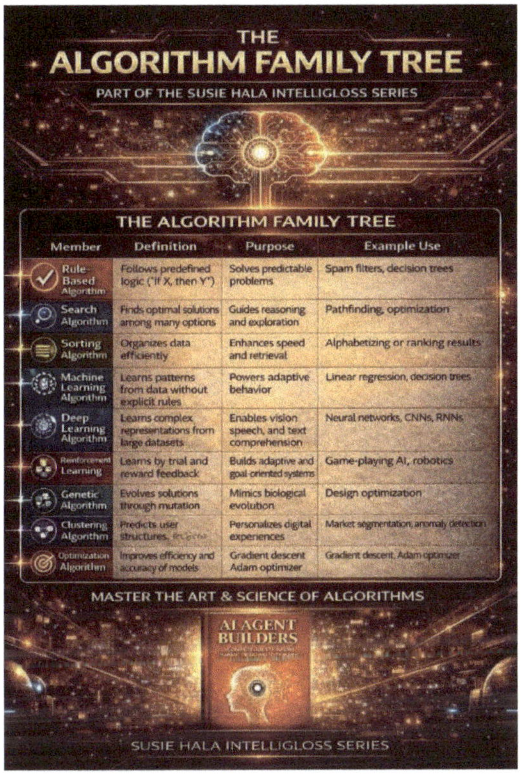

Analogy for Everyday Readers

Imagine AI as a chef in a kitchen:

- The **Data Family** provides the ingredients.
- The **Knowledge Family** gives the recipes.
- The **Algorithm Family** is the *cooking process* — mixing, heating, tasting, and adjusting until the dish is perfect.

Just as cooking methods determine the quality of food, algorithms determine the quality of intelligence.

Algorithm Efficiency and Energy Use

Not all algorithms are equal.
Some are **fast but shallow**, while others are **deep but energy-intensive**.
Training large AI models requires algorithms that can handle billions of calculations per second — powered by the **Watts Family** (energy) and executed through the **Chip Family** (hardware).

The design of efficient algorithms directly affects sustainability in AI — minimizing power consumption while maximizing accuracy and speed.

Algorithms and Prompt Engineering

For prompt engineers, algorithms explain *how* the AI arrives at its answers.
When a model gives inconsistent or off-topic results, it's often due to:

Misinterpretation of input signals (input encoding),

Bias in training algorithms, or

Overfitting to certain data patterns.

Knowing this helps you craft prompts that guide the AI's decision-making — not just its output.

Quick Takeaway: The Algorithm Family is the reasoning heart of AI.
It transforms information into understanding and enables machines to think, learn, and evolve like digital problem-solvers.

Token Family Introduction

The Token Family represents one of the most important bridges between human language and artificial intelligence. While humans communicate using words, sentences, and meaning, AI systems do not understand language in the same way. Instead, they rely on tokens—small units of text that allow machines to process, analyze, and generate language step by step.

A token can be a word, part of a word, a character, or even punctuation. When a student types a sentence into an AI system, that sentence is not read as a whole idea. It is first broken down into tokens. These tokens become the input that the AI model uses to recognize patterns, predict outcomes, and generate responses.

The Token Family works closely with several other foundational families in artificial intelligence. It connects directly with the Data Family, which provides the text used for training, and the Neural Network Family, which processes token patterns to produce intelligent outputs. It also plays a key role in the AI Translator Architecture Family, where tokens are transformed, analyzed, and reassembled into meaningful responses.

Understanding tokens helps students see what is happening behind the scenes when they interact with AI tools. Instead of viewing AI as a "magic system," they begin to understand that every response is built from sequences of tokens processed through mathematical models.

In simple terms, if language is what humans speak, tokens are what AI understands.

Token Family Breakdown Chart

Component	Role	Description	Example
Tokenization	Input Conversion	The process of breaking text into smaller units (tokens) that AI can process	"Artificial Intelligence" → "Artificial" + "Intelligence"
Tokens	Language Units	The individual pieces of text used by AI models for understanding and generation	"AI", "learn", "ing", "."
Subword Tokens	Efficiency Units	Words split into smaller parts to handle unknown or complex vocabulary	"unbelievable" → "un", "believ", "able"
Character Tokens	Fine-Grained Units	Text broken down into individual characters for detailed processing	"AI" → "A" + "I"
Vocabulary (Token Set)	Token Library	The complete set of tokens an AI model recognizes and uses	GPT models have thousands to millions of tokens
Encoding	Token Mapping	Converting tokens into numerical representations for computation	"AI" → [1234, 5678] (example IDs)
Decoding	Output Reconstruction	Converting numerical outputs back into readable text	[1234, 5678] → "AI system"
Context Window	Memory Limit	The number of tokens an AI can process at one time	Example: 8,000 tokens ≈ several pages of text
Token Embeddings	Meaning Representation	Mathematical vectors that capture relationships between tokens	"king" and "queen" have similar embeddings
Token Prediction	Language Generation	The process of predicting the next token in a sequence	"AI is" → predicts "powerful"

The Token Family reminds us that behind every intelligent response is a structured sequence of tokens working together. What feels like natural conversation to humans is, for AI, a carefully processed stream of language units transformed into meaning.

The AI Ecosystem Family

The AI Ecosystem Family is a connected group of artificial intelligence technologies, systems, behaviors, and applications that work together to help machines perform intelligent tasks. This ecosystem includes core AI systems, AI agents, agentic AI, AI autonomy, autonomous AI workers, and generative AI. Each part plays a different role in how modern AI systems think, learn, create, make decisions, solve problems, and interact with the world.

At the center of the ecosystem is artificial intelligence itself — the broad field focused on building machines and software that can perform tasks that normally require human intelligence. AI agents act as the systems that carry out goals and actions. Agentic AI describes the ability of

AI systems to plan, reason, adapt, and pursue objectives with limited human guidance. AI autonomy represents the level of independence an AI system has while making decisions and taking actions. AI autonomous workers apply these capabilities to perform real-world tasks like digital employees or assistants. Generative AI adds the ability to create new content such as text, images, music, video, code, and designs.

The AI Ecosystem Family demonstrates that modern artificial intelligence is no longer just one single technology. Instead, it is an interconnected environment of systems, tools, intelligence, automation, creativity, and human collaboration. As AI continues to evolve, these technologies are becoming increasingly integrated into education, business, healthcare, communication, cybersecurity, research, and everyday life.

Understanding the AI Ecosystem Family helps students, educators, and readers see how the different parts of AI connect together to shape the future of intelligent systems and the digital world.

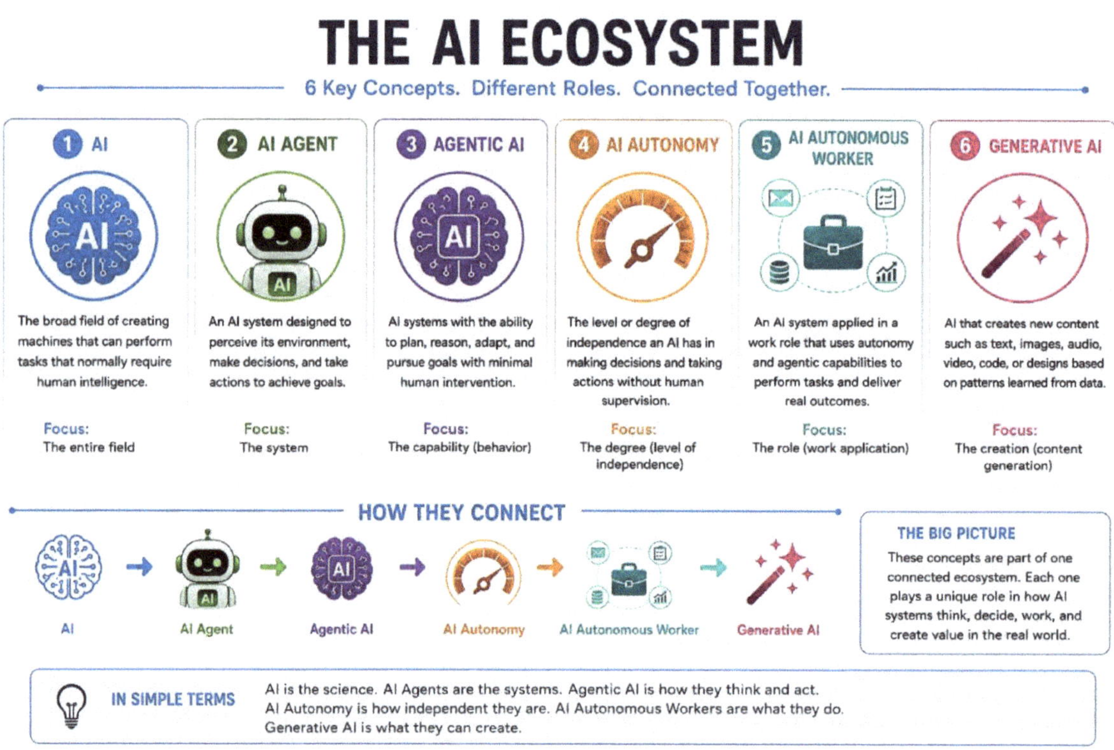

Parameter Family Introduction

The Parameter Family represents the internal learning system of artificial intelligence. While tokens provide the language and data provides the learning material, parameters are what allow AI systems to adjust, improve, and make intelligent decisions over time.

In simple terms, parameters are numerical values inside an AI model that change as the system learns. These values are not visible to users, but they play a critical role in how the model understands patterns, relationships, and meaning. Every time an AI system is trained, it adjusts its parameters to better predict outcomes and generate accurate responses.

Parameters exist throughout neural networks, where they act as the connections between artificial neurons. Each connection has a weight, which determines how important a particular piece of information is. During training, these weights are continuously adjusted based on data, allowing the system to improve its performance.

The Parameter Family works closely with the Data Family, which provides the information needed for learning, and the Neural Network Family, which organizes how parameters are structured and applied. It also supports the Token Family by helping the model interpret and predict sequences of language.

Understanding parameters helps students recognize that AI is not simply programmed with fixed rules. Instead, it learns by adjusting internal values that guide how it processes information. These adjustments are what allow AI systems to evolve from simple pattern recognition to complex reasoning and decision-making.

In essence, if data is what AI learns from, parameters are how AI learns.

Parameter Family Breakdown Chart

Component	Role	Description	Example
Parameters	Learning Values	Numerical values inside an AI model that are adjusted during training	Millions or billions of values inside a model
Weights	Connection Strength	Values that determine how strongly one neuron influences another	A higher weight = stronger influence
Bias	Adjustment Factor	A value added to help the model shift and fine-tune outputs	Helps improve accuracy in predictions
Training Process	Learning Mechanism	The process of adjusting parameters using data to improve performance	Model improves after analyzing many examples
Loss Function	Error Measurement	Measures how far the model's prediction is from the correct answer	Lower loss = better performance

Component	Role	Description	Example
Optimization Algorithm	Adjustment Strategy	Method used to update parameters efficiently	Gradient Descent adjusts weights step by step
Gradient	Direction of Change	Indicates how parameters should change to reduce error	Shows whether to increase or decrease a value
Backpropagation	Learning Process	System that sends error signals backward to update parameters	Adjusts earlier layers based on output error
Hyperparameters	Control Settings	External settings that guide how training happens (not learned)	Learning rate, batch size
Model Size	Capacity Indicator	The total number of parameters in a model	Larger models = more learning capacity

The Parameter Family is the hidden engine of learning in artificial intelligence. While users interact with outputs, it is the continuous adjustment of parameters behind the scenes that makes intelligent behavior possible.

Data Family Introduction

The Data Family represents the foundation of learning in artificial intelligence. Every AI system depends on data to develop knowledge, recognize patterns, and make decisions. Without data, artificial intelligence cannot learn, adapt, or function effectively.

Data can take many forms, including text, images, audio, video, and numerical information. These inputs provide the raw material that AI systems analyze during training. By studying large amounts of data, AI models begin to identify patterns, relationships, and structures that allow them to make predictions and generate responses.

The quality and diversity of data play a critical role in how well an AI system performs. Accurate, balanced, and relevant data helps models produce reliable results, while poor or biased data can lead to incorrect or unfair outcomes. This is why data collection, preparation, and evaluation are essential steps in the development of responsible AI systems.

The Data Family works closely with the Parameter Family, which adjusts internal values based on data, and the Neural Network Family, which processes and organizes data through layers of computation. It also supports the Token Family when dealing with language, as text data is converted into tokens for analysis.

Understanding the Data Family helps students recognize that AI does not "know" things on its own. Instead, it learns from the information it is given. The more meaningful and well-prepared the data, the more capable the AI system becomes.

In simple terms, data is the source of knowledge, and it is the starting point for all artificial intelligence.

Data Family Breakdown Chart

Component	Role	Description	Example
Data	Learning Material	Raw information used by AI systems to learn patterns and relationships	Text, images, audio, numbers
Dataset	Organized Collection	A structured group of data used for training and evaluation	A folder of labeled images
Training Data	Learning Input	Data used to teach the AI model during training	Thousands of sentences for a language model
Validation Data	Performance Check	Data used to tune the model during training without directly learning from it	Helps prevent overfitting
Test Data	Final Evaluation	Data used to measure how well the model performs after training	New unseen examples
Structured Data	Organized Format	Data arranged in tables with clear categories	Spreadsheets, databases
Unstructured Data	Flexible Format	Data without a predefined structure	Text documents, images, videos
Labeled Data	Guided Learning	Data tagged with correct answers to guide training	Image labeled "cat" or "dog"
Unlabeled Data	Self-Learning Input	Data without labels, used in unsupervised learning	Raw text without categories
Data Quality	Accuracy Measure	The reliability and correctness of data	Clean, complete, and consistent data
Data Bias	Imbalance Issue	When data does not represent all groups fairly	Skewed or incomplete datasets
Data Preprocessing	Preparation Step	Cleaning and organizing data before training	Removing errors, formatting text

The Data Family reminds us that artificial intelligence is only as strong as the information it learns from. High-quality data leads to meaningful insights, while poor data can limit or misguide intelligent systems.

Memory Family Introduction

The Memory Family represents how artificial intelligence systems store, retain, and retrieve information. Just as humans rely on memory to recall past experiences, learn new concepts, and make decisions, AI systems depend on memory to access previously processed information and maintain context.

In artificial intelligence, memory is not a single component but a collection of mechanisms that allow systems to handle information over time. Some forms of memory are short-term, holding information temporarily while a task is being completed. Other forms are long-term, storing learned knowledge that can be used across different tasks and interactions.

Memory plays a critical role in enabling AI systems to understand sequences, maintain context in conversations, and improve decision-making. For example, when a user interacts with a language model, the system uses memory to keep track of previous words, sentences, or prompts in order to generate coherent and relevant responses.

The Memory Family works closely with the Data Family, which provides the information to be stored, and the Parameter Family, which encodes learned knowledge within the model. It also supports the Neural Network Family by enabling systems to process sequences and retain important patterns over time.

Understanding the Memory Family helps students see that AI is not simply reacting to individual inputs in isolation. Instead, it relies on stored information and contextual awareness to produce meaningful and consistent outputs.

In simple terms, if data is what AI learns from, memory is how AI remembers and uses what it has learned.

Memory Family Breakdown Chart

Component	Role	Description	Example
Memory	Information Storage	The ability of an AI system to store and access information	Retaining previous inputs in a task
Short-Term Memory	Temporary Storage	Holds information for immediate processing	Keeping track of words in a sentence
Long-Term Memory	Persistent Storage	Stores learned knowledge for future use	Knowledge embedded in model parameters
Context Memory	Conversation Tracking	Maintains information within a specific interaction	Remembering earlier parts of a prompt
Working Memory	Active Processing	Handles information currently being used in computation	Processing a sequence step by step
External Memory	Extended Storage	Memory stored outside the model for retrieval	Databases, vector stores
Internal Memory	Embedded Knowledge	Information stored within the model itself	Learned patterns inside neural networks
Sequence Memory	Order Awareness	Tracks the order of inputs over time	Understanding sentence structure

Component	Role	Description	Example
Retrieval Mechanism	Access System	Retrieves stored information when needed	Searching relevant past data
Attention Mechanism	Focus System	Highlights important parts of memory for processing	Focusing on key words in a sentence
Memory Capacity	Storage Limit	The amount of information the system can handle at once	Context window size

The Memory Family shows that intelligence is not just about processing information in the moment, but about retaining, organizing, and using knowledge over time to create meaningful understanding.

Knowledge Family Introduction

The Knowledge Family represents how artificial intelligence organizes, connects, and uses information to create understanding. While data provides raw information and memory stores it, knowledge is what gives that information meaning and structure.

In artificial intelligence, knowledge is not simply a collection of facts. It is the result of identifying relationships, patterns, and connections within data. AI systems use knowledge to recognize concepts, make decisions, and generate meaningful responses. This allows machines to move beyond simple data processing and toward more intelligent behavior.

Knowledge can be represented in different ways within AI systems. Some forms are structured, such as databases and knowledge graphs, where relationships between concepts are clearly defined. Other forms are learned implicitly through neural networks, where patterns are encoded within parameters and used to guide predictions.

The Knowledge Family works closely with the Data Family, which provides the information needed to build knowledge, and the Memory Family, which stores and retrieves that information. It also connects with the Parameter Family, where learned knowledge is embedded within the model, and the Neural Network Family, which processes and organizes that knowledge.

Understanding the Knowledge Family helps students recognize that AI systems do not simply memorize information. Instead, they learn how pieces of information relate to one another, allowing them to interpret meaning, solve problems, and respond intelligently.

In simple terms, if data is information and memory stores it, knowledge is the understanding that makes it useful.

Knowledge Family Breakdown Chart

Component	Role	Description	Example
Knowledge	Understanding System	Organized information that allows AI to interpret meaning and make decisions	Recognizing relationships between concepts
Facts	Basic Information	Individual pieces of information stored within a system	"Water freezes at 0°C"
Relationships	Connection Mapping	Links between pieces of information that create meaning	"Teacher teaches student"
Knowledge Representation	Structure System	Methods used to organize and store knowledge in AI	Knowledge graphs, semantic networks
Knowledge Graph	Network Mapping	A structured representation of entities and their relationships	Google Knowledge Graph
Semantic Understanding	Meaning Interpretation	The ability to understand meaning behind words and data	Understanding synonyms and context
Inference	Reasoning Process	Drawing conclusions based on known information	If A = B and B = C, then A = C
Rules	Decision Framework	Logical guidelines used to make decisions	If temperature < 0°C → freeze
Ontology	Concept Framework	A structured system defining categories and relationships	Classification of animals
Explicit Knowledge	Direct Information	Clearly defined and stored knowledge	Rules, databases
Implicit Knowledge	Learned Patterns	Knowledge learned through experience and data	Patterns learned by neural networks
Knowledge Integration	System Coordination	Combining information from multiple sources	Merging text, images, and data

The Knowledge Family transforms information into understanding, allowing artificial intelligence to move beyond data and memory into meaningful reasoning and intelligent decision-making.

AI Model Family Introduction

The AI Model Family represents the core system within artificial intelligence that performs tasks such as prediction, classification, and content generation. It is the part of AI that users interact with, whether they are asking questions, generating images, or analyzing data.

An AI model is a trained system that has learned patterns from data. During training, the model processes large amounts of information and adjusts its internal parameters to improve accuracy.

Once trained, the model can take new input and produce meaningful output based on what it has learned.

AI models can take many forms depending on their purpose. Some models are designed to recognize images, others to understand language, and others to make decisions or predictions. Large Language Models (LLMs), for example, are designed to process and generate human language by predicting sequences of tokens.

The AI Model Family works closely with the Data Family, which provides the learning material, and the Parameter Family, which stores learned patterns. It also relies on the Neural Network Family for structure and the Chip and Infrastructure Families for execution and deployment.

Understanding the AI Model Family helps students see that AI is not just a concept, but a working system that has been trained to perform specific tasks. It is the engine that transforms input into output.

In simple terms, if AI is the system, the model is the part that actually does the thinking and producing.

AI Model Family Breakdown Chart

Component	Role	Description	Example
AI Model	Core System	The trained system that performs tasks	Chatbot, image generator
Training	Learning Process	Process of teaching the model using data	Learning from datasets
Inference	Output Generation	Using the trained model to produce results	Answering a question
Model Architecture	Structural Design	Defines how the model is built	Neural networks, transformers
Parameters	Learned Values	Internal values adjusted during training	Billions of weights
Input Data	Entry Information	Data provided to the model for processing	User prompt
Output Data	Result	The response or prediction generated	AI-generated text
Model Types	Functional Categories	Different kinds of models for different tasks	Classification, generation
Fine-Tuning	Model Adjustment	Improving a model for specific tasks	Custom-trained AI
Pretrained Model	Base System	A model trained on large datasets before use	General-purpose AI

Component	Role	Description	Example
Evaluation	Performance Check	Measuring how well the model performs	Accuracy, loss metrics

The AI Model Family represents the working core of artificial intelligence, where learned patterns are transformed into meaningful actions, predictions, and responses.

Neural Network Family Introduction

The Neural Network Family represents the structural foundation of how artificial intelligence learns and processes information. Inspired by the human brain, neural networks are systems of interconnected units, often called neurons, that work together to analyze data, recognize patterns, and make decisions.

In artificial intelligence, a neural network is made up of layers. The input layer receives data, the hidden layers process that data, and the output layer produces a result. As information flows through these layers, the network applies mathematical transformations that allow it to detect patterns and relationships within the data.

Neural networks rely heavily on the Parameter Family, where weights and biases determine how strongly information flows between neurons. During training, these parameters are adjusted to improve the network's performance. The more the network learns, the better it becomes at recognizing patterns and making accurate predictions.

The Neural Network Family works closely with the Data Family, which provides the information needed for learning, and the Memory and Knowledge Families, which help store and organize learned information. It also supports the Token Family when processing language, allowing AI systems to interpret sequences of tokens in meaningful ways.

Understanding neural networks helps students see that AI is not simply following instructions. Instead, it is learning from examples and improving over time through layered processing and pattern recognition.

In simple terms, neural networks are the systems that allow AI to think, learn, and make sense of information.

Neural Network Family Breakdown Chart

Component	Role	Description	Example
Neural Network	Learning Structure	A system of interconnected neurons that processes data and learns patterns	Image recognition system

Component	Role	Description	Example
Neuron (Node)	Processing Unit	A basic unit that receives input, processes it, and passes output forward	A single calculation point
Input Layer	Data Entry Point	The first layer that receives raw data	Pixels of an image
Hidden Layers	Processing Layers	Intermediate layers that transform data and detect patterns	Feature detection layers
Output Layer	Result Generator	The final layer that produces predictions or decisions	"Cat" vs "Dog" classification
Weights	Signal Strength	Values that determine how strongly inputs influence outputs	Higher weight = stronger impact
Bias	Adjustment Value	Helps shift outputs to improve learning accuracy	Fine-tuning predictions
Activation Function	Decision Function	Determines whether a neuron should activate based on input	ReLU, Sigmoid
Forward Propagation	Data Flow	The process of passing input data through the network to produce output	Input → Hidden → Output
Backpropagation	Learning Process	Adjusts weights and biases based on error to improve performance	Correcting mistakes
Loss Function	Error Measurement	Calculates how far the output is from the correct answer	Prediction vs actual
Deep Neural Network	Advanced Structure	A network with many hidden layers for complex learning	Deep learning models

The Neural Network Family provides the structure that allows artificial intelligence to transform data into understanding, making it possible for machines to learn from experience and improve over time.

Dual Language System in Artificial Intelligence

Definition

The Dual Language System in Artificial Intelligence refers to the way AI communicates using two different forms of language at the same time: human language for interaction and machine language for internal processing.

Key Components

Human Language (Natural Language)
This is the language people use to communicate with AI, such as English, Spanish, Tongan, or Fijian. It includes words, sentences, and questions that users type or speak.

Machine Language (Numerical Representation)
This is how AI understands information internally. Words are converted into numbers called tokens and processed using mathematical models and algorithms.

How It Works (Step-by-Step)

A user enters a question in human language

The AI converts the words into numerical tokens

The AI processes the tokens using a neural network

The AI generates a response based on patterns and probabilities

The response is converted back into human language

Example

User Input:
"What is Artificial Intelligence?"

AI Process:

Converts words into numbers

Analyzes patterns from training data

Predicts the best possible answer

Output:
"Artificial Intelligence is the ability of machines to perform tasks that normally require human intelligence."

Why This Matters

Understanding the dual language system helps students realize that:

AI does not "think" like humans

AI translates language into math and back into language

Every interaction with AI is based on patterns, not emotions or understanding

Applications

Chatbots and virtual assistants

Language translation systems

Search engines

Voice recognition tools

Challenges

Misinterpretation of human language

Bias in language data

Lack of true understanding or reasoning

Summary

Artificial Intelligence works by translating human language into machine-readable data and then converting the results back into human language. This dual system allows AI to interact with people while operating through mathematical processes behind the scenes.

AI Translator Architecture Family Introduction

The AI Translator Architecture Family represents the system that transforms input into meaningful output in artificial intelligence. It acts as the bridge between what humans provide and what AI produces. Whether a user types a question, uploads an image, or speaks a command, this architecture is responsible for interpreting that input and generating a response.

In artificial intelligence, translation does not only mean converting one language to another. It refers to the broader process of transforming one form of information into another. For example, text can be translated into a response, speech can be converted into text, and images can be interpreted into descriptions. This transformation process is at the core of how modern AI systems function.

The AI Translator Architecture is built on multiple foundational families. It relies on the Token Family to break input into manageable units, the Neural Network Family to process patterns, and the Parameter Family to guide learning. It also uses knowledge and memory to maintain context and produce coherent results.

At the center of this architecture is the ability to encode and decode information. Encoding transforms input into a format the model can understand, while decoding converts processed information back into human-readable output. This continuous transformation allows AI systems to interact with users in a natural and meaningful way.

Understanding the AI Translator Architecture Family helps students see that AI is not simply responding randomly. Instead, it is systematically translating input into output through structured processes and learned patterns.

In simple terms, if tokens are the language pieces and neural networks are the brain, the AI Translator Architecture is the system that turns understanding into communication.

AI Translator Architecture Family Breakdown Chart

Component	Role	Description	Example
AI Translator Architecture	Transformation System	Converts input into meaningful output	Question → Answer
Input Processing	Data Intake	Receives and prepares user input for analysis	Text prompt entered by a user
Encoding	Input Conversion	Transforms input into numerical representations	Words → token IDs
Context Building	Meaning Formation	Organizes input into a structured understanding	Sentence context tracking
Sequence Processing	Order Handling	Maintains the correct order of information	Word sequence in a sentence
Attention Mechanism	Focus System	Identifies important parts of input data	Highlighting key words
Representation Layer	Feature Mapping	Converts data into internal representations for processing	Embeddings
Decoding	Output Generation	Converts processed data back into human-readable form	Token IDs → words
Output Generation	Response Creation	Produces the final answer or result	AI-generated response
Multimodal Translation	Cross-Format Processing	Translates between different types of data	Image → text description
Feedback Loop	Improvement Cycle	Uses results to refine future outputs	Model learning over time

The AI Translator Architecture Family shows that artificial intelligence is not just about understanding information, but about transforming it into meaningful communication that humans can use and interact with.

AI Architecture Family Introduction

The AI Architecture Family represents the overall design and structure of an artificial intelligence system. While individual families such as Data, Parameters, and Neural Networks explain how AI learns and processes information, the AI Architecture Family shows how all these components are organized and work together as a complete system.

In artificial intelligence, architecture refers to the blueprint that defines how data flows through a system, how components interact, and how decisions are produced. It determines how input is received, how it is processed, and how output is generated. A well-designed architecture allows AI systems to operate efficiently, scale to large problems, and produce reliable results.

AI architectures can vary depending on the type of system being built. Some are designed for image recognition, others for language processing, and others for decision-making or automation. Despite these differences, most architectures share common elements such as input layers, processing layers, memory components, and output mechanisms.

The AI Architecture Family connects all foundational families. It integrates the Data Family for input, the Token Family for language processing, the Neural Network Family for computation, the Parameter Family for learning, and the Memory and Knowledge Families for storing and organizing information. It also works closely with the AI Translator Architecture Family to transform input into meaningful output.

Understanding the AI Architecture Family helps students see the "big picture" of artificial intelligence. Instead of viewing AI as separate parts, they begin to understand it as a coordinated system where each component plays a specific role.

In simple terms, if individual families are the parts of AI, the AI Architecture Family is the blueprint that brings everything together into one working system.

AI Architecture Family Breakdown Chart

Component	Role	Description	Example
AI Architecture	System Blueprint	The overall design that defines how an AI system is structured and operates	ChatGPT system design
Input Layer	Data Entry Point	Receives raw input from users or external sources	Text prompt, image upload
Preprocessing Layer	Data Preparation	Cleans and organizes input data before processing	Tokenization, normalization
Processing Core	Computation Engine	The main system where data is analyzed and transformed	Neural networks, transformers
Parameter System	Learning Core	Stores adjustable values that guide learning and predictions	Model weights and biases
Memory System	Context Storage	Maintains and retrieves information during processing	Context window, external memory
Knowledge System	Understanding Layer	Organizes relationships and meaning within the system	Knowledge graphs, learned patterns
Decision Layer	Output Logic	Determines the final output based on processed data	Selecting the best response
Output Layer	Result Delivery	Presents results to the user in a usable format	Text, image, or audio response
Feedback Loop	Improvement System	Uses outcomes to refine future performance	Model updates and retraining
Scalability System	Expansion Capability	Allows the system to handle increasing data and complexity	Cloud-based AI systems
Integration Layer	System Connection	Connects AI with external tools and platforms	APIs, databases, applications

The AI Architecture Family reveals that artificial intelligence is not a single technology, but a coordinated system of interconnected components working together to transform data into intelligent outcomes.

Chip Family Introduction

The Chip Family represents the physical hardware that powers artificial intelligence systems. While software components such as data, algorithms, and neural networks define how AI works, none of these systems can function without the computing chips that perform the actual calculations.

Chips are specialized electronic components designed to process information at extremely high speeds. In artificial intelligence, these chips handle the complex mathematical operations required for training models and generating outputs. Every prediction, calculation, and response produced by an AI system is executed by hardware within the Chip Family.

Different types of chips are used depending on the needs of the system. Central Processing Units (CPUs) handle general-purpose tasks, while Graphics Processing Units (GPUs) are optimized for parallel processing, making them ideal for training neural networks. More specialized chips, such as Tensor Processing Units (TPUs) and Neural Processing Units (NPUs), are designed specifically for AI workloads, enabling faster and more efficient computation.

The Chip Family works closely with the Neural Network Family, which defines the structure of computation, and the Parameter Family, which stores the values being processed. It also connects to the Infrastructure Family, where large-scale systems of chips are organized in data centers and cloud environments.

Understanding the Chip Family helps students recognize that artificial intelligence is not purely abstract. It depends on physical machines that require power, resources, and engineering to operate. These chips are the engines that bring AI models to life.

In simple terms, if AI is the intelligence, chips are the machines that make that intelligence possible.

Chip Family Breakdown Chart

Component	Role	Description	Example
Chip (Processor)	Computation Engine	Electronic hardware that performs calculations required for AI	CPU, GPU
CPU (Central Processing Unit)	General Processor	Handles a wide range of computing tasks	Running basic applications
GPU (Graphics Processing Unit)	Parallel Processor	Processes many calculations at once, ideal for AI training	Training neural networks
TPU (Tensor Processing Unit)	AI Accelerator	Specialized chip designed for machine learning tasks	Google TPU
NPU (Neural Processing Unit)	Edge AI Processor	Optimized for running AI on devices like phones	Smartphone AI features
AI Accelerator	Performance Booster	Hardware designed to speed up AI computations	Dedicated AI chips
Memory (Hardware)	Data Storage	Stores data and instructions for processing	RAM, VRAM
Parallel Processing	Speed Mechanism	Ability to perform multiple calculations simultaneously	GPUs processing thousands of operations
Throughput	Processing Capacity	Amount of data processed over time	High-performance computing systems

Component	Role	Description	Example
Latency	Response Time	Time it takes to process a request	Faster chips = lower latency
Power Consumption	Energy Usage	Amount of energy required to run the chip	High-performance GPUs use more power
Edge Devices	Local Processing	Devices that run AI locally without cloud support	Phones, smart cameras

The Chip Family reminds us that behind every intelligent system is powerful hardware performing millions or billions of calculations, turning abstract models into real-world functionality.

Watts Family Introduction

The Watts Family represents the measurement of power used by artificial intelligence systems. While the Chip Family provides the hardware that performs computations, the Watts Family explains how much energy those systems consume while operating.

A watt is a unit of power that measures the rate at which energy is used. In artificial intelligence, watts help us understand how much electricity is required to run processors, train models, and generate responses. Every time an AI system processes data, performs calculations, or produces output, it consumes power.

Different AI systems require different levels of power depending on their size and complexity. Small systems, such as those running on mobile devices, use relatively low amounts of power. In contrast, large-scale AI models operating in data centers can require significant amounts of electricity, especially during training, where billions of calculations are performed continuously.

The Watts Family works closely with the Chip Family, which determines how efficiently computations are performed, and the Infrastructure Family, where large networks of machines operate together. It also connects to the overall design of AI systems, as more efficient models can reduce power consumption while maintaining performance.

Understanding the Watts Family helps students recognize that artificial intelligence is not only about intelligence and computation, but also about energy use and resource management. As AI continues to grow, managing power efficiently becomes an important part of building responsible and sustainable systems.

In simple terms, if chips perform the work, watts measure how much power it takes to do that work.

Watts Family Breakdown Chart

Component	Role	Description	Example
Watt (W)	Power Measurement	Unit that measures the rate of energy use	A device using 100 watts
Power Consumption	Energy Usage Rate	Amount of power used during operation	AI model running on GPUs
Energy Efficiency	Performance Balance	How effectively a system uses power to perform tasks	More output with less power
High-Performance Computing	Intensive Power Use	Systems that require large amounts of power for complex tasks	AI training clusters
Idle Power	Standby Usage	Power consumed when systems are not actively processing	Servers waiting for requests
Peak Power	Maximum Usage	Highest level of power used during heavy workloads	Training large AI models
Thermal Output	Heat Generation	Heat produced as a result of power usage	Cooling systems in data centers
Cooling Systems	Temperature Control	Systems used to manage heat from high power usage	Air or liquid cooling
Power Supply	Energy Source	Provides electricity to AI systems	Electrical grid, batteries
Edge Power Usage	Local Energy Use	Power consumption on smaller devices	Smartphones, IoT devices
Data Center Power	Large-Scale Usage	Power required for large AI operations	Server farms running AI models
Sustainable Energy	Efficiency Goal	Use of renewable energy to reduce environmental impact	Solar-powered data centers

The Watts Family highlights that intelligence comes with a cost—every AI system requires power, and understanding that power is essential for building efficient and sustainable technologies.

Watts Family (AI Power Usage Scale)

Definition

The **Watts Family** represents the real-time power usage of artificial intelligence systems, measured in watts (W). It shows how much power AI systems consume at a given moment as they process data and perform computations.

Watts Scale

1 Watt
10 Watts
100 Watts
500 Watts
1,000 Watts (1 Kilowatt)
10,000 Watts (10 Kilowatts)
100,000 Watts (100 Kilowatts)
1,000,000 Watts (1 Megawatt)
10,000,000 Watts (10 Megawatts)
100,000,000+ Watts (100+ Megawatts)

Key Characteristics

Measured in real-world electrical power

Higher watt values indicate higher processing demand

Used to represent the scale of AI systems from small devices to large infrastructures

Closely connected to the Chip Family, Energy Family, and Infrastructure Family

Examples

Low watts → small devices and basic AI functions

Medium watts → computers and advanced applications

High watts → data centers and large AI systems

Summary

The **Watts Family** provides a numerical representation of how much power artificial intelligence systems use in real time, helping to illustrate the scale and intensity of AI operations.

Student Insight

Watts show how much power AI is using right now.

AI Energy Family Introduction

The AI Energy Family represents the total amount of energy consumed by artificial intelligence systems over time. While the Watts Family measures the rate at which power is used at any given moment, the Energy Family focuses on the accumulated energy required to perform tasks, run systems, and sustain operations.

In artificial intelligence, energy is used every time a model is trained, a system processes data, or a response is generated. Large-scale AI systems, especially those operating in data centers, can consume significant amounts of energy due to the continuous processing of massive datasets and complex computations.

Energy is typically measured over time using units such as kilowatt-hours (kWh), which reflect how much power has been used during a specific period. For example, running a high-performance AI system for several hours or days results in a total energy cost that goes beyond the moment-to-moment power usage measured in watts.

The AI Energy Family works closely with the Watts Family, which provides the rate of power consumption, and the Chip Family, which determines how efficiently computations are performed. It also connects to the Infrastructure Family, where large-scale systems operate continuously and require long-term energy management.

Understanding the AI Energy Family helps students recognize that artificial intelligence has real-world resource implications. It is not only about performance and speed, but also about sustainability, efficiency, and responsible use of technology.

In simple terms, if watts measure how fast energy is used, energy measures how much is used over time.

AI Energy Family Breakdown Chart

Component	Role	Description	Example
Energy	Total Consumption	The total amount of power used over a period of time	Running an AI system for hours or days
Kilowatt-hour (kWh)	Energy Measurement	Unit used to measure energy consumption over time	1 kWh = using 1,000 watts for 1 hour
Energy Usage	Consumption Tracking	Total energy required for AI operations	Training a large model
Training Energy	Learning Cost	Energy used during model training processes	Weeks of GPU usage
Inference Energy	Response Cost	Energy used when AI generates outputs	Answering a user prompt
Energy Efficiency	Optimization Goal	Reducing energy use while maintaining performance	Efficient AI models

Component	Role	Description	Example
Energy Scaling	Growth Impact	Increase in energy use as systems grow larger	Bigger models = more energy
Data Center Energy	Infrastructure Demand	Total energy used by large AI facilities	Server farms operating 24/7
Cooling Energy	Temperature Control	Energy required to cool systems and prevent overheating	Air conditioning in data centers
Renewable Energy	Sustainability Source	Use of clean energy to power AI systems	Solar, wind-powered data centers
Carbon Impact	Environmental Effect	Emissions associated with energy consumption	AI training carbon footprint
Energy Management	Resource Control	Strategies to monitor and reduce energy use	Efficient scheduling, hardware optimization

The AI Energy Family reminds us that artificial intelligence operates within the physical world, where every computation consumes energy and every system has an impact on resources and sustainability.

Energy Family (Total Power Consumption of Artificial Intelligence)

Definition

The **Energy Family** represents the total amount of electricity used by artificial intelligence systems over time. It is measured in watt-hours (Wh) or kilowatt-hours (kWh) and shows how much energy AI systems consume while running.

Energy Scale

1 Watt-hour (Wh)
10 Watt-hours (Wh)
100 Watt-hours (Wh)
500 Watt-hours (Wh)
1,000 Watt-hours (1 Kilowatt-hour, kWh)
10,000 Watt-hours (10 kWh)
100,000 Watt-hours (100 kWh)
1,000,000 Watt-hours (1 Megawatt-hour, MWh)
10,000,000 Watt-hours (10 MWh)
100,000,000+ Watt-hours (100+ MWh)

Key Characteristics

Measured over time (not instant like watts)

Represents total electricity consumption

Increases the longer AI systems run

Directly related to cost and energy usage

Closely connected to Watts Family, Chip Family, and Infrastructure Family

Examples

Low energy → short AI tasks or small devices

Medium energy → daily AI usage on computers

High energy → training AI models and running data centers

Summary

The **Energy Family** provides a numerical representation of the total electricity consumed by artificial intelligence systems over time, helping to illustrate the overall cost and impact of AI operations.

Student Insight

Energy shows how much total power AI has used over time.

AI Infrastructure Family Introduction

The AI Infrastructure Family represents the large-scale systems and environments that support, power, and connect artificial intelligence technologies. While individual components such as chips, data, and models explain how AI works, infrastructure explains where and how these systems operate in the real world.

AI infrastructure includes data centers, cloud platforms, networking systems, and storage environments that allow artificial intelligence to function at scale. These systems provide the computing power, data access, and connectivity needed to train models, process information, and deliver results to users around the world.

Modern AI systems rely heavily on cloud-based infrastructure, where thousands of machines work together to handle massive workloads. This allows AI to scale efficiently, making it possible to process large datasets, run complex models, and serve millions of users simultaneously. Infrastructure also ensures reliability, security, and continuous availability of AI services.

The AI Infrastructure Family works closely with the Chip Family, which provides the hardware, the Watts and Energy Families, which manage power consumption, and the Data Family, which supplies the information being processed. It also supports the AI Architecture Family by providing the environment where all system components are deployed and connected.

Understanding the AI Infrastructure Family helps students recognize that artificial intelligence is not contained within a single device. Instead, it operates across global systems that require coordination, resources, and engineering to function effectively.

In simple terms, if AI is the system and chips are the engines, infrastructure is the environment that allows everything to run at scale.

AI Infrastructure Family Breakdown Chart

Component	Role	Description	Example
AI Infrastructure	System Environment	The physical and digital systems that support AI operations	Global AI platforms
Data Center	Processing Hub	Facilities that house servers and computing equipment	Large server farms
Cloud Computing	Scalable Platform	Remote systems that provide computing resources over the internet	AWS, Azure, Google Cloud
Servers	Compute Units	Machines that process data and run AI models	Rack-mounted servers
Networking	Connectivity System	Systems that allow communication between machines	Internet, fiber networks
Storage Systems	Data Management	Systems that store large volumes of data	Databases, cloud storage
Distributed Computing	Workload Sharing	Splitting tasks across multiple machines for efficiency	Parallel processing across clusters
Edge Infrastructure	Local Processing	Running AI closer to the user or device	Smart devices, IoT systems
Load Balancing	Traffic Control	Distributes workloads to prevent overload	Managing user requests
Security Systems	Protection Layer	Safeguards data and systems from threats	Encryption, firewalls
Redundancy	Reliability System	Backup systems to ensure continuous operation	Failover servers

Component	Role	Description	Example
Scalability	Growth Capability	Ability to expand resources as demand increases	Adding more servers dynamically

The AI Infrastructure Family reveals that artificial intelligence operates on a global scale, relying on interconnected systems that provide the power, storage, and connectivity needed to support intelligent technologies.

AI Agent Family Introduction

The AI Agent Family represents systems that can take action, make decisions, and perform tasks on behalf of users or other systems. Unlike traditional AI models that only respond to input, AI agents are designed to operate with a level of autonomy, allowing them to plan, execute, and adapt to achieve specific goals.

An AI agent receives input from its environment, processes that information, and takes actions based on predefined objectives or learned behaviors. These actions can include answering questions, automating workflows, retrieving information, or interacting with other systems. Some agents operate in simple environments, while others function in complex systems that require continuous decision-making.

AI agents often combine multiple foundational families. They use the Data Family to gather information, the Memory and Knowledge Families to retain and understand context, and the Neural Network and Parameter Families to process and learn from interactions. They also rely on the AI Architecture and Infrastructure Families to operate reliably at scale.

Modern AI agents can work independently or as part of larger systems. For example, a customer support agent can respond to inquiries automatically, while a more advanced agent can complete multi-step tasks such as scheduling, research, or system management.

Understanding the AI Agent Family helps students see that artificial intelligence is not only about generating responses, but also about taking meaningful action in real-world scenarios.

In simple terms, if AI models think and respond, AI agents act and execute.

AI Agent Family Breakdown Chart

Component	Role	Description	Example
AI Agent	Action System	An AI system that can make decisions and perform tasks	Virtual assistant

Component	Role	Description	Example
Environment	Operating Context	The space where the agent interacts and gathers information	Web, apps, databases
Input Perception	Data Intake	Receives information from the environment	User query or sensor input
Decision Engine	Action Selection	Determines what action to take based on input	Choosing a response or task
Action Execution	Task Performance	Carries out decisions in the environment	Sending an email, retrieving data
Goal System	Objective Setting	Defines what the agent is trying to achieve	Complete a task or solve a problem
Planning Module	Strategy Builder	Breaks down tasks into steps	Multi-step problem solving
Feedback Loop	Learning Cycle	Improves performance based on outcomes	Adjusting actions over time
Autonomy Level	Independence Scale	Degree of independence in decision-making	Fully automated vs assisted
Multi-Agent System	Collaboration Network	Multiple agents working together	Coordinated AI systems

Ingredient Family Introduction

The Ingredient Family represents the essential components that come together to create an artificial intelligence system. Just as a recipe requires specific ingredients to produce a final dish, AI systems rely on a combination of foundational elements working together to function effectively.

Artificial intelligence is not built from a single component. It requires data to learn from, algorithms to guide processing, models to perform tasks, hardware to execute computations, and energy to power the entire system. Each of these elements plays a critical role, and the absence of any one component would prevent the system from operating properly.

The Ingredient Family provides a simplified way for students to understand AI as a system made up of interconnected parts. Instead of viewing AI as complex or mysterious, learners can begin to see it as something constructed from identifiable and understandable components.

This family connects directly with all other foundational families, including Data, Algorithm, Neural Network, Parameter, Chip, and Energy Families. It serves as an overview that brings these elements together into a unified perspective.

Understanding the Ingredient Family helps students recognize that artificial intelligence is built, not magical. It is the result of carefully combining the right components in the right way.

In simple terms, if AI is the final product, the Ingredient Family represents everything needed to build it.

Ingredient Family Breakdown Chart

Component	Role	Description	Example
Data	Learning Input	Provides the information AI uses to learn patterns	Text, images, audio
Algorithms	Instruction Set	Guides how data is processed and decisions are made	Sorting, classification
AI Models	Execution System	Performs tasks such as prediction or generation	Language models
Neural Networks	Processing Structure	Organizes how data is processed through layers	Deep learning models
Parameters	Learning Adjustments	Fine-tune how the model learns and makes predictions	Weights and biases
Tokens	Language Units	Breaks text into smaller pieces for processing	Words or subwords
Hardware (Chips)	Computation Engine	Executes calculations required by AI systems	GPUs, CPUs
Energy	Power Source	Supplies the energy needed to run systems	Electricity usage
Infrastructure	Support System	Provides the environment for AI to operate at scale	Cloud systems, data centers
Memory	Storage System	Stores and retrieves information for processing	Context memory
Knowledge	Understanding Layer	Represents meaning and relationships within data	Knowledge graphs

The Ingredient Family shows that artificial intelligence is built from a combination of essential components, each playing a vital role in creating intelligent systems.

The Frontend and Backend Family of Artificial Intelligence

How AI Systems Connect User Interaction to Intelligent Processing

Introduction

Every artificial intelligence system operates through two essential layers: the frontend and the backend. These layers work together to transform human interaction into intelligent responses, allowing AI systems to function smoothly and effectively.

The frontend is the part of the system that users see and interact with. It includes screens, input tools, and the display of results. Whether a user is typing a question, speaking a command, or uploading an image, all interaction begins at the frontend.

Behind the scenes, the backend serves as the processing engine of the system. It receives input from the frontend, manages data, connects to the AI model, and performs the computations needed to generate a response. The backend is where the intelligence of the system operates, using models, algorithms, and infrastructure to interpret and respond to user requests.

This visual illustrates how these two layers work together as a complete system. It shows the flow of information from user input to AI processing and back to the user as a result. By understanding this structure, students can see that AI is not a single tool, but a coordinated system of layers working together.

In simple terms, the frontend is where interaction happens, and the backend is where intelligence is created.

Every AI system has two sides: what you see and what actually does the thinking.

AI Qubit Family Introduction

The AI Qubit Family represents the foundation of quantum computing as it relates to artificial intelligence. While traditional computing relies on bits, which can exist as either 0 or 1, quantum computing uses qubits, which can exist in multiple states simultaneously.

A qubit is the basic unit of quantum information. Unlike classical bits, qubits can take advantage of properties such as superposition and entanglement, allowing quantum systems to process complex computations more efficiently in certain scenarios. This opens new possibilities for solving problems that are difficult or impossible for traditional computers.

In the context of artificial intelligence, qubits have the potential to accelerate learning processes, optimize large-scale systems, and improve complex simulations. Although quantum AI is still in development, it represents a future direction where computational power can expand beyond current limitations.

The AI Qubit Family connects with the Chip Family, as quantum processors are specialized hardware, and with the Algorithm Family, where new types of quantum algorithms are designed. It also relates to the Parameter and Neural Network Families, as researchers explore quantum-enhanced learning models.

Understanding the AI Qubit Family helps students see that artificial intelligence is continuously evolving. It introduces the idea that the foundations of computing themselves can change, leading to new forms of intelligence and problem-solving.

In simple terms, if bits are the foundation of today's computing, qubits represent the foundation of tomorrow's possibilities.

AI Qubit Family Breakdown Chart

Component	Role	Description	Example
Qubit	Quantum Unit	Basic unit of quantum information	Quantum bit in a quantum computer
Superposition	Multi-State Ability	Ability to exist in multiple states at once	0 and 1 simultaneously
Entanglement	Connection Property	Linking qubits so they influence each other	Paired quantum states
Quantum Gate	Operation System	Performs operations on qubits	Quantum logic gates
Quantum Circuit	Processing Structure	Sequence of quantum operations	Quantum algorithms
Quantum Processor	Hardware Engine	Specialized chip for quantum computing	Quantum computer hardware

Component	Role	Description	Example
Quantum Algorithm	Computation Method	Algorithm designed for quantum systems	Optimization problems
Quantum Speedup	Performance Advantage	Faster processing for certain problems	Complex simulations
Quantum Noise	Stability Challenge	Errors caused by environmental interference	Qubit instability
Quantum Error Correction	Stability Solution	Techniques to reduce errors in quantum systems	Fault-tolerant computing

The AI Qubit Family introduces a new frontier in computing, where the limits of traditional systems are expanded, opening the door to more powerful and advanced forms of artificial intelligence.

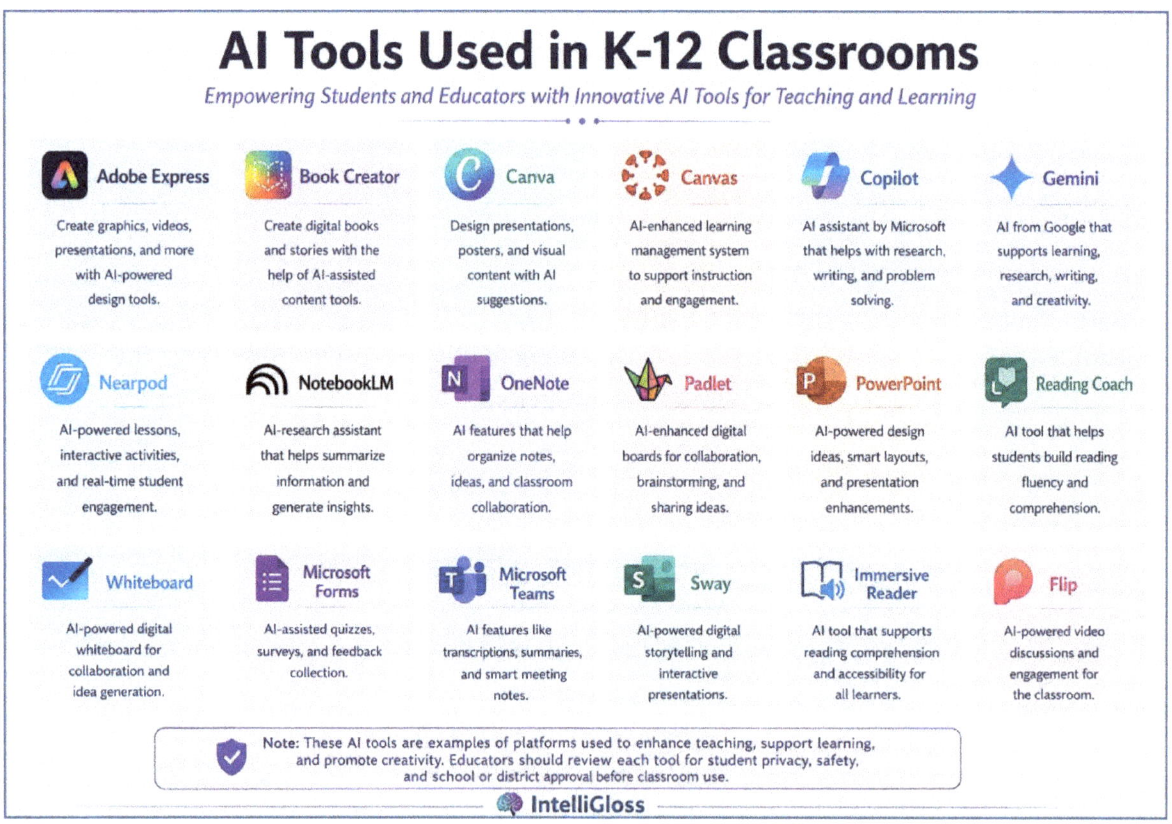

TABLE OF CONTENTS

Introduction

Welcome to the AGI Generation

Every generation experiences a moment that changes history. Some generations witnessed the invention of electricity. Others watched airplanes connect continents, computers transform workplaces, and the internet reshape communication across the globe. Today's students are growing up during another historic turning point—the emergence of Artificial General Intelligence (AGI).

Unlike earlier forms of artificial intelligence that perform specific tasks, AGI represents the vision of intelligent systems capable of learning, adapting, solving problems, and applying knowledge across many different subjects. Whether AGI arrives gradually or through major breakthroughs, one thing is certain: today's students will be the first generation to live, learn, work, and lead in a world where increasingly intelligent machines become part of everyday life.

This does not mean that machines will replace people. Instead, it means that people who understand artificial intelligence will be better prepared to work alongside it. The future will belong to individuals who can combine human creativity, critical thinking, ethical decision-making, communication, and compassion with the incredible capabilities of intelligent technologies.

Education is entering a new era. Memorizing facts alone will no longer be enough. Students will need to ask thoughtful questions, evaluate information carefully, solve complex problems, work effectively with others, and continue learning throughout their lives. Teachers will guide students in developing these essential skills while helping them understand how to use AI responsibly, safely, and ethically. Parents will also play an important role by encouraging curiosity, character, and responsible technology use both inside and outside the classroom.

This book was written to help prepare readers for that future. Rather than focusing only on how AGI works, it explores how young people can grow into confident, knowledgeable, and responsible citizens in an intelligent world. Along the way, readers will discover how education, careers, leadership, innovation, ethics, and lifelong learning are evolving as artificial intelligence becomes an increasingly important part of society.

The AGI Generation is not defined by age alone. It is defined by mindset. It is a generation willing to embrace change, learn continuously, think independently, collaborate across cultures, and use technology to improve the lives of others. The greatest achievements of the future will not come from machines acting alone. They will come from people who know how to guide technology with wisdom, integrity, and purpose.

Throughout this book, you will explore how intelligent systems are changing education, transforming careers, creating new opportunities for innovation, and presenting important ethical questions that every future leader should understand. More importantly, you will discover that the future is not something that simply happens—it is something each generation helps create through its choices, values, and actions.

Whether you are a student preparing for your future, an educator inspiring the next generation, a parent supporting lifelong learning, or simply someone who wants to understand where our world is headed, this journey begins with one important idea: the future of AGI is ultimately a human story. Technology may provide extraordinary tools, but people will determine how those tools are used to build stronger communities, expand knowledge, solve global challenges, and improve life for everyone.

The future is already beginning.

The AGI Generation will help write its next chapter.

Welcome to the journey.

Chapter 1

Meet the AGI Generation

Every generation grows up during a time that shapes the way people think, learn, work, and live. Some generations witnessed the arrival of electricity in homes. Others experienced the invention of television, the first personal computers, the internet, and smartphones. Each of these technologies changed society in ways that few people could have imagined when they first appeared. Today, another transformation is taking place. It is the rise of artificial intelligence, and eventually, Artificial General Intelligence (AGI). The students sitting in classrooms today are growing up during this remarkable period of change. They are becoming the first true AGI Generation.

Being part of the AGI Generation does not simply mean using technology every day. It means growing up in a world where intelligent systems are becoming trusted partners in education, healthcare, transportation, scientific research, engineering, business, entertainment, and countless other areas of life. Unlike previous generations that had to learn about new technologies after entering adulthood, today's students are watching intelligent machines become more capable while they are still in school. This gives them an opportunity that no generation before them has ever experienced. They have the chance to understand intelligent technology from the very beginning and help shape how it develops in the future.

Artificial intelligence is already influencing daily life in ways many people do not notice. Recommendation systems suggest music, movies, books, and videos. Navigation apps help drivers avoid traffic. Translation tools allow people from different countries to communicate almost instantly. Digital assistants answer questions, organize schedules, and help people complete everyday tasks. Hospitals use AI to assist doctors in analyzing medical images. Scientists use AI to study climate patterns, discover new medicines, and explore space. Farmers use intelligent systems to monitor crops and improve harvests. Teachers use educational AI tools to personalize instruction and provide students with additional learning opportunities. While many people simply see these tools as convenient technology, students of the AGI Generation have the opportunity to understand the ideas behind them and eventually improve them.

For thousands of years, education focused primarily on passing knowledge from one generation to the next. Students learned mathematics, science, language, history, and the arts because these subjects helped societies grow stronger. Those subjects remain just as important today, but education is expanding to include digital literacy, computational thinking, data understanding, artificial intelligence, cybersecurity, and ethical technology use. Future graduates will not only need to understand how the world has worked in the past, but also how intelligent technologies will influence the future. Learning about AI is no longer limited to computer scientists. It is becoming valuable knowledge for doctors, teachers, engineers, artists, business owners, government leaders, healthcare professionals, and many other careers.

One reason this generation is so important is that AGI has the potential to become one of the most influential technologies ever developed. While today's AI systems usually specialize in specific tasks, researchers continue exploring ways to build systems capable of learning across many different subjects, adapting to unfamiliar situations, solving new kinds of problems, and working alongside people in increasingly flexible ways. Whether AGI develops quickly or gradually over many years, today's students are likely to witness its progress throughout their lifetimes. Understanding its possibilities, as well as its limitations, will help them become thoughtful users instead of passive observers.

Growing up during a technological revolution also brings responsibility. Every important invention throughout history has offered both opportunities and challenges. Electricity transformed homes but required safety standards. Automobiles created faster transportation but also introduced traffic laws and driver's education. The internet connected billions of people while creating new concerns about privacy, misinformation, and cybersecurity. Artificial intelligence is no different. Powerful technologies require knowledgeable people who understand how to use them wisely. The AGI Generation will play an important role in creating rules, designing systems, protecting human rights, and ensuring that intelligent machines benefit society rather than causing unnecessary harm.

One of the most exciting characteristics of the AGI Generation is curiosity. Young people naturally ask questions about how things work. They explore new apps, experiment with technology, solve puzzles, and imagine creative possibilities. Curiosity has always been one of humanity's greatest strengths. Every scientific discovery, medical breakthrough, engineering achievement, and technological innovation began because someone was curious enough to ask a question that others had not considered. Artificial intelligence does not replace curiosity. Instead, it gives curious learners new tools to investigate ideas, analyze information, and discover answers more efficiently than ever before.

Curiosity alone, however, is not enough. Students must also develop wisdom. Information is becoming easier to find, but understanding remains a uniquely human skill. Intelligent systems can organize facts, generate explanations, recognize patterns, and perform calculations with incredible speed, but people must still determine whether information is accurate, fair, ethical, and useful. The ability to think critically will become one of the defining characteristics of successful students in the AGI era. Instead of accepting every answer immediately, learners will need to compare sources, ask thoughtful questions, evaluate evidence, and understand different perspectives before reaching conclusions.

Another defining quality of the AGI Generation is adaptability. Throughout history, jobs have changed whenever new technologies appeared. Farmers learned to operate tractors instead of relying entirely on manual labor. Office workers learned to use computers instead of typewriters. Businesses adopted the internet to reach customers around the world. Today's students will likely experience similar changes throughout their careers. Some jobs will evolve, others will disappear, and entirely new professions will emerge. The individuals who succeed will not necessarily be those who memorize the most information. They will be those who continue learning, adapt to changing technologies, and confidently develop new skills throughout their lives.

Learning has become a lifelong journey rather than something that ends with graduation. Previous generations often completed their formal education before beginning careers that remained relatively stable for decades. The AGI Generation will experience a different reality. New technologies may appear every few years, requiring workers to update their knowledge regularly. This continuous learning should not be viewed as a burden. Instead, it represents an opportunity to keep growing, discovering new interests, and contributing to society in meaningful ways. The willingness to learn continuously may become one of the greatest competitive advantages in the future workplace.

Equally important is the ability to collaborate. Although AI systems are becoming increasingly capable, the future will depend on cooperation between people and intelligent machines rather than competition between them. Students will learn how to ask better questions, interpret AI-generated information, verify results, and combine machine-generated insights with human judgment. Successful professionals will understand that technology performs best when guided by thoughtful people who understand both its strengths and its limitations. Human creativity, empathy, leadership, communication, and ethical reasoning will remain essential qualities that technology cannot replace.

The AGI Generation also has the opportunity to become one of the most globally connected generations in history. Students today can communicate with classmates, educators, researchers, and professionals from around the world within seconds. They can access educational resources from universities, museums, libraries, and scientific organizations that were once available only to a small number of people. Artificial intelligence makes it even easier to translate languages, organize information, and connect ideas across cultures. These opportunities encourage students to think beyond their own communities and recognize that many of the world's greatest challenges require international cooperation and shared knowledge.

Perhaps the most inspiring aspect of belonging to the AGI Generation is realizing that the future has not yet been written. Every important technology is shaped by the people who design it, improve it, regulate it, and decide how it should be used. Today's students are not simply preparing for the future—they are preparing to build it. Some will become engineers who create new intelligent systems. Others will become teachers who inspire future innovators. Some will become doctors who use AI to improve patient care, scientists who make groundbreaking discoveries, entrepreneurs who launch new businesses, artists who combine creativity with technology, or public leaders who develop thoughtful policies that guide responsible innovation.

The choices students make today will influence the intelligent world of tomorrow. Every lesson learned, every question asked, every skill developed, and every ethical decision made contributes to the future they will help create. The AGI Generation has the opportunity to become one of the most educated, connected, creative, and innovative generations in human history. That opportunity carries both excitement and responsibility.

This book is designed to help students, educators, parents, and lifelong learners understand that Artificial General Intelligence is not only about advanced technology. It is also about people. It is about preparing minds to think critically, hearts to lead compassionately, and communities to use powerful tools responsibly. As you continue reading, remember that the story of AGI is still being written. The next chapter of that story may one day be written by someone sitting in a classroom today.

The AGI Generation has already begun. The future is waiting for leaders who are ready to learn, ready to adapt, and ready to shape an intelligent world that benefits everyone.

Chapter 1 – Part 2

The Opportunity to Shape an Intelligent Future

Every generation inherits a world created by those who came before it, but every generation also leaves behind a new world for those who follow. The AGI Generation is unique because it may become the first generation to guide the development of machines that can learn, reason across many subjects, and assist people in ways that were once imagined only in science fiction. This responsibility extends far beyond writing computer programs or building robots. It includes making thoughtful decisions about how intelligent systems should be designed, how they should be used, and how they can improve the lives of people everywhere. Students may not realize it today, but many of them will become the scientists, engineers, educators, healthcare professionals, entrepreneurs, artists, lawmakers, and community leaders who shape the future of AGI. The lessons they learn now will help prepare them for opportunities that have not yet been invented.

One of the greatest strengths students can develop is the ability to solve problems. Throughout history, societies have advanced because people looked at difficult challenges and refused to accept that they could not be solved. Diseases that once claimed millions of lives now have treatments because researchers continued searching for answers. Transportation became faster because inventors imagined new ways to travel. Communication became nearly instant because engineers developed technologies that connected the world. Artificial General Intelligence has the potential to become another powerful tool for solving problems, but only if people learn how to direct it wisely. Intelligent systems may analyze enormous amounts of information, recognize hidden patterns, and generate possible solutions, but people must still decide which solutions are practical, ethical, and beneficial. The partnership between human judgment and machine intelligence will become one of the defining characteristics of the future.

As students prepare for this future, they should understand that intelligence is much more than earning high grades or memorizing facts. True intelligence includes curiosity, creativity, resilience, empathy, communication, and sound judgment. A student who asks thoughtful questions often learns more than one who simply memorizes answers. A student who works well with others frequently solves more complex problems than someone working alone. A student who demonstrates honesty and integrity earns trust that cannot be replaced by technology. These qualities have always mattered, and they will become even more valuable in an intelligent world. Machines may process information at incredible speed, but they do not replace the character that allows people to build trust, inspire others, and lead with wisdom.

The AGI Generation will also discover that mistakes are valuable teachers. Many people fear making mistakes because they believe failure means they are not capable. In reality, nearly every important invention was improved through repeated testing, revision, and learning from errors. Scientists perform experiments that sometimes fail before making groundbreaking discoveries. Engineers redesign products many times before they become reliable. Writers revise manuscripts repeatedly before publishing them. Software developers continuously improve computer programs by correcting problems they discover along the way. Students should view mistakes as opportunities to learn rather than reasons to give up. This growth mindset encourages perseverance and prepares learners for a future in which continuous improvement is part of everyday life.

Another important lesson for the AGI Generation is understanding that technology changes rapidly, but human values remain remarkably consistent. People still value honesty, kindness, respect, fairness, responsibility, and compassion regardless of how advanced technology becomes. Intelligent machines may assist with difficult calculations, generate creative ideas, or recommend solutions, but they cannot replace the importance of treating others with dignity and respect. The future will need individuals who understand both advanced technology and timeless human values. Combining these two strengths will allow society to enjoy the benefits of innovation while protecting the principles that make communities strong.

Communication will become another essential skill for students entering the AGI era. Even as intelligent systems become more capable of understanding language, people will still need to express ideas clearly, listen carefully, collaborate respectfully, and explain complex concepts in ways that others can understand. Whether presenting scientific discoveries, leading business teams, teaching classrooms, or helping patients understand medical information, effective communication builds understanding and strengthens relationships. Students who learn to communicate thoughtfully will be prepared to lead teams that include both people and intelligent technologies.

Leadership itself is changing. In the past, many leaders were expected to have all the answers. The leaders of the AGI Generation may instead become individuals who ask meaningful questions, encourage teamwork, evaluate evidence, and guide ethical decision-making. They will recognize that leadership is not about controlling others but about helping people achieve common goals. Intelligent technologies can provide valuable information, but leadership still requires courage, humility, accountability, and the ability to make thoughtful decisions when facing uncertainty. Future leaders will need to balance innovation with responsibility, ensuring that technological progress benefits everyone rather than only a small group of people.

The workplace of tomorrow will likely look very different from today's workplaces. Many routine tasks may become increasingly automated, allowing people to spend more time solving creative problems, designing new ideas, caring for others, conducting research, and making strategic decisions. Students entering future careers should prepare themselves not only to work with AI systems but also to supervise them, evaluate their performance, and improve how they operate. Instead of asking whether AI will replace people, students should ask how people and AI can accomplish more together than either could achieve alone. This partnership will define many professions in the decades ahead.

The AGI Generation also has an opportunity to improve society in ways previous generations could scarcely imagine. Intelligent systems may help scientists develop cleaner energy sources, improve food production, monitor environmental changes, reduce waste, and discover new treatments for diseases. They may assist teachers in creating personalized learning experiences that help every student succeed. They may support emergency responders during natural disasters by analyzing information quickly and coordinating rescue efforts. While these possibilities are exciting, they will require thoughtful people to ensure that AI systems are designed fairly, tested carefully, and used responsibly. Technology alone does not create a better world. People create a better world by deciding how technology should be applied.

Preparing for the future also means developing digital responsibility. Students should learn to protect personal information, recognize misleading content, verify sources, and understand that not everything generated by AI is automatically correct. Intelligent systems can occasionally produce inaccurate or incomplete information. Responsible users verify important facts before making decisions, especially when information affects health, education, finances, or public safety. Becoming a thoughtful digital citizen means understanding both the strengths and limitations of technology while using it responsibly and respectfully.

Education itself is becoming more personalized because of advances in AI. Instead of every student following exactly the same learning path, intelligent educational tools may help identify individual strengths, areas for improvement, and preferred learning styles. Some students learn best through reading, while others benefit from visual demonstrations, hands-on activities, discussions, or interactive simulations. AI has the potential to help teachers provide additional support without replacing the essential role of educators. Great teachers do far more than deliver information. They inspire confidence, encourage curiosity, recognize individual potential, and help students become responsible members of society. The relationship between teachers and students will continue to be one of the most valuable parts of education.

Families will also play an important role in preparing young people for an intelligent future. Parents and guardians help children develop habits that no machine can teach, including honesty, perseverance, kindness, patience, responsibility, and respect for others. Conversations around the dinner table, encouragement during difficult assignments, and guidance through life's challenges all contribute to building confident learners. As AI becomes more common in homes, families can help students understand when technology is useful and when human conversation, personal reflection, and face-to-face relationships are even more important. Strong families help students develop the balance needed to use technology wisely without allowing it to replace meaningful human connections.

Perhaps the most exciting truth about the AGI Generation is that no one knows exactly what the future will look like. Many careers that today's students will hold have not yet been invented. New industries will emerge. Scientific discoveries will create opportunities that are difficult to imagine today. Intelligent technologies will continue to evolve, opening doors to challenges and possibilities that will require creative thinkers from every background and profession. This uncertainty should not create fear. Instead, it should inspire curiosity. Every generation faces an unknown future, but the AGI Generation enters that future with access to more knowledge, more educational resources, and more opportunities for collaboration than any generation before it.

As you continue reading this book, remember that Artificial General Intelligence is ultimately a story about people. It is about students who choose to learn, teachers who choose to inspire, families who choose to support lifelong education, and communities that choose to use technology responsibly. AGI may become one of humanity's greatest technological achievements, but its success will depend on the wisdom, character, and leadership of the people who guide it.

The AGI Generation is more than a group of students born during a particular period in history. It is a generation defined by curiosity, adaptability, integrity, compassion, and the courage to embrace change. These students will inherit powerful technologies, but they will also inherit the responsibility to ensure that those technologies strengthen education, improve healthcare, protect the environment, expand scientific discovery, and create opportunities that benefit all people.

History will remember this generation not simply because it lived during the rise of AGI, but because of what it chose to do with the opportunities that AGI created. The future is not waiting for someone else to build it. The future is being shaped every day by students who are learning, questioning, imagining, and preparing themselves to become thoughtful leaders in an intelligent world.

The AGI Generation has already begun, and every student has the opportunity to become part of its remarkable story.

Chapter 1 Summary

Meet the AGI Generation

The AGI Generation is the first generation of students growing up during the rapid development of artificial intelligence and the future emergence of Artificial General Intelligence (AGI). Unlike previous generations that adapted to technology later in life, today's students are learning, communicating, and solving problems alongside intelligent systems from an early age.

This chapter explained that AGI is more than a technological milestone—it is a new chapter in human history that will influence education, careers, healthcare, science, engineering, business, and everyday life. Students of the AGI Generation have the opportunity to become active participants in shaping this future rather than simply observing it.

The chapter emphasized that while AI will continue becoming more capable, human qualities such as curiosity, creativity, critical thinking, empathy, integrity, communication, leadership, and ethical decision-making will remain essential. Technology may become more intelligent, but people will always be responsible for deciding how it should be used.

Students also learned that lifelong learning will become increasingly important. Because technology continues to evolve, successful individuals will develop the habit of continuously learning new skills, adapting to change, and embracing innovation throughout their lives.

Finally, the chapter encouraged readers to see themselves as future leaders, innovators, scientists, educators, entrepreneurs, healthcare professionals, artists, engineers, and responsible citizens who can help ensure that AGI benefits humanity. The future is not predetermined. It will be shaped by the decisions, values, and actions of today's students.

Chapter 1 Reflection

Thinking About Your Place in the AGI Generation

1. What does being part of the AGI Generation mean to you?
2. Which human qualities do you believe will become even more valuable as AI becomes more advanced? Explain your answer.
3. Why is lifelong learning important in a world where technology changes rapidly?

4. Think about a career that interests you. How do you think AI or AGI could help professionals in that field?
5. How can students use artificial intelligence responsibly while continuing to develop their own thinking skills?
6. What responsibilities do future leaders have when creating or using intelligent technologies?
7. Describe one way you can prepare yourself today for the intelligent world of tomorrow.
8. After reading this chapter, what excites you the most about the future? What concerns you the most?

Chapter 1 Worksheet

Meet the AGI Generation

Part A – Vocabulary

Write a definition for each term in your own words.

1. Artificial General Intelligence (AGI)
2. Adaptability
3. Critical Thinking
4. Lifelong Learning
5. Ethics
6. Innovation
7. Collaboration
8. Leadership
9. Creativity
10. Responsibility

Part B – Short Answer

Answer each question using complete sentences.

1. Why is today's generation called the AGI Generation?
2. Name three human skills that AI cannot easily replace.
3. Why is curiosity important for future innovators?
4. How can AI help improve education?
5. Why should people verify information produced by AI?
6. How can students prepare for careers that do not yet exist?
7. Why will communication continue to be important in the future?
8. Explain why technology should always be guided by human values.

Part C – Critical Thinking

Write one or two paragraphs for each question.

1. Imagine you graduate twenty years from now. Describe what you think your workplace may look like if AGI becomes common.
2. If you were designing an AGI system for your school, what would it do? How would it help students and teachers?
3. What ethical rules would you include before allowing your AGI system to be used?

Part D – Personal Challenge

Create your own "Future Readiness Plan."

List:

• Three new skills you want to learn.

• Three habits you want to improve.

• Three careers that interest you.

• Three ways you can become a responsible user of AI.

Chapter 1 Quiz

Multiple Choice

Choose the best answer.

1. What makes today's students part of the AGI Generation?

A. They use only smartphones.

B. They are growing up during the development of advanced artificial intelligence.

C. They only study computer science.

D. They no longer need teachers.

2. Which human quality will remain important in an AI-powered world?

A. Curiosity

B. Empathy

C. Ethical decision-making

D. All of the above

3. Lifelong learning means:

A. Learning ends after graduation.

B. Continuing to learn throughout life.

C. Memorizing everything in school.

D. Avoiding new technology.

4. Why is critical thinking important when using AI?

A. AI is always perfect.

B. People should evaluate information before accepting it.

C. AI never makes mistakes.

D. Students should never question technology.

5. Which career may benefit from AI?

A. Doctors

B. Teachers

C. Engineers

D. All of the above

True or False

6. _____ AGI is expected to influence many areas of society.
7. _____ Human values become less important as AI improves.
8. _____ Students should continue developing creativity and communication skills.
9. _____ Technology should always be used responsibly.
10. _____ The future will be shaped by the choices made by today's students.

Short Answer

11. Explain why adaptability is an important skill.
12. Describe one responsibility every future AI leader should have.
13. Give one example of how AI could improve education.
14. Why should students continue learning after graduation?
15. In your own words, explain what it means to be part of the AGI Generation.

Chapter 1 Quiz

Multiple Choice

Choose the best answer.

1. What makes today's students part of the AGI Generation?

A. They use only smartphones.

B. They are growing up during the development of advanced artificial intelligence.

C. They only study computer science.

D. They no longer need teachers.

2. Which human quality will remain important in an AI-powered world?

A. Curiosity

B. Empathy

C. Ethical decision-making

D. All of the above

3. Lifelong learning means:

A. Learning ends after graduation.

B. Continuing to learn throughout life.

C. Memorizing everything in school.

D. Avoiding new technology.

4. Why is critical thinking important when using AI?

A. AI is always perfect.

B. People should evaluate information before accepting it.

C. AI never makes mistakes.

D. Students should never question technology.

5. Which career may benefit from AI?

A. Doctors

B. Teachers

C. Engineers

D. All of the above

True or False

6. _____ AGI is expected to influence many areas of society.
7. _____ Human values become less important as AI improves.
8. _____ Students should continue developing creativity and communication skills.
9. _____ Technology should always be used responsibly.
10. _____ The future will be shaped by the choices made by today's students.

Short Answer

11. Explain why adaptability is an important skill.
12. Describe one responsibility every future AI leader should have.
13. Give one example of how AI could improve education.
14. Why should students continue learning after graduation?
15. In your own words, explain what it means to be part of the AGI Generation.

Chapter 2 – Part 1

Growing Up with Intelligent Machines

For most of human history, children grew up learning how to use the tools created by earlier generations. They learned how to write with pencils, calculate with paper, read printed books, and later use calculators and computers. Each new invention changed education a little at a time. Today's students, however, are growing up during a much larger transformation. They are becoming the first generation to live in a world where intelligent machines are becoming part of everyday life. This does not mean robots will replace people or that computers will make every decision. Instead, it means that artificial intelligence is becoming another tool that helps people solve problems, communicate, learn, and create. Understanding how to live and work alongside these intelligent systems is becoming an important part of modern education.

Many students interact with artificial intelligence long before they realize it. When a music app recommends a new song, AI is working behind the scenes. When a video streaming service suggests a movie, AI analyzes viewing habits to predict what someone might enjoy. Navigation apps calculate the fastest route by studying traffic conditions in real time. Email programs identify unwanted messages before they reach the inbox. Online stores recommend products based on previous purchases. Translation software helps people communicate across languages. Even smartphones use AI to recognize voices, organize photographs, improve camera images, and predict the next word while someone is typing. These examples show that artificial intelligence is already woven into everyday life. Most people simply use these tools without stopping to think about the technology that makes them possible.

As AI continues to improve, students will encounter intelligent systems in even more places. Schools are beginning to explore AI-powered tutoring programs that provide additional practice when students struggle with a topic. Libraries are organizing digital information more efficiently through intelligent search systems. Hospitals use AI to assist physicians in reviewing medical images. Scientists rely on AI to organize enormous amounts of research data that would take humans years to examine. Farmers use intelligent sensors to monitor crops and conserve water. Engineers design safer buildings with the help of computer simulations. Emergency responders analyze weather information to prepare for storms and natural disasters. These examples remind us that AI is not limited to one profession. It is becoming a valuable tool across nearly every field of study.

Growing up with intelligent machines also changes how students learn. In previous generations, finding information often required visiting a library, searching through books, and spending hours locating reliable sources. Those research skills remain valuable today, but intelligent technologies now allow students to search vast collections of information within seconds. This new capability saves time, but it also creates a new responsibility. Students must learn how to evaluate information carefully. Not every answer generated by an AI system is complete, accurate, or appropriate for every situation. Responsible learners compare multiple sources, verify important facts, and use their own judgment before accepting information as true. Learning how to think remains more important than simply finding answers quickly.

One of the greatest opportunities for the AGI Generation is learning how to ask better questions. Artificial intelligence often produces stronger responses when people provide thoughtful instructions and clear explanations. This means that curiosity becomes an even more valuable skill. Instead of asking simple questions, students can learn to ask deeper questions that explore causes, relationships, possibilities, and solutions. For example, instead of asking, "What is climate change?" a student might ask, "How can artificial intelligence help scientists reduce the effects of climate change while protecting communities?" Questions like these encourage investigation, creativity, and meaningful discussion. The quality of learning often begins with the quality of the questions students ask.

Another important change involves creativity. Some people mistakenly believe that AI will replace creativity, but the opposite may be true. Intelligent systems can generate ideas, organize information, create images, suggest designs, or draft written material, yet people still provide imagination, purpose, taste, emotion, and originality. An artist decides what story to tell. A teacher decides how to inspire students. A scientist decides which questions deserve investigation. A business owner decides which problems should be solved. AI can become a helpful assistant during the creative process, but human imagination remains the driving force behind meaningful innovation. Students who learn to combine creativity with intelligent technology will be well prepared for future opportunities.

Growing up with intelligent machines also teaches students the importance of digital responsibility. Technology should always be used in ways that respect other people. Students should protect their personal information, respect privacy, avoid spreading misinformation, and understand that technology can have both positive and negative effects depending on how it is used. Every new invention throughout history has required people to develop new habits and new responsibilities. The same is true for AI. Learning how to use intelligent systems ethically is just as important as learning how they operate.

As students become more familiar with AI, they may notice that intelligent systems sometimes make mistakes. A chatbot may misunderstand a question. A recommendation system may suggest something unrelated. A translation tool may choose the wrong word. These examples remind us that AI is a tool rather than a perfect source of knowledge. Human judgment remains essential. Students should never assume that a computer is always correct simply because it produces an answer quickly. Instead, they should develop habits of verification, reflection, and careful thinking. These habits strengthen learning and build confidence when using advanced technologies.

Teachers remain at the center of education, even as classrooms adopt new technologies. Great teachers do much more than explain lessons. They encourage curiosity, build confidence, answer difficult questions, recognize individual strengths, and create learning environments where students feel safe to explore new ideas. AI can support these efforts by providing additional practice, helping organize educational materials, or identifying concepts that need more review. However, technology cannot replace the encouragement, wisdom, empathy, and personal guidance that teachers provide every day. The strongest classrooms of the future will likely combine outstanding educators with thoughtfully designed AI tools that help every student succeed.

Families also play an important role in helping students grow up with intelligent machines. Parents and guardians can encourage healthy technology habits by discussing online safety, balancing screen time with other activities, and showing children how to use AI as a learning partner rather than a shortcut. Conversations at home about honesty, responsibility, respect, and kindness remain just as important as conversations about technology. Strong values provide the foundation that allows students to use powerful tools wisely throughout their lives.

Growing up with intelligent machines is not about depending on technology for every answer. It is about learning how to use technology thoughtfully while continuing to develop the uniquely human abilities that have always driven progress. Curiosity, integrity, creativity, collaboration, communication, and critical thinking will remain valuable no matter how advanced AI becomes. Students who develop these qualities while learning to work alongside intelligent systems will be prepared not only for future careers but also for lives filled with meaningful contributions to their families, communities, and the world.

The AGI Generation has the extraordinary opportunity to witness one of the greatest technological transformations in history. More importantly, this generation has the chance to guide that transformation with wisdom and purpose. Every lesson learned today prepares students to become tomorrow's innovators, educators, healthcare professionals, engineers, scientists, artists, entrepreneurs, and leaders. Growing up with intelligent machines is not simply about watching technology evolve. It is about growing into the kind of people who can ensure that technology always serves humanity in positive, responsible, and inspiring ways.

Chapter 2 – Part 2

Growing Up with Intelligent Machines

As intelligent technologies become more common, students are beginning to experience a world that looks different from the one their parents and grandparents knew while growing up. In previous generations, learning often happened only inside classrooms, libraries, or through conversations with family members and teachers. Today, knowledge is available almost everywhere. A student can watch a science demonstration from another country, take part in a virtual museum tour, practice speaking a new language with an AI assistant, or explore the surface of Mars through interactive simulations—all from a classroom or home computer. These opportunities allow learning to continue beyond the school day and encourage students to become lifelong explorers of knowledge rather than simply receivers of information.

Having access to so much information is exciting, but it also creates new responsibilities. Students must learn how to separate reliable information from inaccurate or misleading content. Artificial intelligence can generate answers quickly, yet speed does not always guarantee accuracy. Sometimes an AI system may misunderstand a question, rely on incomplete information, or produce an answer that sounds convincing but contains errors. For this reason, successful students learn to verify important facts by checking trusted sources, asking teachers for guidance, comparing information from multiple references, and thinking carefully before accepting an answer as true. Developing these habits helps students become thoughtful learners instead of passive consumers of information.

One of the most important skills for the AGI Generation will be learning how to work with AI instead of depending on AI. There is a significant difference between the two. Working with AI means using intelligent tools to organize ideas, discover information, analyze data, and improve learning while continuing to think independently. Depending on AI means allowing technology to do all the thinking, problem-solving, and decision-making. Students who rely entirely on AI may complete assignments more quickly, but they risk missing the opportunity to strengthen their own knowledge and abilities. The purpose of education has always been to develop human understanding, confidence, and judgment. AI should support those goals rather than replace them.

Consider the example of learning mathematics. An AI tutoring system may explain how to solve an equation, provide additional practice problems, and identify areas where a student needs more help. These are valuable learning supports. However, the student still needs to understand the reasoning behind the solution, practice independently, and develop confidence in solving similar problems without assistance. The same idea applies to writing, science, history, art, and every other subject. Intelligent tools can become excellent learning partners, but genuine understanding develops through practice, curiosity, reflection, and effort.

Another important change students will experience involves teamwork. Future workplaces will likely include teams made up of people with different backgrounds, skills, and experiences who also use intelligent technologies as part of their daily work. Students should begin preparing for this environment by learning how to communicate respectfully, listen to different viewpoints, share ideas openly, and solve problems together. Collaboration has always been valuable, but it becomes even more important in a world where people and intelligent systems work side by side. AI may contribute information or analyze data, but successful teams still depend on trust, cooperation, and strong relationships among people.

Growing up with intelligent machines also encourages students to think more globally. A student working on a science project may collaborate online with classmates in another state or even another country. Language translation tools make communication easier than ever before, allowing people from different cultures to exchange ideas and learn from one another. As intelligent technologies continue to improve, opportunities for international cooperation will expand. Future scientists may work together across continents to develop new medicines. Engineers may collaborate to create cleaner energy systems. Educators may share innovative teaching methods that help students around the world succeed. The AGI Generation will likely become one of the most internationally connected generations in history.

Although technology creates many opportunities, students should also remember the importance of maintaining healthy relationships away from screens. Face-to-face conversations, family meals, outdoor activities, sports, music, art, volunteering, and community service continue to play essential roles in personal growth. These experiences help people develop empathy, emotional intelligence, leadership, and communication skills that cannot be fully learned through technology alone. Artificial intelligence can support learning and productivity, but it should never replace meaningful human relationships. Strong friendships, supportive families, caring teachers, and engaged communities remain the foundation of a healthy and balanced life.

Ethics will become an increasingly important topic as intelligent technologies become more powerful. Students should begin asking thoughtful questions whenever they use AI. Is the information accurate? Does it respect people's privacy? Is it fair to everyone? Could someone be harmed by the way this technology is used? Responsible citizens understand that every technological advancement brings choices. The goal is not simply to build more advanced machines but to ensure those machines improve society while respecting human rights, dignity, and fairness. Ethical thinking allows students to become responsible innovators who consider both the benefits and possible consequences of new technologies.

The careers available to today's students may be very different from those available when they graduate. New industries will appear as AI continues to evolve. Some careers will involve designing intelligent systems, while others will focus on managing, improving, teaching, regulating, or safely using them. Many professions that exist today will also change. Doctors may spend more time caring for patients while AI assists with analyzing medical data. Teachers may personalize instruction more effectively with AI-powered educational tools. Engineers may design safer bridges, buildings, and transportation systems with the help of intelligent simulations. Farmers may use AI to improve crop production while protecting natural resources. Artists may combine traditional creativity with advanced digital tools to produce entirely new forms of expression. Nearly every profession will continue to value human creativity, ethical judgment, communication, and leadership.

This means students should focus on building strong foundational skills rather than preparing for only one specific job. Reading, writing, mathematics, science, communication, collaboration, creativity, and critical thinking will remain valuable regardless of how technology changes. Adaptability—the ability to learn new skills and adjust to changing situations—may become one of the most important abilities of all. A person who enjoys learning and is willing to grow throughout life will be better prepared for opportunities that do not yet exist.

The AGI Generation also has an opportunity to solve challenges that previous generations could not solve alone. Intelligent systems may help scientists understand diseases more quickly, improve disaster response, reduce pollution, protect endangered ecosystems, discover new materials, and make education more accessible to students around the world. However, these achievements will depend on people who understand both technology and humanity. Future innovators must ask not only, "Can we build this?" but also, "Should we build it?" and "How can we use it to improve people's lives?" These questions remind us that wisdom is just as important as intelligence.

Students should never underestimate the value of imagination. Many of today's technologies began as ideas that seemed impossible. Flying across oceans, speaking instantly with someone on another continent, carrying powerful computers in our pockets, and exploring distant planets were once considered dreams. Every major innovation began because someone imagined a better future and worked persistently to make it a reality. Artificial General Intelligence will also continue to develop because people are willing to imagine possibilities beyond what currently exists. The students reading this book may become the individuals who make the next great breakthrough in medicine, education, engineering, environmental protection, or scientific discovery.

As technology continues to advance, one truth remains unchanged: people give technology its purpose. A computer does not decide what goals humanity should pursue. A machine does not determine what is fair, compassionate, or just. Those decisions belong to people. Students who develop strong character, respect for others, curiosity, integrity, and a commitment to lifelong learning will help ensure that intelligent technologies strengthen society instead of weakening it. The future depends not only on smarter machines but also on wiser people.

Growing up with intelligent machines is one of the greatest educational opportunities in history. Never before have young people had access to so much knowledge, so many learning tools, and so many opportunities to collaborate with others across the world. These resources make it possible to dream bigger, learn faster, and solve problems that once seemed impossible. At the same time, they remind students that knowledge carries responsibility. Every choice made while using AI contributes to the kind of future society will create.

The AGI Generation is not defined simply by the technologies it uses. It is defined by the character of the people who choose to use those technologies with wisdom, compassion, honesty, and purpose. The students of today are becoming the leaders of tomorrow. They will inherit powerful intelligent systems, but they will also inherit the responsibility to guide those systems in ways that improve education, strengthen communities, advance scientific discovery, protect the environment, and create opportunities for future generations.

Growing up with intelligent machines is not the end of the human story. It is the beginning of a new chapter—one in which human intelligence and artificial intelligence work together to build a future filled with discovery, innovation, cooperation, and hope. Every student has a role to play in writing that chapter, and the journey has already begun.

Chapter 2 Summary

Growing Up with Intelligent Machines

Today's students are growing up during one of the most significant technological transformations in history. Artificial intelligence is becoming part of everyday life, helping people communicate, learn, solve problems, improve healthcare, conduct scientific research, and perform countless other tasks. As AI continues to advance toward more capable intelligent systems, students will have opportunities that no previous generation has experienced.

This chapter explained that intelligent machines are tools designed to assist people, not replace human intelligence. Students learned that AI is already being used in smartphones, navigation systems, online learning platforms, healthcare, agriculture, transportation, business, and education. Understanding how these systems work will help students become confident and responsible users of technology.

The chapter also emphasized that human thinking remains essential. While AI can organize information, recognize patterns, and generate ideas quickly, students must continue developing critical thinking, creativity, communication, ethical decision-making, and problem-solving skills.

These human abilities allow people to evaluate information, make wise decisions, and use technology responsibly.

Readers learned the importance of asking thoughtful questions, verifying AI-generated information, protecting personal privacy, and maintaining healthy relationships with family, friends, teachers, and their communities. Artificial intelligence should be viewed as a learning partner that supports education rather than replacing independent thinking.

Finally, the chapter encouraged students to prepare for a future where people and intelligent machines work together. Success in the AGI era will depend not only on technological knowledge but also on lifelong learning, adaptability, collaboration, integrity, compassion, and responsible leadership. The AGI Generation has an extraordinary opportunity to help build a future where intelligent technology improves lives while remaining guided by human values.

Chapter 2 Reflection

Growing Up with Intelligent Machines

Take time to think about what you learned in this chapter. Write complete answers using your own ideas and experiences.

1. What intelligent technologies do you already use during a typical day?
2. How has AI changed the way students learn compared to previous generations?
3. Why is it important to verify information generated by AI instead of automatically trusting every answer?
4. Explain the difference between working with AI and depending on AI.
5. Which human skill do you think will become most valuable in the future? Why?
6. How can families help students use AI responsibly at home?
7. Imagine your future career. How do you think intelligent machines may assist you in your work?
8. After reading this chapter, what is one new habit you would like to develop to become a responsible member of the AGI Generation?

Personal Reflection Activity

Write one paragraph describing how you hope to use artificial intelligence to improve your education, career, family, or community while continuing to develop your own knowledge, creativity, and character.

Chapter 2 Quiz

Multiple Choice

Choose the best answer.

1. Artificial intelligence is best described as:

A. A replacement for all human workers

B. A tool that can assist people with many different tasks

C. A machine that never makes mistakes

D. A technology used only by scientists

2. Which of the following is an example of AI in everyday life?

A. GPS navigation

B. Streaming recommendations

C. Voice assistants

D. All of the above

3. Why should students verify AI-generated information?

A. AI may occasionally produce inaccurate or incomplete information.

B. AI is always correct.

C. Teachers no longer matter.

D. Books should never be used.

4. Which human quality remains essential in an AI-powered world?

A. Ethical decision-making

B. Creativity

C. Critical thinking

D. All of the above

5. Lifelong learning means:

A. Learning only during school years.

B. Continuing to develop knowledge and skills throughout life.

C. Never changing careers.

D. Avoiding new technology.

True or False

6. _____ AI can support education, but teachers remain essential.
7. _____ Students should depend completely on AI to complete schoolwork.
8. _____ Human relationships continue to be important even as technology advances.
9. _____ Adaptability helps people prepare for future changes.
10. _____ The AGI Generation should use technology responsibly.

Short Answer

11. Explain why human judgment is still necessary when using AI.
12. Name two ways AI is helping improve education.
13. Why is collaboration an important future skill?
14. What is one responsibility every digital citizen should practice?
15. Describe one way you can prepare yourself for an AI-powered future.

Chapter 2 Answer Key

Multiple Choice

1. **B**
2. **D**
3. **A**
4. **D**
5. **B**

True or False

6. **True**
7. **False**
8. **True**
9. **True**
10. **True**

Short Answer (Sample Responses)

11. Human judgment helps people evaluate information, recognize mistakes, make ethical decisions, and determine whether AI-generated answers are accurate and appropriate.
12. AI can personalize learning, provide tutoring, identify learning gaps, organize educational resources, and assist teachers with lesson preparation.
13. Collaboration allows people to combine different ideas, skills, and experiences while working effectively with both other people and intelligent technologies.
14. Responsible digital citizens should protect personal information, verify facts, respect others online, use AI honestly, and think carefully before sharing information.
15. Students can prepare by strengthening critical thinking, communication, creativity, adaptability, ethical decision-making, technology skills, and committing to lifelong learning.

Chapter 3 – Part 1

Learning Beyond Memorization

For thousands of years, education has been one of humanity's greatest tools for building civilizations. Every generation has passed its knowledge to the next through storytelling, books, classrooms, experiments, and personal experience. Students have memorized multiplication tables, historical dates, scientific formulas, grammar rules, and vocabulary because remembering important information has always been part of learning. Memorization continues to have value today, but the world is changing. The rapid growth of artificial intelligence is encouraging educators to rethink what students should learn and how they should learn it. In the age of Artificial General Intelligence (AGI), education is expanding beyond memorizing facts toward developing the ability to think, create, solve problems, communicate, and continue learning throughout life.

Imagine trying to memorize every book in a large library. It would be impossible. Yet modern computers can store enormous amounts of information and retrieve it within seconds. Artificial intelligence can search millions of documents, recognize patterns, summarize articles, translate languages, and answer questions much faster than any person could search through books manually. If intelligent systems can quickly locate information, does memorization still matter? The answer is yes—but not in the same way it once did. Students still need foundational knowledge because understanding begins with knowing important facts and concepts. However, education is now placing greater emphasis on what students can do with that knowledge rather than simply how much they can remember.

Think about learning to ride a bicycle. Reading a book about bicycles is helpful, but no one truly learns to ride without practice. The same idea applies to education. Memorizing scientific terms does not automatically create a scientist. Memorizing historical dates does not automatically create a historian. Memorizing mathematical formulas does not automatically create an engineer. True learning happens when students apply knowledge to real situations, ask meaningful questions, solve unfamiliar problems, and explain ideas clearly to others. Knowledge becomes powerful when it is understood, not simply remembered.

This shift is changing classrooms around the world. Teachers are increasingly encouraging students to investigate real-world problems, participate in discussions, complete projects, work in teams, and think critically about complex issues. Instead of asking only, "What is the correct answer?" educators also ask, "How did you reach that conclusion?" and "Can you explain your reasoning?" These questions help students develop confidence in their own thinking. They also prepare students for a future where many problems will not have simple answers printed at the back of a textbook.

Critical thinking is becoming one of the most valuable skills in modern education. Critical thinking means carefully examining information before accepting it as true. It involves asking questions, looking for evidence, comparing different viewpoints, recognizing assumptions, and drawing thoughtful conclusions. Artificial intelligence can generate answers very quickly, but students must still evaluate whether those answers are accurate, complete, fair, and appropriate. A thoughtful learner understands that speed is useful, but wisdom requires careful analysis. Developing critical thinking allows students to become informed decision-makers instead of simply accepting whatever they are told.

Another important skill is creativity. Creativity is often misunderstood as something that belongs only to artists, musicians, or writers. In reality, creativity exists in every profession. Scientists use creativity when designing experiments. Engineers use creativity when inventing new technologies. Doctors use creativity when developing treatment plans for complex patients. Teachers use creativity when helping students understand difficult concepts. Entrepreneurs use creativity when solving problems that others have overlooked. Artificial intelligence can assist with generating ideas, organizing information, and exploring possibilities, but human imagination gives those ideas purpose and direction. Students who strengthen their creativity will be prepared to contribute original solutions in every field they enter.

Communication is another skill growing in importance. Throughout history, great discoveries have become meaningful only when people could explain them clearly. A brilliant scientific discovery has little impact if no one understands it. A creative invention cannot improve society if people cannot learn how to use it. Strong communication includes speaking, writing, listening, presenting ideas, asking thoughtful questions, and respecting different perspectives. As AI becomes more common, people who can explain complex ideas in simple language will become increasingly valuable. The ability to communicate clearly builds trust, encourages teamwork, and helps communities solve problems together.

Learning beyond memorization also encourages curiosity. Curious students rarely stop with the first answer they receive. They continue asking why, how, what if, and what comes next. Curiosity has driven nearly every important discovery in human history. Explorers crossed oceans because they wondered what lay beyond the horizon. Scientists studied the stars because they wanted to understand the universe. Engineers developed airplanes because they imagined humans flying through the sky. Curiosity transforms ordinary learning into extraordinary discovery. Artificial intelligence provides powerful tools for exploring questions, but curiosity provides the motivation to begin asking them in the first place.

Modern education is also teaching students how to become problem solvers. Every community faces challenges that require thoughtful solutions. Some problems involve protecting the environment. Others involve improving healthcare, transportation, education, agriculture, or public safety. Solving these problems requires more than memorized information. Students must analyze situations, gather evidence, consider multiple solutions, predict possible outcomes, and work together with others. Artificial intelligence can assist by organizing information and identifying patterns, but people must decide which solutions best serve individuals and society. Problem-solving combines knowledge, creativity, communication, and ethical judgment into one of the most valuable skills students can develop.

Ethics has become another essential part of learning in the AGI era. Powerful technology should always be guided by responsible people. Students must learn to ask questions that go beyond technical ability. Just because something can be built does not always mean it should be built. Responsible innovators think about privacy, fairness, safety, transparency, and the well-being of others before making important decisions. Ethical thinking helps students understand that every invention has consequences. By developing strong values alongside strong technical skills, the AGI Generation can help create intelligent systems that improve lives while protecting human dignity.

One of the most exciting aspects of learning today is that education is becoming more personalized. Students do not all learn in exactly the same way. Some understand concepts best through reading. Others prefer visual demonstrations, hands-on activities, discussions, experiments, or creative projects. AI-powered educational tools may help teachers identify different learning needs and provide additional support where necessary. However, personalized learning does not mean students work alone. Teachers remain the guides who inspire curiosity, encourage perseverance, answer difficult questions, and help students build confidence. Technology supports learning, but meaningful education continues to be built upon strong relationships between teachers and students.

As classrooms continue evolving, students should recognize that education is no longer focused only on preparing for the next test. It is preparing them for a lifetime of learning. New technologies will continue to appear throughout their careers, making adaptability one of the greatest strengths they can develop. Students who enjoy learning, welcome challenges, and remain curious throughout life will be ready for opportunities that cannot yet be predicted. Memorizing information may help someone pass an examination, but learning how to think, communicate, create, and solve problems prepares them for success long after graduation.

The AGI Generation stands at the beginning of a remarkable educational transformation. Students are not leaving traditional learning behind; they are building upon it. Foundational knowledge remains essential, but it is now joined by skills that help people apply knowledge wisely, creatively, and responsibly. This combination of knowledge and human understanding will allow today's students to become tomorrow's innovators, educators, scientists, engineers, healthcare professionals, entrepreneurs, and leaders. The future will belong not simply to those who know the most facts, but to those who know how to use knowledge to improve the world.

Chapter 3 – Part 2

Learning Beyond Memorization

As education continues to evolve, one of the biggest changes students will experience is a shift from simply collecting information to understanding how information connects across many different subjects. In the past, school subjects were often taught separately. Mathematics was studied during one class period, science during another, history later in the day, and language arts in between. Each subject was important on its own, but the modern world increasingly asks people to combine knowledge from many areas at the same time. Solving real-world problems rarely involves only one subject. Building a cleaner energy system requires science, engineering, mathematics, environmental studies, economics, communication, and teamwork. Developing a new medicine requires biology, chemistry, computer science, ethics, and healthcare. Artificial intelligence is encouraging education to become more connected because intelligent systems often analyze information from many different fields simultaneously.

Students who learn to make these connections become stronger thinkers. For example, imagine studying the history of ancient civilizations. Instead of memorizing only names and dates, students might explore how geography influenced settlement, how mathematics helped engineers construct buildings, how trade encouraged the exchange of ideas, and how communication shaped cultures over time. By connecting different subjects, learning becomes more meaningful because students begin to see how knowledge works together rather than existing as separate pieces. This deeper understanding helps learners remember concepts naturally because they understand the reasons behind them.

Artificial intelligence can support this type of connected learning by helping students discover relationships they may not have noticed before. A student researching ocean pollution, for example, may quickly locate scientific studies, environmental reports, historical information, engineering solutions, and economic data. AI can organize these resources efficiently, but students still decide which information is trustworthy, which evidence is most convincing, and which solutions appear most practical. The technology helps organize knowledge, while human thinking gives that knowledge meaning.

Another important goal of education is developing confidence. Confidence does not come from always knowing the correct answer. Instead, it develops when students are willing to face unfamiliar challenges without giving up. Every difficult math problem solved, every science experiment completed, every speech delivered, and every essay revised builds confidence through experience. Students gradually discover that learning is not about avoiding mistakes but about improving through effort. Artificial intelligence may provide hints, explanations, or additional examples, but personal confidence grows when learners overcome obstacles through persistence and practice.

This understanding changes how students should view mistakes. Many learners become discouraged when they answer a question incorrectly or struggle with a difficult assignment. However, mistakes often reveal exactly where learning is taking place. When a student discovers an error, the brain has an opportunity to correct misunderstanding and build stronger knowledge. Scientists often say that experiments producing unexpected results can be just as valuable as successful ones because they reveal new information. Engineers test prototypes repeatedly before creating reliable products. Authors revise their writing many times before publishing a finished book. Learning is a process of continuous improvement, and mistakes are often stepping stones toward mastery.

The AGI Generation should also recognize the importance of asking questions that have no single correct answer. Throughout school, students often encounter questions with clear solutions. What is seven multiplied by eight? What is the capital of a particular country? What year did an important historical event occur? These questions remain valuable because they build foundational knowledge. However, the future will increasingly present questions that require investigation, discussion, and thoughtful reasoning. How can artificial intelligence improve healthcare while protecting patient privacy? How should communities balance technological innovation with environmental protection? What responsibilities should developers have when designing powerful AI systems? Questions like these encourage students to think deeply, examine different viewpoints, and develop informed opinions based on evidence.

Collaboration becomes especially important when solving these kinds of complex challenges. No single person possesses all the knowledge required to solve every problem. Great discoveries often happen because people with different skills work together. A medical researcher may understand biology, while a computer scientist develops intelligent software and an engineer designs advanced equipment. Each person contributes valuable expertise. Students who learn to cooperate respectfully, listen carefully, and appreciate different perspectives will be well prepared for future careers where teamwork is essential. Artificial intelligence may support these teams by organizing information or analyzing data, but successful collaboration will always depend on human communication and mutual respect.

The ability to adapt is another defining characteristic of successful learners. Technology changes rapidly, and the careers available ten or twenty years from now may look very different from those that exist today. Some professions will evolve by incorporating intelligent systems into everyday work, while entirely new careers will appear that cannot yet be imagined. Instead of fearing change, students can prepare by becoming adaptable learners. Adaptability means remaining open to new ideas, learning new skills, and viewing change as an opportunity for growth. A curious and flexible learner is more likely to succeed in an environment where knowledge continues to expand.

Reading also remains one of the most powerful learning tools available. Even as intelligent technologies become more advanced, reading develops imagination, concentration, vocabulary, comprehension, and critical thinking. Books allow students to explore different cultures, historical periods, scientific discoveries, and human experiences. They encourage readers to think carefully, visualize ideas, and make connections between concepts. Artificial intelligence may help locate information quickly, but reading deeply helps students understand ideas at a much richer level. The strongest learners of the future will combine modern technology with strong reading habits.

Writing is equally important. Writing encourages students to organize their thoughts, explain their reasoning, defend their conclusions, and communicate ideas clearly. Whether composing essays, scientific reports, business proposals, or creative stories, writing strengthens thinking because it requires careful organization and reflection. AI may assist by suggesting improvements or identifying grammatical errors, but students should continue developing their own ability to express ideas with clarity and originality. Strong writers become strong thinkers because writing forces the mind to examine ideas carefully before sharing them with others.

Learning beyond memorization also means becoming an independent learner. Independent learners do not wait for someone else to tell them what to study. They ask questions, explore topics that interest them, seek reliable information, and continue learning even after assignments are complete. This habit of self-directed learning will become increasingly valuable throughout adulthood. As technology continues advancing, successful professionals will regularly update their knowledge, explore emerging discoveries, and adapt to new opportunities. Lifelong learning is no longer simply an educational goal—it is becoming an essential part of personal and professional success.

Perhaps the greatest lesson for the AGI Generation is that education is ultimately about preparing people, not simply preparing workers. Schools help students become knowledgeable citizens, thoughtful neighbors, ethical leaders, caring family members, and responsible members of society. Artificial intelligence can support learning in remarkable ways, but education continues to focus on developing character as well as knowledge. Honesty, kindness, perseverance, responsibility, respect, and compassion cannot be downloaded into the human mind. They are developed through daily choices, meaningful relationships, and a commitment to doing what is right.

As you continue your educational journey, remember that memorizing information is only the beginning of learning. True education teaches you how to ask meaningful questions, think independently, solve difficult problems, communicate clearly, collaborate with others, and continue growing throughout your life. These abilities will remain valuable regardless of how advanced technology becomes.

The AGI Generation has the opportunity to redefine what it means to be educated. Knowledge will always matter, but wisdom comes from knowing how to apply that knowledge to improve lives, strengthen communities, and solve the challenges of tomorrow. Students who embrace curiosity, creativity, critical thinking, adaptability, and lifelong learning will not simply prepare for the future—they will help create it.

Chapter 3 Summary

Learning Beyond Memorization

Education has always included memorizing important facts, formulas, vocabulary, and historical events. These foundational skills remain valuable because they help students build knowledge and understand the world around them. However, in the age of Artificial General Intelligence (AGI), education is expanding beyond memorization to emphasize deeper understanding, critical thinking, creativity, communication, collaboration, and lifelong learning.

This chapter explained that modern students have access to more information than any previous generation. Artificial intelligence can quickly organize, summarize, and retrieve information, but students must still evaluate whether that information is accurate, reliable, ethical, and useful. The ability to think independently has become just as important as the ability to remember facts.

Students also learned that real-world problems rarely belong to a single subject. Solving challenges in healthcare, environmental science, engineering, business, and education often requires knowledge from multiple disciplines. Learning how to connect ideas across different subjects helps students develop stronger problem-solving abilities and a deeper understanding of how the world works.

The chapter emphasized that mistakes are a natural and valuable part of learning. Every mistake provides an opportunity to improve understanding, strengthen skills, and build confidence. Instead of fearing failure, students should see challenges as opportunities for growth and continuous improvement.

Readers also explored the importance of communication, reading, writing, collaboration, adaptability, and independent learning. These skills prepare students to work successfully with intelligent technologies while continuing to develop the uniquely human qualities that AI cannot replace.

Finally, the chapter reminded students that education is not simply about preparing for tests or careers. It is about preparing thoughtful, ethical, curious, and responsible citizens who can use knowledge wisely to improve their communities and contribute positively to an intelligent world.

Chapter 3 Reflection

Learning Beyond Memorization

Take time to think about the ideas presented in this chapter. Write complete answers using your own thoughts and experiences.

1. Why is memorization still important even though AI can quickly find information?
2. Describe a time when understanding a concept was more helpful than simply memorizing it.
3. Why do you think critical thinking is becoming more valuable in the age of AI?
4. How can making mistakes actually improve learning?
5. Which human skill discussed in this chapter do you believe will help you the most in your future career? Explain why.

6. Why is it important to connect ideas from different school subjects when solving real-world problems?
7. How can AI help students learn without replacing their own thinking?
8. What does lifelong learning mean to you after reading this chapter?

Personal Reflection

Imagine yourself ten years from now. Describe the skills, habits, and attitudes you hope to develop that will help you succeed in a world where people and intelligent machines work together.

Chapter 3 Worksheet

Learning Beyond Memorization

Part A – Vocabulary

Define each term using your own words.

1. Memorization
2. Critical Thinking
3. Creativity
4. Adaptability
5. Collaboration
6. Lifelong Learning
7. Independent Learning
8. Communication
9. Problem Solving
10. Human Judgment

Part B – Comprehension Questions

Answer each question using complete sentences.

1. Why is education changing in the AGI era?
2. How does understanding differ from memorization?
3. Why should students verify information produced by AI?
4. Give two examples of how different school subjects work together to solve real-world problems.
5. Why are communication skills important for future careers?
6. How do mistakes help students become stronger learners?

7. What does it mean to become an independent learner?
8. Why should education focus on developing both knowledge and character?

Part C – Critical Thinking

Answer each question in one or two well-developed paragraphs.

1. Imagine your school removes all memorization from every class. What would students gain, and what important skills might they lose?
2. Describe a real-world problem that requires science, mathematics, communication, teamwork, and ethical decision-making to solve.
3. Explain how AI can support education while teachers continue serving as the leaders of the classroom.

Part D – Personal Learning Plan

Create your own "Learning Beyond Memorization" action plan.

Write down:

• Five skills you want to strengthen this year.

• Three subjects you would like to understand more deeply.

• Three ways you can improve your critical thinking.

• Three habits that will help you become a lifelong learner.

• One personal goal you will accomplish before the end of the school year.

Chapter 3 Worksheet

Learning Beyond Memorization

Part A – Vocabulary

Define each term using your own words.

1. Memorization
2. Critical Thinking
3. Creativity

4. Adaptability
5. Collaboration
6. Lifelong Learning
7. Independent Learning
8. Communication
9. Problem Solving
10. Human Judgment

Part B – Comprehension Questions

Answer each question using complete sentences.

1. Why is education changing in the AGI era?
2. How does understanding differ from memorization?
3. Why should students verify information produced by AI?
4. Give two examples of how different school subjects work together to solve real-world problems.
5. Why are communication skills important for future careers?
6. How do mistakes help students become stronger learners?
7. What does it mean to become an independent learner?
8. Why should education focus on developing both knowledge and character?

Part C – Critical Thinking

Answer each question in one or two well-developed paragraphs.

1. Imagine your school removes all memorization from every class. What would students gain, and what important skills might they lose?
2. Describe a real-world problem that requires science, mathematics, communication, teamwork, and ethical decision-making to solve.
3. Explain how AI can support education while teachers continue serving as the leaders of the classroom.

Part D – Personal Learning Plan

Create your own "Learning Beyond Memorization" action plan.

Write down:

• Five skills you want to strengthen this year.

• Three subjects you would like to understand more deeply.

• Three ways you can improve your critical thinking.

• Three habits that will help you become a lifelong learner.

• One personal goal you will accomplish before the end of the school year.

Chapter 3 Quiz

Multiple Choice

Choose the best answer.

1. What is the main message of this chapter?

A. Memorization is no longer useful.

B. Education should focus only on AI.

C. Students should combine knowledge with thinking, creativity, and problem solving.

D. Technology replaces learning.

2. Critical thinking helps students:

A. Accept every answer without questioning it.

B. Evaluate information carefully before making decisions.

C. Avoid learning difficult subjects.

D. Memorize faster.

3. Which skill is important for solving real-world problems?

A. Collaboration

B. Creativity

C. Communication

D. All of the above

4. Lifelong learning means:

A. Learning ends after graduation.

B. Continuing to develop knowledge and skills throughout life.

C. Memorizing every textbook.

D. Avoiding new technology.

5. AI should be viewed as:

A. A replacement for human thinking.

B. A learning partner that supports education.

C. A substitute for teachers.

D. A system that never makes mistakes.

True or False

6. _____ Understanding is more valuable than memorizing facts alone.
7. _____ Students should stop asking questions because AI has all the answers.
8. _____ Reading and writing continue to strengthen thinking skills.
9. _____ Making mistakes can help students learn and improve.
10. _____ Character remains important even as technology becomes more advanced.

Short Answer

11. Explain the difference between memorization and understanding.
12. Why is adaptability important in an AI-powered world?
13. Describe one way AI can support classroom learning.
14. Why should students become independent learners?
15. In your own words, explain what it means to learn beyond memorization.

Chapter 3 Answer Key

Multiple Choice

1. **C**
2. **B**
3. **D**
4. **B**
5. **B**

True or False

6. **True**
7. **False**
8. **True**
9. **True**
10. **True**

Short Answer (Sample Responses)

11. Memorization involves remembering information, while understanding means knowing how to explain, apply, analyze, and use that knowledge in different situations.
12. Adaptability helps people adjust to changing technologies, new careers, new ideas, and lifelong learning opportunities.
13. AI can provide personalized tutoring, generate practice activities, organize information, identify learning gaps, and support teachers with instructional resources.
14. Independent learners continue exploring knowledge on their own, ask thoughtful questions, seek reliable information, and continue learning throughout life.
15. Learning beyond memorization means developing critical thinking, creativity, communication, collaboration, ethical decision-making, and problem-solving skills so knowledge can be applied wisely in real-life situations.

Chapter 4 – Part 1

The New Skills Every Student Will Need

Education has always prepared young people for the future, but the future has never changed as quickly as it is changing today. Throughout history, students learned the knowledge and skills needed for the world they expected to enter as adults. Farmers learned about agriculture, merchants learned about trade, craftsmen mastered specialized skills, and later generations learned how to work with machines, computers, and the internet. Today, students are preparing for a future that is still being created. Artificial intelligence is advancing rapidly, new careers are appearing, and intelligent technologies are becoming part of nearly every profession. Because of these changes, students will need more than academic knowledge alone. They will need a new collection of human skills that will help them succeed in an intelligent world.

One of the most valuable skills students can develop is adaptability. Adaptability is the ability to adjust when situations change. Throughout life, people experience new schools, new jobs, new technologies, and new responsibilities. Those who adapt well are more likely to see change as an opportunity rather than as a problem. The AGI Generation will almost certainly experience careers that continue evolving throughout their working lives. Software will improve, industries will transform, and entirely new professions will emerge. Students who remain curious, flexible, and willing to learn will be prepared to grow alongside these changes instead of being overwhelmed by them.

Adaptability does not mean abandoning everything that has been learned. Instead, it means building upon existing knowledge while remaining open to new ideas. Imagine a bridge that is strong enough to support heavy traffic but flexible enough to move slightly during strong winds or earthquakes. That flexibility makes the bridge safer, not weaker. In the same way, adaptable learners remain confident while adjusting to new situations. They understand that learning never truly ends and that every new experience provides another opportunity to improve.

Another essential skill is critical thinking. In an age where information is available almost instantly, students must know how to evaluate what they read, hear, and see. Critical thinking involves asking thoughtful questions, examining evidence, comparing different viewpoints, and reaching conclusions based on facts rather than assumptions. Artificial intelligence can produce answers quickly, but students should always ask whether those answers are accurate, complete, and appropriate. Developing strong critical thinking skills allows people to become informed decision-makers who understand not only what to think about but also how to think carefully before making important choices.

Closely connected to critical thinking is problem-solving. Every profession depends on people who can recognize challenges, analyze situations, and develop practical solutions. A nurse solving a patient's medical concern, an engineer designing a safer bridge, a teacher helping a struggling student, or an entrepreneur creating a new business all rely on problem-solving skills. AI may assist by analyzing information or suggesting possible solutions, but people remain responsible for making final decisions. Students who enjoy solving puzzles, exploring different approaches, and learning from mistakes are developing abilities that will serve them throughout their lives.

Communication continues to be one of the most important skills in every career. Regardless of how advanced technology becomes, people must still explain ideas, listen carefully, ask meaningful questions, write clearly, and work respectfully with others. Good communication builds trust and reduces misunderstandings. It also allows teams to solve problems more effectively. As intelligent systems become common in schools and workplaces, people who can explain complicated ideas in simple language will become increasingly valuable. Teachers, doctors, scientists, business leaders, engineers, and public officials all depend on communication to help others understand important information.

Listening is an important part of communication that is sometimes overlooked. Many people think communication means speaking well, but effective communicators also know how to listen carefully. Listening allows people to understand different perspectives, recognize concerns, and learn from the experiences of others. Students who become active listeners often build stronger friendships, perform better during group projects, and become more effective leaders. Intelligent machines may process spoken language, but they do not replace the human ability to listen with empathy and genuine understanding.

Creativity is another skill that will become increasingly valuable. Creativity is not limited to painting, music, or writing stories. It is the ability to imagine new possibilities, improve existing ideas, and develop original solutions. Every invention in history began as someone's idea. The first airplane, the first personal computer, and the first smartphone all started with individuals who imagined something that did not yet exist. Artificial intelligence can help generate possibilities, but people provide the imagination, purpose, and vision that turn ideas into meaningful innovations. Students who practice creative thinking learn to ask, "What if?" instead of assuming that every problem has only one solution.

Closely connected to creativity is curiosity. Curious students are lifelong learners because they enjoy discovering how things work. They ask questions, perform experiments, read widely, and explore topics beyond classroom assignments. Curiosity transforms learning from a task into an adventure. Some of the world's greatest discoveries began with simple questions that many people ignored. Why do planets move the way they do? How can diseases be treated more effectively? What causes weather patterns to change? Students who remain curious throughout life are more likely to discover opportunities that others overlook.

The AGI Generation will also need strong collaboration skills. Modern challenges often require teams with different areas of expertise working together toward a common goal. Scientists collaborate with engineers. Doctors work with nurses, pharmacists, and researchers. Teachers cooperate with parents, counselors, and administrators. Business leaders work alongside designers, marketers, and technology specialists. Artificial intelligence may contribute valuable information, but successful teamwork depends on respect, trust, cooperation, and shared responsibility. Students who learn to contribute ideas while appreciating the strengths of others will be prepared for future workplaces built upon collaboration.

Another essential quality is resilience. Resilience is the ability to recover from setbacks and continue moving forward after disappointment or difficulty. Every successful person encounters obstacles. Athletes lose competitions before winning championships. Scientists conduct experiments that fail before making important discoveries. Authors revise books many times before publication. Entrepreneurs experience setbacks before building successful companies. Students who develop resilience understand that temporary failure does not define their future. Instead, challenges become opportunities to improve skills, gain experience, and build confidence.

As students prepare for the intelligent world ahead, they should remember that technology continues to change, but strong character remains timeless. Qualities such as honesty, responsibility, kindness, respect, integrity, and compassion have guided successful leaders for generations. Artificial intelligence may become increasingly capable, but it cannot replace the trust that develops when people consistently demonstrate good character. Communities become stronger when individuals choose to use knowledge responsibly and treat others with fairness and respect.

Education in the AGI era is no longer focused only on preparing students for their first job after graduation. It is preparing them for decades of learning, adapting, growing, and leading. The students who succeed will not necessarily be those who memorize the most information. They will be the individuals who combine knowledge with curiosity, communication, creativity, resilience, adaptability, collaboration, and ethical decision-making. These human skills will remain valuable regardless of how intelligent technology becomes because they reflect the qualities that allow people to improve their communities and contribute meaningfully to society.

The AGI Generation has an exciting opportunity. Instead of fearing rapid technological change, students can prepare themselves by strengthening the abilities that intelligent machines cannot replace. These abilities will help them become thoughtful leaders, responsible innovators, trusted professionals, and compassionate citizens who understand that technology achieves its greatest value when guided by human wisdom.

Chapter 4 – Part 2

The New Skills Every Student Will Need

As technology becomes more intelligent, one surprising truth is becoming clear: the most valuable skills of the future may be the ones that make us the most human. Computers can perform calculations in a fraction of a second, organize enormous amounts of information, and recognize patterns that people might overlook. However, they do not experience emotions, build meaningful relationships, or understand the personal experiences that shape every individual. This is why emotional intelligence is becoming one of the most important skills students can develop. Emotional intelligence is the ability to recognize, understand, and manage emotions while also understanding the feelings of others. It helps people communicate respectfully, solve disagreements peacefully, and build strong relationships in school, at work, and in their communities.

Imagine two students working together on an important science project. Both students are intelligent and hardworking, but they disagree about how to complete the assignment. One student becomes frustrated and refuses to listen to other ideas. The second student remains calm, asks questions, and tries to understand the other person's point of view before suggesting a solution. Which student is more likely to build a successful partnership? In many situations, emotional intelligence becomes just as important as academic knowledge. Future employers, educators, and community leaders will continue looking for individuals who can cooperate respectfully, solve conflicts, and encourage teamwork.

Decision-making is another essential skill that students will need throughout their lives. Every day people make decisions, both large and small. Some choices involve school assignments, friendships, or managing time. Later in life, decisions may involve careers, finances, healthcare, family responsibilities, or business opportunities. Artificial intelligence may provide useful information to support these choices, but people remain responsible for making the final decision. Good decision-making requires gathering reliable information, considering different options, thinking about possible consequences, and selecting the choice that best reflects personal values and ethical principles. Students who practice thoughtful decision-making today will become more confident leaders tomorrow.

Time management is also becoming increasingly important in an age filled with constant information and digital distractions. Students have access to educational videos, social media, games, streaming entertainment, online discussions, and countless other activities competing for their attention. Learning how to organize time wisely helps students balance schoolwork, family responsibilities, hobbies, exercise, friendships, and personal interests. Successful learners understand that every hour spent wisely contributes to long-term success. Managing time effectively also reduces stress because important responsibilities are completed before they become overwhelming.

Self-discipline supports good time management. Self-discipline means choosing to do what is important even when it is difficult or less enjoyable in the moment. A student who studies for tomorrow's exam instead of postponing preparation demonstrates self-discipline. An athlete who continues practicing after making mistakes demonstrates self-discipline. A musician who rehearses regularly instead of waiting until the day before a performance demonstrates self-discipline. These habits build confidence because they show students that success often comes from consistent effort rather than natural talent alone.

Digital citizenship has become another important life skill. As students spend more time using computers, smartphones, and online learning tools, they also become members of digital communities. Responsible digital citizens understand that their actions online affect real people. They protect personal information, respect copyright, avoid cyberbullying, communicate politely, verify information before sharing it, and use technology honestly. Artificial intelligence creates exciting opportunities, but it also increases the importance of responsible online behavior. Every message, image, video, or piece of information shared online contributes to a person's digital reputation. Students should remember that responsible behavior online reflects the same values expected in face-to-face interactions.

Another skill that will become increasingly valuable is adaptability in learning itself. New technologies, scientific discoveries, and professional practices will continue appearing throughout students' lives. Graduating from school will no longer mark the end of education. Instead, it will represent the beginning of continuous learning. Professionals in medicine regularly study new treatments. Engineers learn new design methods. Teachers update instructional strategies. Business leaders study changing markets. Lifelong learning allows individuals to remain knowledgeable, competitive, and prepared for new opportunities. Students who enjoy learning today will find it easier to adapt to tomorrow's changing world.

Leadership is also evolving. Many people imagine leaders as individuals who simply give instructions or supervise others. Modern leadership is much broader than that. Effective leaders inspire confidence, encourage cooperation, solve problems, accept responsibility, and help others succeed. They understand that leadership is based on service rather than authority. In classrooms, leadership may involve helping classmates understand difficult concepts or encouraging others during group projects. In future workplaces, leadership may involve guiding teams through technological changes while ensuring that every person feels respected and valued. Intelligent machines can provide information, but leadership remains deeply human because it depends upon trust, integrity, empathy, and vision.

Ethical leadership is especially important in the AGI era. Future leaders may help make decisions about how intelligent systems are designed, tested, and used in society. They will need to think carefully about fairness, privacy, transparency, accountability, and public safety. For example, if an AI system helps doctors diagnose illnesses, leaders must ensure that the technology works accurately for people from different backgrounds and communities. If AI assists schools with educational decisions, fairness and equal opportunity must remain priorities. Students who develop strong ethical values today will be better prepared to make responsible decisions tomorrow.

Financial literacy is another valuable life skill that students should begin developing. Understanding how money works helps people make informed decisions about saving, budgeting, investing, and spending responsibly. As AI becomes more common in banking, business, and personal finance, individuals will benefit from understanding both technology and basic financial principles. Intelligent systems may provide recommendations, but people must still decide how to manage resources wisely to achieve their personal goals and support their families.

One quality that connects all these skills is confidence. Confidence grows through preparation, experience, and persistence. It does not mean believing that mistakes will never happen. Instead, confidence means believing that challenges can be overcome through learning and effort. Students who continue asking questions, practicing new skills, accepting constructive feedback, and working toward meaningful goals gradually develop confidence that lasts throughout life. Every successful scientist, teacher, engineer, entrepreneur, healthcare professional, artist, and leader once began as a learner willing to improve one step at a time.

The future workplace will reward individuals who combine technical knowledge with strong human skills. Employers will continue looking for people who communicate effectively, solve problems creatively, collaborate respectfully, adapt to change, manage projects responsibly, and demonstrate ethical leadership. AI may automate some routine tasks, but it will also create opportunities for people to focus on work that requires imagination, compassion, judgment, and innovation. Students who develop these abilities will remain valuable regardless of how technology evolves.

Perhaps the most encouraging message for the AGI Generation is that every one of these skills can be learned and strengthened. No one is born with perfect communication skills, outstanding leadership abilities, or exceptional resilience. These qualities develop through practice, experience, reflection, and a willingness to improve. Every classroom discussion, group project, volunteer activity, athletic competition, musical performance, science experiment, and family responsibility provides another opportunity to grow. Learning extends far beyond textbooks because every life experience teaches valuable lessons.

As the world enters the age of Artificial General Intelligence, education continues to serve the same important purpose it has always served: helping people become capable, responsible, and compassionate human beings. The tools may become more advanced, but the mission remains unchanged. Schools prepare students not only for careers but also for citizenship, leadership, service, and lifelong learning.

The AGI Generation has the opportunity to become one of the most skilled generations in history. By combining academic knowledge with adaptability, emotional intelligence, communication, creativity, ethical leadership, resilience, curiosity, and lifelong learning, today's students can build futures filled with opportunity and purpose. These are the skills that will help them lead confidently in an intelligent world while ensuring that technology always remains a tool that serves humanity.

When future historians look back at this generation, they may not remember it simply because intelligent machines became more powerful. They may remember it because a generation of students learned that the greatest strength in an AI-powered world was not found inside a computer, but inside the human mind and heart.

Chapter 4 Summary

The New Skills Every Student Will Need

The world is changing rapidly because of advances in artificial intelligence, automation, and digital technology. While academic subjects such as mathematics, science, language arts, and history remain essential, students must also develop human skills that will help them succeed in an intelligent world. These skills prepare students not only for future careers but also for leadership, responsible citizenship, and lifelong learning.

This chapter introduced several important skills that will become increasingly valuable during the AGI era. Adaptability helps students adjust to new technologies, changing careers, and unexpected challenges. Critical thinking allows learners to evaluate information carefully before making decisions. Creativity encourages innovation by helping students imagine new ideas and solve problems in original ways. Communication and collaboration strengthen teamwork and build meaningful relationships in school, the workplace, and the community.

Students also learned about emotional intelligence, which includes understanding emotions, managing stress, showing empathy, and working respectfully with others. These qualities help build trust and improve leadership. Decision-making, time management, and self-discipline were presented as important life skills that allow students to make responsible choices and achieve long-term goals.

The chapter explained the importance of digital citizenship by encouraging students to use technology responsibly, protect privacy, communicate respectfully, and verify information before sharing it. Lifelong learning was introduced as a mindset that prepares people to continue developing new knowledge and skills throughout their lives.

Finally, the chapter emphasized that strong character remains one of the greatest strengths a person can possess. Honesty, integrity, kindness, compassion, responsibility, and ethical leadership will continue guiding successful individuals regardless of how advanced technology becomes. The AGI Generation will succeed by combining technical knowledge with these timeless human values.

Chapter 4 Reflection

The New Skills Every Student Will Need

Take time to think about the lessons from this chapter. Answer each question using complete sentences and your own ideas.

1. Which future-ready skill discussed in this chapter do you believe is your greatest strength? Why?
2. Which skill would you most like to improve over the next year? Explain your answer.
3. Why is emotional intelligence just as important as academic intelligence?
4. Describe a time when adaptability helped you overcome a challenge.
5. Why should future leaders understand both technology and ethics?
6. How does self-discipline help students achieve their goals?
7. In what ways can digital citizenship make the internet a safer place for everyone?
8. Why do you think lifelong learning will become even more important as AI continues to evolve?

Personal Reflection

Imagine yourself twenty years from now. Describe the personal qualities and skills you hope people will recognize in you. Explain how those qualities will help you contribute positively to your family, career, and community in an AI-powered world.

Chapter 4 Worksheet

The New Skills Every Student Will Need

Part A – Vocabulary

Define each term using your own words.

1. Adaptability
2. Emotional Intelligence
3. Critical Thinking
4. Collaboration
5. Creativity
6. Self-Discipline
7. Digital Citizenship
8. Ethical Leadership
9. Lifelong Learning
10. Resilience

Part B – Comprehension Questions

Answer using complete sentences.

1. Why is adaptability considered one of the most important future skills?
2. How does critical thinking help students use AI responsibly?
3. Why is communication important even when intelligent machines become more advanced?
4. Explain the difference between creativity and memorization.
5. How does emotional intelligence improve teamwork?
6. Why should students continue learning after graduation?
7. What responsibilities do ethical leaders have when using AI?
8. How does self-discipline contribute to long-term success?

Part C – Critical Thinking

Write one or two paragraphs for each question.

1. Imagine two students have the same academic grades. One has excellent communication and teamwork skills while the other struggles to work with others. Which student is likely to be more successful in the workplace? Explain your reasoning.
2. If you were creating a new high school curriculum for the AGI Generation, which five human skills would you require every student to develop? Explain why you chose them.
3. Describe a future career that combines artificial intelligence with strong human skills such as empathy, creativity, leadership, or communication.

Part D – My Future Skills Plan

Create your own personal development plan.

Write:

- Five human skills you want to strengthen.
- Three leadership qualities you admire.
- Three habits you will practice every week.
- Three examples of responsible digital citizenship.
- One long-term goal you hope to achieve by continuing to learn throughout your life.

Chapter 4 Quiz

Multiple Choice

Choose the best answer.

1. According to this chapter, future success depends on:

A. Memorizing more facts than everyone else.

B. Combining academic knowledge with strong human skills.

C. Avoiding technology.

D. Letting AI make every decision.

2. Adaptability means:

A. Refusing to change.

B. Adjusting to new situations and continuing to learn.

C. Memorizing every new technology.

D. Working alone.

3. Emotional intelligence includes:

A. Understanding and managing emotions.

B. Showing empathy toward others.

C. Building healthy relationships.

D. All of the above.

4. Which skill helps students evaluate AI-generated information?

A. Critical Thinking

B. Memorization

C. Guessing

D. Speed Reading

5. Lifelong learning means:

A. Education ends after high school.

B. Continuing to develop knowledge and skills throughout life.

C. Avoiding new ideas.

D. Learning only when required by an employer.

True or False

6. _____ Strong communication skills remain valuable in the AGI era.
7. _____ Artificial intelligence replaces the need for ethical leadership.
8. _____ Self-discipline helps students reach long-term goals.
9. _____ Digital citizens should protect privacy and communicate respectfully online.
10. _____ Human character becomes less important as technology improves.

Short Answer

11. Why is adaptability important for future careers?
12. Explain why emotional intelligence is important in teamwork.
13. Describe one example of responsible digital citizenship.
14. Why does lifelong learning prepare people for an AI-powered future?
15. In your own words, explain why human skills remain valuable even as artificial intelligence becomes more capable.

Chapter 4 Answer Key

Multiple Choice

1. **B**
2. **B**
3. **D**
4. **A**
5. **B**

True or False

6. **True**
7. **False**
8. **True**
9. **True**
10. **False**

Short Answer (Sample Responses)

11. Adaptability allows people to adjust to new technologies, changing industries, evolving careers, and unexpected challenges while continuing to grow throughout life.
12. Emotional intelligence helps people understand emotions, communicate respectfully, resolve conflicts peacefully, and build strong relationships with teammates and coworkers.
13. Responsible digital citizenship includes protecting personal information, verifying facts before sharing them, respecting others online, avoiding cyberbullying, and using AI honestly and ethically.
14. Lifelong learning helps people continue developing new knowledge and skills as technology, careers, and society continue to evolve.
15. Human skills such as creativity, communication, empathy, leadership, ethical judgment, collaboration, and critical thinking guide how technology is used. These qualities allow

people to make wise decisions, solve complex problems, and ensure that AI benefits individuals and society.

Chapter 5 – Part 1

Working Alongside Artificial Intelligence

For many years, people have asked an important question: **Will artificial intelligence replace human workers?** It is a question that often appears in news reports, television programs, classrooms, and conversations around the world. Some people worry that intelligent machines will take over every job, while others believe AI will create exciting new opportunities. The truth is more balanced than either extreme. Throughout history, technology has changed the way people work, but it has also created entirely new industries, careers, and opportunities that earlier generations could not have imagined. The AGI Generation will not simply witness these changes—they will become the professionals who help shape them.

Long before computers existed, most people worked on farms. Families planted crops, cared for animals, and produced much of what they needed to survive. As machines became more advanced during the Industrial Revolution, factories introduced equipment that could perform many physical tasks faster than people. Some jobs disappeared, but new careers appeared in manufacturing, engineering, transportation, and business. Decades later, computers transformed offices by replacing typewriters, filing cabinets, and paper records with digital systems. Once again, some jobs changed dramatically, but new professions such as software development, information technology, cybersecurity, digital marketing, and computer engineering emerged. History shows that technological progress changes work rather than ending the need for human workers.

Artificial intelligence represents another major transformation. Unlike earlier machines that mainly performed physical work, AI assists with thinking tasks. It can organize information, recognize patterns, translate languages, summarize reports, analyze medical images, recommend products, predict equipment failures, and answer questions within seconds. These abilities allow people to complete many routine tasks more efficiently. However, efficiency alone does not replace human judgment. Someone must still decide which goals matter, evaluate the quality of results, communicate with other people, solve unexpected problems, and make ethical decisions. These responsibilities continue to depend upon human intelligence.

Understanding the difference between **automation** and **augmentation** is important. Automation occurs when technology performs a task with little or no human involvement. For example, an automatic washing machine cleans clothes after the user selects the settings. Modern factories use robotic equipment to perform repetitive manufacturing tasks with remarkable precision. Automatic inventory systems track products in warehouses. These technologies reduce repetitive work and improve efficiency.

Augmentation is different. Augmentation means technology helps people perform their jobs better rather than replacing them. A doctor may use AI to review thousands of medical images more quickly, but the physician still speaks with the patient, considers medical history, explains treatment options, and makes the final diagnosis. A teacher may use AI to generate practice activities for different learning levels, but the teacher still motivates students, answers questions, encourages curiosity, and builds relationships that technology cannot replace. An engineer may use intelligent software to test hundreds of design possibilities, but the engineer decides which design best meets safety requirements and community needs. In these situations, people and intelligent systems become partners.

Healthcare offers one of the clearest examples of this partnership. Hospitals produce enormous amounts of information every day, including laboratory results, medical images, patient records, research findings, and treatment recommendations. AI can analyze this information much faster than any individual could accomplish alone. It may identify patterns that help doctors recognize diseases earlier or recommend possible treatment options based on similar cases. However, healthcare involves much more than analyzing data. Patients often feel worried, frightened, or uncertain. They need healthcare professionals who listen carefully, answer questions with compassion, respect cultural differences, and provide emotional support. Technology contributes valuable information, but healing remains a deeply human experience built upon trust and empathy.

Education is another profession where AI will likely become an important partner rather than a replacement. Every classroom contains students with different strengths, interests, learning styles, and goals. Some students master new concepts quickly, while others benefit from additional explanations and practice. AI-powered educational tools may help teachers identify learning gaps, recommend personalized activities, and organize instructional materials more efficiently. These tools save valuable time, allowing teachers to focus on what matters most: inspiring curiosity, encouraging confidence, guiding discussions, and helping students become thoughtful citizens. Great teachers do much more than deliver information. They help students discover their potential and believe in their ability to succeed.

Engineering also demonstrates the growing partnership between people and intelligent systems. Modern engineers use advanced software to simulate earthquakes, analyze traffic patterns, design energy-efficient buildings, and test thousands of possible solutions before constructing a final product. Artificial intelligence can rapidly evaluate enormous amounts of technical information, helping engineers identify problems that might otherwise remain hidden. Yet engineering decisions also involve public safety, environmental responsibility, financial planning, and long-term community needs. Human engineers combine technical expertise with ethical judgment to ensure that technology improves people's lives safely and responsibly.

Business leaders are discovering similar opportunities. AI can study customer preferences, forecast market trends, organize financial information, and improve supply chain operations. These capabilities help businesses make informed decisions more quickly. However, successful businesses depend on much more than data. They depend on leadership, customer relationships, innovation, teamwork, communication, and ethical decision-making. Customers continue choosing businesses they trust. Employees continue working hardest for leaders who treat them with fairness and respect. AI strengthens business operations, but people create the culture that determines long-term success.

The legal profession is another example of changing work. Lawyers spend countless hours reviewing documents, researching previous court decisions, and preparing legal arguments. AI can assist by organizing large collections of legal information, identifying relevant cases, and summarizing complex documents. This allows attorneys to spend more time advising clients, negotiating agreements, and representing people fairly within the legal system. The law requires careful interpretation, ethical reasoning, and understanding of human circumstances—qualities that depend upon thoughtful professionals rather than computer programs alone.

Agriculture has also entered the age of intelligent technology. Farmers use drones, sensors, satellite images, and AI systems to monitor crops, predict weather conditions, identify plant diseases, and manage irrigation more efficiently. These tools help conserve water, reduce waste, and improve harvests while protecting natural resources. Even with these technological advances, farming continues to require experience, observation, planning, and decision-making. Farmers understand their land, respond to changing environmental conditions, and make choices that affect both food production and environmental sustainability.

As students consider future careers, they should recognize that nearly every profession will evolve alongside intelligent technology. Instead of asking whether AI will eliminate a particular job, a more useful question is, **"How will this profession change, and what new skills will people need?"** This question encourages students to prepare for growth rather than fear change. Every career will continue requiring human qualities such as communication, creativity, adaptability, collaboration, integrity, and leadership. These abilities allow professionals to work effectively with intelligent systems while continuing to serve other people.

One of the greatest opportunities for the AGI Generation is learning how to become excellent partners with artificial intelligence. This partnership requires technical knowledge, but it also requires wisdom. Students must understand when AI can improve efficiency, when human judgment should guide important decisions, and when ethical concerns require careful discussion. Developing this balance will prepare future professionals to use intelligent technology responsibly while maintaining the human values that strengthen every community.

Working alongside artificial intelligence does not reduce the importance of human beings. Instead, it highlights the qualities that make people unique. Machines may become increasingly capable of processing information, but people continue imagining new possibilities, building meaningful relationships, leading organizations, caring for others, solving unexpected problems, and making decisions guided by ethics and compassion. These abilities have always driven human progress, and they will become even more valuable as intelligent technology continues to advance.

The workplace of tomorrow will not belong to humans alone or machines alone. It will belong to teams where human intelligence and artificial intelligence complement one another. Students who understand both technology and humanity will be prepared to lead this new era with confidence, responsibility, and purpose.

Chapter 5 – Part 2

Working Alongside Artificial Intelligence

As students prepare for the future, one of the most exciting realities they should understand is that many of the careers they will one day pursue have not yet been invented. Every major technological revolution has created occupations that did not exist before. A century ago, there were no software engineers, cybersecurity analysts, drone operators, app developers, cloud architects, or social media managers. As technology advanced, entirely new industries emerged, creating millions of jobs around the world. Artificial intelligence and the future development of Artificial General Intelligence (AGI) will likely continue this pattern by opening doors to careers that today's students are only beginning to imagine.

Some future professionals may specialize in designing intelligent systems that help doctors detect diseases earlier. Others may develop AI tools that improve farming, reduce pollution, protect endangered wildlife, or make transportation safer. Some students may become AI ethics advisors who ensure that intelligent systems are fair, transparent, and respectful of human rights. Others may become AI education specialists who help schools integrate intelligent technology into classrooms in ways that strengthen learning rather than replace it. As AI continues evolving, opportunities will expand across nearly every profession, creating exciting pathways for students who combine technical knowledge with strong human skills.

Entrepreneurship will also become an important opportunity for the AGI Generation. Throughout history, entrepreneurs have recognized problems and created new solutions that improve people's lives. Artificial intelligence provides future business owners with powerful tools for research, planning, communication, customer service, and product development. A young entrepreneur may use AI to analyze market trends, design marketing materials, organize finances, or communicate with customers around the world. However, successful businesses are built upon much more than technology. Entrepreneurs must still understand people, recognize customer needs, build trust, solve problems creatively, and lead teams effectively. Technology can accelerate innovation, but human vision remains the driving force behind every successful business.

One of the greatest advantages students can develop is the ability to learn new skills quickly. The future workplace will reward people who are curious and willing to grow. Instead of expecting one career to remain unchanged for forty years, many professionals may experience several career transitions throughout their lives. An engineer may become an entrepreneur. A teacher may become an educational technology consultant. A healthcare worker may specialize in AI-assisted medicine. A graphic designer may learn to create interactive digital experiences using intelligent creative tools. Students who enjoy learning will discover that every new skill opens the door to additional opportunities.

The ability to work with people from different backgrounds will also become increasingly valuable. Modern organizations often include employees from different cultures, countries, languages, and professional experiences. Artificial intelligence can help translate conversations, organize projects, and share information more efficiently, making international collaboration easier than ever before. Even so, successful teamwork still depends on respect, patience, understanding, and effective communication. Students who learn to appreciate different perspectives will be prepared to contribute to organizations serving communities across the globe.

Innovation depends on asking questions that others have not yet considered. Some of history's greatest inventors succeeded because they looked at familiar problems from entirely new perspectives. They did not simply accept that existing methods were the only possibilities. They asked how work could become safer, faster, simpler, or more effective. Artificial intelligence can generate ideas and analyze enormous amounts of information, but innovation still begins with human curiosity. Students should never stop asking questions such as, "How can this be improved?" "What problem still needs solving?" or "How could technology help people live healthier, safer, or happier lives?" These questions often become the starting point for future discoveries.

Working alongside AI also requires responsibility. Powerful technologies should always be used thoughtfully and ethically. Students must understand that technology affects real people. A decision made by an AI system may influence someone's education, healthcare, finances, transportation, or employment. Because of this, future professionals must carefully evaluate AI-generated recommendations instead of accepting them automatically. Human oversight helps ensure that intelligent systems remain accurate, fair, transparent, and aligned with society's values. Responsible professionals understand that efficiency should never come at the expense of fairness, safety, or human dignity.

Another important workplace skill is the ability to explain technology in ways that everyone can understand. Many people will use AI without having technical backgrounds. Doctors will explain AI-assisted diagnoses to patients. Teachers will introduce AI learning tools to students and parents. Business leaders will explain new technologies to employees. Government officials will discuss AI policies with the public. Professionals who communicate clearly help others feel confident instead of confused. This ability to translate complex ideas into plain language builds trust and encourages responsible technology adoption throughout society.

Students should also understand that success in the future will not be measured only by income or job titles. True success includes making meaningful contributions to other people's lives. A nurse comforting a frightened patient, a teacher encouraging a struggling student, an engineer designing safer roads, or a scientist developing cleaner energy all contribute to society in valuable ways. Artificial intelligence can support these efforts, but people continue providing compassion, encouragement, leadership, and ethical judgment. These qualities give work deeper meaning and strengthen communities.

Resilience will continue to play an important role throughout every career. Technology changes quickly, and not every new idea succeeds immediately. Businesses sometimes fail before becoming successful. Scientific research often requires years of experimentation. Engineers redesign products many times before they are ready for public use. Students who develop resilience learn to view setbacks as opportunities for improvement rather than reasons to quit. This mindset encourages continuous growth and prepares future professionals to adapt confidently to changing circumstances.

One exciting possibility created by AI is the opportunity for more people to focus on work requiring imagination, empathy, strategy, and human connection. As intelligent systems assist with repetitive tasks, professionals may spend more time mentoring others, solving creative challenges, conducting research, designing innovative products, and strengthening relationships with customers and communities. Instead of replacing meaningful work, AI has the potential to shift human effort toward activities that require uniquely human abilities.

The AGI Generation also has the opportunity to become responsible stewards of technology. Stewardship means caring for something so it benefits both present and future generations. Students who become responsible stewards of AI will think carefully about how intelligent systems affect education, healthcare, business, the environment, public safety, and society as a whole. They will recognize that technological progress should improve people's lives while protecting fairness, privacy, security, and opportunity for everyone. This balance between innovation and responsibility will become one of the defining leadership qualities of the future.

Preparing for tomorrow's workplace begins today. Every classroom assignment, science experiment, group discussion, volunteer project, athletic competition, and creative activity helps students strengthen skills they will use throughout their careers. Reading develops understanding. Writing strengthens communication. Mathematics builds logical reasoning. Science encourages investigation. History teaches lessons from the past. The arts inspire creativity. Physical education builds perseverance and teamwork. Every subject contributes something valuable because future careers require well-rounded individuals rather than experts in only one area.

Perhaps the most encouraging message for today's students is that they do not need to compete against artificial intelligence. Instead, they should learn how to collaborate with it. Just as calculators became valuable tools for mathematicians and computers became essential tools for businesses, AI will become another powerful tool that helps people accomplish more than they could alone. Students who understand both technology and human values will be prepared to lead organizations, strengthen communities, solve global challenges, and inspire future generations.

The future workplace will be filled with intelligent machines, but it will always need thoughtful people. It will need educators who inspire learning, healthcare professionals who provide compassionate care, engineers who design responsibly, scientists who pursue discovery, entrepreneurs who create opportunity, artists who spark imagination, and leaders who place people at the center of every decision.

Working alongside artificial intelligence is not about replacing human potential—it is about expanding it. By combining knowledge, character, creativity, curiosity, ethical judgment, and lifelong learning with the capabilities of intelligent technology, the AGI Generation has the opportunity to build one of the most innovative, compassionate, and successful societies in human history.

Chapter 5 Summary

Working Alongside Artificial Intelligence

Artificial intelligence is transforming the way people work across nearly every profession. Rather than replacing all human workers, AI is becoming a powerful tool that helps people perform their jobs more efficiently, make better decisions, and solve more complex problems. Throughout history, technological advances have changed occupations while also creating entirely new careers, and the AGI era is expected to continue this pattern.

This chapter explained the difference between **automation** and **augmentation**. Automation allows machines to perform repetitive tasks with little human involvement, while augmentation helps people improve their work by combining human judgment with intelligent technology. Students learned that successful professionals of the future will know how to collaborate with AI rather than compete against it.

The chapter explored how AI is changing many industries, including healthcare, education, engineering, agriculture, business, law, and scientific research. In each profession, AI provides valuable assistance by organizing information, analyzing data, and increasing efficiency. However, human qualities such as empathy, ethical decision-making, creativity, communication, leadership, and critical thinking remain essential because they cannot be replaced by technology.

Students also learned that many future careers have not yet been created. Adaptability, lifelong learning, entrepreneurship, collaboration, and problem-solving will prepare them to succeed in an evolving workplace. Responsible professionals will understand not only how to use AI effectively but also how to ensure that technology serves people fairly, safely, and ethically.

The chapter concluded by emphasizing that the future workplace will belong to teams where human intelligence and artificial intelligence work together. The AGI Generation has an opportunity to build careers that combine technical knowledge with compassion, integrity, creativity, and responsible leadership to improve the lives of people around the world.

Chapter 5 Reflection

Working Alongside Artificial Intelligence

Think carefully about what you learned in this chapter. Answer each question using complete sentences and your own ideas.

1. Why do you think many people worry that AI will replace human workers?
2. Explain the difference between automation and augmentation in your own words.
3. Which career mentioned in this chapter interests you the most? Why?
4. Why will human qualities such as empathy and communication continue to be valuable in future workplaces?
5. If AI could perform many routine tasks, how would you choose to spend your extra time at work?
6. Why is lifelong learning important for future careers?
7. How can future professionals ensure that AI is used ethically and responsibly?
8. After reading this chapter, what skills do you believe you should begin strengthening today?

Personal Reflection

Imagine your future career twenty years from now. Describe how you and AI might work together to solve problems, help people, and improve your community. Explain how your human skills would complement intelligent technology.

Chapter 5 Worksheet

Working Alongside Artificial Intelligence

Part A – Vocabulary

Define each term using your own words.

1. Artificial Intelligence (AI)
2. Automation
3. Augmentation
4. Entrepreneurship
5. Adaptability
6. Collaboration
7. Ethical Leadership
8. Lifelong Learning
9. Innovation
10. Human Judgment

Part B – Comprehension Questions

Answer each question using complete sentences.

1. Why does technology often create new jobs while changing existing ones?
2. Explain the difference between automation and augmentation.
3. Why is human judgment still necessary when using AI?
4. Give three examples of careers that may work alongside AI.
5. Why are communication and teamwork important in future workplaces?
6. How can entrepreneurship benefit from AI?
7. Why should professionals continue learning throughout their careers?
8. What responsibilities do future AI professionals have toward society?

Part C – Critical Thinking

Answer each question in one or two paragraphs.

1. Imagine you are the principal of a school introducing AI into classrooms. How would you ensure that teachers remain the leaders of learning while using AI effectively?
2. Think about a profession you admire. Describe how AI could improve that career without replacing the people who perform it.
3. Explain why society needs both technological innovation and ethical leadership as AI becomes more powerful.

Part D – Career Planning Activity

Create your own "Future Career Roadmap."

Include:

• Three careers that interest you.

• Five human skills you want to strengthen.

• Three technology skills you hope to learn.

• Three ways AI might assist you in your future career.

• One personal goal that will help you become a responsible professional.

Chapter 5 Quiz

Multiple Choice

Choose the best answer.

1. According to this chapter, the future workplace will most likely involve:

A. Humans working without technology.

B. AI replacing every profession.

C. People and AI working together.

D. Technology eliminating education.

2. Automation refers to:

A. People solving problems creatively.

B. Machines performing repetitive tasks automatically.

C. Teachers replacing computers.

D. Students memorizing information.

3. Augmentation means:

A. Technology helps people perform their jobs better.

B. AI replaces all workers.

C. Machines make every important decision.

D. Technology eliminates teamwork.

4. Which human quality remains essential in future careers?

A. Empathy

B. Communication

C. Ethical decision-making

D. All of the above

5. Why is lifelong learning important?

A. Technology never changes.

B. Careers remain exactly the same.

C. New knowledge and skills will continue to emerge.

D. Students stop learning after graduation.

True or False

6. _____ AI can improve efficiency while people continue making important decisions.
7. _____ Human creativity remains valuable even in an AI-powered workplace.
8. _____ Every future career will require exactly the same skills.
9. _____ Responsible professionals should think about the ethical use of AI.
10. _____ Many future careers have not yet been invented.

Short Answer

11. Explain the difference between automation and augmentation.
12. Name two careers that may benefit from AI in the future.
13. Why are communication skills important when working with AI?
14. Describe one responsibility of future AI leaders.
15. In your own words, explain what it means to work alongside artificial intelligence.

Chapter 5 Answer Key

Multiple Choice

1. **C**
2. **B**
3. **A**
4. **D**
5. **C**

True or False

6. **True**
7. **True**
8. **False**

9. **True**
10. **True**

Short Answer (Sample Responses)

11. Automation allows machines to perform repetitive tasks with little human involvement, while augmentation uses AI to help people perform their work more effectively while keeping humans responsible for important decisions.
12. Sample answers include doctors, teachers, engineers, scientists, farmers, lawyers, architects, business managers, healthcare professionals, and educators.
13. Communication helps professionals explain AI-generated information clearly, work effectively with teams, build trust, and help others understand how intelligent technology supports their work.
14. Future AI leaders should ensure that intelligent systems are fair, transparent, safe, accurate, ethical, and beneficial to society while respecting privacy and human rights.
15. Working alongside artificial intelligence means combining human creativity, ethical judgment, communication, empathy, leadership, and critical thinking with AI's ability to analyze information, automate routine tasks, and support better decision-making.

Chapter 6 – Part 1

The Future Classroom

Walk into a classroom today, and you may see students using laptops, tablets, interactive displays, educational websites, and digital learning platforms. Walk into a classroom twenty years from now, and you may still see many of these same tools, but they will likely be far more intelligent, personalized, and connected than ever before. Artificial intelligence is already beginning to transform education by helping teachers organize lessons, personalize instruction, identify learning gaps, and provide students with additional learning opportunities. As Artificial General Intelligence (AGI) continues to develop in the future, classrooms may become even more flexible, interactive, and responsive to the needs of every learner.

Despite these exciting technological advances, one important truth remains unchanged: schools exist to help people grow. Education is not simply about delivering information. It is about helping students become knowledgeable, responsible, creative, ethical, and confident individuals. Technology can support this mission, but it cannot replace the human relationships that make learning meaningful. The future classroom will likely become a partnership where teachers, students, families, and intelligent technologies work together to create richer educational experiences.

For generations, teachers have faced a common challenge. Every classroom contains students who learn at different speeds and in different ways. Some students quickly understand new ideas after one explanation, while others need additional examples or extra practice before concepts become clear. Some students learn best through reading, while others understand more effectively by watching demonstrations, participating in discussions, building models, or completing hands-on activities. Meeting the needs of every learner has always required patience, creativity, and careful planning.

Artificial intelligence has the potential to make personalized learning more practical than ever before. Intelligent educational systems can analyze how students answer questions, identify concepts that need additional review, recommend appropriate practice activities, and provide immediate feedback. Instead of every student completing exactly the same assignment in exactly the same way, future classrooms may allow each learner to receive instruction that matches individual strengths, interests, and learning needs. Students who master a concept quickly may move on to more challenging activities, while students needing additional support receive extra guidance without feeling left behind.

Personalized learning does not mean students learn alone. Teachers remain at the center of the educational experience because they understand their students as individuals rather than simply as data. A teacher notices when a student appears discouraged, celebrates improvement, encourages participation, and helps build confidence after setbacks. These human interactions create trust, motivation, and a sense of belonging that technology cannot duplicate. AI may provide valuable information, but teachers transform information into meaningful learning experiences through encouragement, understanding, and inspiration.

Imagine a science classroom studying ecosystems. An AI learning assistant might generate interactive simulations showing how changes in rainfall affect forests, rivers, and wildlife. Students could experiment with different environmental conditions, observe the results, and ask questions during the simulation. While the technology provides visual demonstrations, the teacher guides discussions, encourages critical thinking, and helps students connect scientific concepts to real-world environmental challenges. The lesson becomes more engaging because technology supports exploration while the teacher provides context and deeper understanding.

Artificial intelligence may also help teachers save valuable time. Educators spend many hours preparing lessons, organizing classroom materials, reviewing assignments, and tracking student progress. Intelligent tools can assist by organizing educational resources, suggesting instructional activities, creating practice exercises, and identifying topics that require additional review. When routine administrative tasks become more efficient, teachers gain more time to interact directly with students, answer questions, provide individual support, and design creative learning experiences.

Assessment may also evolve in the future classroom. Traditional quizzes and examinations remain useful for measuring certain types of knowledge, but education increasingly recognizes that students should also demonstrate understanding through projects, presentations, research, teamwork, creative design, and real-world problem solving. AI can help monitor learning progress over time by identifying patterns in student performance rather than relying only on a single test score. Teachers can then use this information to adjust instruction and provide additional support where it is needed most. Assessment becomes less about measuring mistakes and more about encouraging continuous growth.

The future classroom may also become more connected to the world beyond school walls. Students studying astronomy might communicate with scientists working at research centers. History classes could participate in virtual tours of historical landmarks across different countries. Language students might practice conversations with learners from other parts of the world using intelligent translation tools that encourage international collaboration. Engineering students could work together on design challenges with classrooms located thousands of miles away. Technology creates opportunities for learning experiences that extend far beyond traditional textbooks.

Another exciting possibility involves virtual and augmented learning environments. Students may explore the human body from the inside, examine ancient civilizations as though walking through them, travel across the surface of distant planets, or observe microscopic organisms in three-dimensional simulations. These experiences make abstract concepts easier to understand because students actively interact with information rather than simply reading about it. Teachers continue guiding discussions, asking thoughtful questions, and helping students connect these experiences to broader academic concepts.

Collaboration will remain one of the most important parts of education. Future classrooms should encourage students to solve problems together, discuss different viewpoints, share creative ideas, and learn from one another. AI can organize information and support projects, but students continue developing communication, leadership, empathy, and teamwork through direct interaction with classmates. These experiences prepare learners for future workplaces where cooperation between people will remain essential.

The future classroom is not defined by the technology it contains. It is defined by the opportunities it creates for students to become curious thinkers, confident learners, ethical decision-makers, and compassionate members of society. Artificial intelligence offers powerful educational tools, but meaningful learning continues to depend upon dedicated teachers, engaged students, supportive families, and communities that value education.

The AGI Generation has the opportunity to experience one of the most exciting periods in the history of education. Classrooms will continue evolving, but their greatest purpose will remain the same: helping every student discover knowledge, develop character, strengthen skills, and prepare for a lifetime of learning. Technology may transform how education is delivered, but people will continue giving education its heart, its purpose, and its lasting impact.

Chapter 6 – Part 2

The Future Classroom

The classroom of the future will not simply contain more technology. It will encourage students to become more active participants in their own education. For many years, classrooms often focused on listening, taking notes, completing assignments, and preparing for tests. Those activities will continue to have value, but future learning will place greater emphasis on exploration, discussion, investigation, creativity, and real-world problem solving. Students will not be expected to memorize information alone. They will be encouraged to understand ideas deeply, ask meaningful questions, and apply knowledge to situations they may encounter throughout their lives.

Artificial intelligence can support this change by making learning more interactive. Imagine a history lesson where students explore an ancient city through a realistic virtual environment instead of only looking at pictures in a textbook. As students move through streets, buildings, and marketplaces, they ask questions about daily life, architecture, government, trade, and culture. An AI learning assistant can answer questions, provide additional background information, and adjust explanations to match each student's level of understanding. The teacher remains the guide who encourages discussion, connects historical events to modern society, and helps students think critically about the lessons history teaches us.

Science education may become equally exciting. Instead of only reading about volcanoes, students may observe detailed simulations showing how pressure builds beneath Earth's surface before an eruption occurs. Biology students may explore interactive models of the human body that demonstrate how organs work together. Physics students may conduct virtual experiments that would be too expensive, dangerous, or time-consuming in a traditional classroom. These experiences make learning more engaging because students actively investigate ideas instead of simply reading about them. At the same time, teachers help students interpret observations, ask thoughtful questions, and understand the scientific principles behind each activity.

Mathematics may also become more personalized. Every student learns at a different pace, and AI can help identify exactly where additional support is needed. If a learner struggles with fractions, algebra, or geometry, intelligent tutoring systems may provide extra explanations, visual examples, and guided practice until the concept becomes clear. Students who master a topic quickly can move on to more advanced challenges without waiting for the rest of the class. This flexibility allows teachers to spend more time helping students develop confidence while ensuring that no learner feels forgotten or left behind.

Reading and writing will continue to play a central role in education, even as intelligent technologies become more advanced. Reading develops imagination, comprehension, vocabulary, concentration, and critical thinking. Writing teaches students to organize ideas, explain reasoning, communicate clearly, and support conclusions with evidence. AI may assist by identifying grammar mistakes, suggesting revisions, or providing feedback on organization, but students must continue developing their own voices as writers. The ability to communicate clearly will remain valuable in every profession because ideas only become useful when people can understand and apply them.

Teachers in the future classroom may spend less time delivering information and more time mentoring, coaching, and inspiring students. Instead of standing in front of the room for every lesson, educators may guide investigations, facilitate discussions, supervise projects, and help students connect classroom learning to real-world situations. They will encourage curiosity, celebrate progress, and support students when learning becomes challenging. This shift allows teachers to focus on the human side of education—building confidence, encouraging resilience, and helping students discover their strengths.

Students will also take greater responsibility for their own learning. Intelligent educational tools may recommend activities, organize study schedules, and identify areas for improvement, but students must decide to stay curious, complete assignments honestly, ask questions, and continue practicing difficult skills. Responsibility remains one of the foundations of education. AI can provide opportunities to learn, but only students can choose to take advantage of those opportunities through consistent effort and determination.

Parents and families will continue serving as essential partners in education. Learning does not begin when the school day starts or end when students leave the classroom. Families encourage reading, discuss current events, help children develop good study habits, and teach values such as honesty, respect, kindness, and responsibility. As AI becomes more common in education, parents can help children understand when technology is useful and when personal effort, face-to-face conversations, and independent thinking are equally important. Strong partnerships between schools and families create learning environments where students feel supported both academically and emotionally.

The future classroom will also encourage global learning. Students may collaborate with classrooms in other countries to study climate change, compare cultural traditions, solve engineering challenges, or discuss historical events from different perspectives. Intelligent translation tools may help overcome language barriers, allowing learners from different cultures to communicate more easily. These experiences teach students that the world's greatest challenges often require cooperation across nations, cultures, and professions. Global collaboration helps develop empathy, respect, and appreciation for diverse viewpoints while preparing students to become responsible global citizens.

As technology becomes more powerful, ethical education becomes even more important. Students should understand not only how AI works but also how to use it responsibly. They should learn to respect privacy, verify information, avoid plagiarism, recognize bias, and understand that technology should always support fairness and human dignity. Future classrooms will likely include discussions about digital citizenship, cybersecurity, responsible innovation, and the social impact of intelligent systems. These conversations help students become thoughtful users and future leaders of technology rather than passive consumers.

One important lesson every future classroom should teach is that intelligence comes in many forms. Some students excel at mathematics, while others demonstrate exceptional creativity, leadership, artistic ability, communication, or mechanical problem-solving. AI may help identify learning strengths and recommend opportunities for growth, but every student possesses unique talents that deserve recognition and encouragement. Great education helps students discover those strengths while also helping them improve areas that require additional practice. Every learner has the potential to contribute something meaningful to society.

Lifelong learning will become one of the defining characteristics of the AGI Generation. Graduation will no longer represent the end of education. Instead, it will mark the beginning of continuous learning throughout adulthood. New technologies, scientific discoveries, medical advances, and business innovations will require professionals to update their knowledge regularly. Future classrooms can prepare students for this reality by helping them enjoy learning rather than viewing education as something limited to school years. Curiosity becomes a lifelong habit that opens doors to new opportunities and personal growth.

The classroom of tomorrow will likely look different from today's classroom, but its purpose will remain remarkably familiar. Schools will continue helping students discover knowledge, strengthen character, build confidence, and prepare for meaningful lives. Artificial intelligence may provide powerful educational tools, but teachers will continue inspiring learners, families will continue encouraging growth, and students will continue shaping their futures through dedication and hard work.

Perhaps the greatest lesson of the future classroom is that technology should never replace the joy of learning. The excitement of solving a difficult problem, discovering a new idea, completing a challenging project, helping a classmate understand a concept, or achieving a personal goal comes from human effort and determination. AI can support these experiences, but it cannot replace the pride students feel when they realize how much they have learned.

The AGI Generation has the opportunity to experience an educational system unlike any before it. By combining outstanding teachers, supportive families, responsible use of artificial intelligence, and students who are eager to learn, tomorrow's classrooms can become places where curiosity flourishes, creativity grows, knowledge expands, and every learner is encouraged to reach his or her fullest potential.

The future classroom is not simply a room filled with advanced technology. It is a community of learners who use intelligent tools wisely while never losing sight of the qualities that make education truly meaningful: curiosity, compassion, integrity, perseverance, and the lifelong pursuit of knowledge.

Chapter 6 Summary

The Future Classroom

Education is entering an exciting new era where artificial intelligence can help create more personalized, engaging, and effective learning experiences. The future classroom will use intelligent technologies to support both teachers and students, allowing learning to become more flexible while continuing to focus on developing knowledgeable, ethical, and responsible individuals.

This chapter explained that AI can help personalize education by identifying each student's strengths, learning needs, and progress. Intelligent learning systems may recommend activities, provide immediate feedback, and offer additional practice when needed. At the same time, students who master concepts more quickly can continue exploring advanced material without waiting for the rest of the class.

Students learned that teachers will remain the most important part of education. While AI can organize information and assist with instruction, teachers continue inspiring students, building confidence, encouraging curiosity, answering questions, supporting emotional growth, and helping learners develop critical thinking skills. Human relationships remain at the heart of successful education.

The chapter also explored how future classrooms may include virtual simulations, interactive science experiments, global classroom collaborations, AI tutoring systems, and project-based learning that connects students with real-world challenges. These experiences help students understand concepts more deeply by encouraging exploration, creativity, communication, and teamwork.

Readers also discovered the importance of digital citizenship, ethical technology use, lifelong learning, and strong partnerships between schools and families. Students were reminded that technology should support education rather than replace independent thinking, personal responsibility, or meaningful human relationships.

Finally, the chapter emphasized that the classroom of the future is not defined by computers or intelligent machines. It is defined by teachers who inspire learning, students who remain curious, families who encourage growth, and communities that value education. Artificial intelligence becomes one more tool that helps every learner reach his or her full potential while strengthening the qualities that make people uniquely human.

Chapter 6 Reflection

The Future Classroom

Answer each question thoughtfully using complete sentences.

1. How do you imagine your classroom might look ten or twenty years from now?
2. Why do you think teachers will continue to play an important role even if AI becomes much more advanced?
3. Which future classroom technology described in this chapter would help you learn the most? Explain your answer.
4. How can AI personalize learning without replacing student responsibility?
5. Why is it important for students to continue reading and writing even when AI can generate information quickly?
6. What responsibilities do students have when using AI in school?
7. How can parents continue supporting education in an AI-powered world?
8. Why should future classrooms teach ethics along with technology?

Personal Reflection

Imagine you are designing your ideal classroom for the AGI Generation. Describe what it would look like, how students would learn, how teachers would teach, and how AI would support—but not replace—the educational experience.

Chapter 6 Worksheet

The Future Classroom

Part A – Vocabulary

Write your own definition for each term.

1. Personalized Learning
2. Artificial Intelligence
3. Artificial General Intelligence
4. Digital Citizenship
5. Collaboration
6. Lifelong Learning
7. Critical Thinking
8. Interactive Learning
9. Virtual Simulation
10. Ethical Technology

Part B – Comprehension Questions

Answer each question using complete sentences.

1. How can AI personalize education for different students?
2. Why are teachers still essential in future classrooms?
3. Name three ways AI can support classroom instruction.
4. How do virtual learning experiences improve student understanding?
5. Why should students continue developing communication skills?
6. How can global classroom collaboration benefit students?
7. Why is ethical technology use important in education?
8. What does lifelong learning mean in the AGI era?

Part C – Critical Thinking

Write one or two paragraphs for each question.

1. Imagine your school receives unlimited funding to build the classroom of the future. Describe the technology you would include while explaining how teachers remain the leaders of learning.
2. Explain how AI can help struggling students while also challenging advanced learners.
3. Discuss how schools can balance technology with face-to-face communication, teamwork, creativity, and independent thinking.

Part D – My Future Classroom Plan

Design your own classroom.

Include:

• Five technologies you would include.

• Five classroom rules for using AI responsibly.

• Five activities students would complete during a typical week.

• Three ways teachers would encourage creativity.

• Three ways families could participate in student learning.

Chapter 6 Quiz

Multiple Choice

Choose the best answer.

1. According to this chapter, the future classroom will:

A. Replace teachers with AI.

B. Combine teachers, students, families, and AI to improve learning.

C. Eliminate homework.

D. Teach only computer science.

2. Personalized learning means:

A. Every student completes the exact same lesson.

B. Learning is adjusted to meet individual student needs.

C. Students work without teachers.

D. AI completes all assignments.

3. Which classroom activity helps students apply knowledge to real-world situations?

A. Project-based learning

B. Memorizing vocabulary only

C. Copying notes

D. Reading without discussion

4. Why are teachers still essential?

A. They build relationships, inspire students, and guide learning.

B. AI cannot organize information.

C. Technology no longer exists.

D. Students cannot use computers.

5. Which skill remains important even with advanced AI?

A. Communication

B. Collaboration

C. Critical thinking

D. All of the above

True or False

6. _____ AI can help personalize education.
7. _____ Future classrooms should teach ethical technology use.
8. _____ Students no longer need to read or write because AI exists.
9. _____ Families continue playing an important role in education.
10. _____ Lifelong learning prepares students for changing careers and technologies.

Short Answer

11. Explain how AI can support teachers in the classroom.
12. Describe one advantage of virtual learning experiences.
13. Why should students verify AI-generated information?
14. How can schools encourage responsible digital citizenship?
15. In your own words, describe what the future classroom should accomplish.

Chapter 6 Answer Key

Multiple Choice

1. **B**
2. **B**
3. **A**
4. **A**
5. **D**

True or False

6. **True**
7. **True**
8. **False**
9. **True**
10. **True**

Short Answer (Sample Responses)

11. AI can organize instructional materials, identify learning gaps, provide personalized practice, generate educational resources, and reduce routine administrative tasks, allowing teachers to spend more time working directly with students.
12. Virtual learning experiences allow students to explore places, conduct simulations, visualize complex concepts, and investigate situations that may be impossible, expensive, or unsafe to experience in a traditional classroom.
13. Students should verify AI-generated information because AI systems can occasionally produce inaccurate, incomplete, outdated, or misleading responses. Responsible learners compare information using reliable sources and critical thinking.
14. Schools can encourage digital citizenship by teaching students to protect privacy, communicate respectfully online, verify information before sharing it, respect intellectual property, avoid plagiarism, and use AI honestly and ethically.
15. The future classroom should help every student develop knowledge, creativity, critical thinking, communication, ethical decision-making, collaboration, and lifelong learning

skills while using AI as a supportive educational tool rather than a replacement for teachers or independent thinking.

Chapter 7 – Part 1

Innovation Begins with Curiosity

Every great invention in history began with a simple question.

Why does this happen?

How can this be improved?

What if there is a better way?

These questions may sound ordinary, but they have led to extraordinary discoveries. They inspired people to invent the wheel, build bridges, explore the oceans, harness electricity, fly across continents, develop life-saving medicines, and create computers that now connect billions of people around the world. Curiosity has always been the starting point of innovation.

The AGI Generation is entering a world where curiosity will become more valuable than ever before. Artificial intelligence can answer many questions within seconds, organize enormous amounts of information, and help people solve complex problems. Yet AI rarely decides which questions deserve to be asked in the first place. That responsibility belongs to people. The students who ask thoughtful questions today may become the inventors, scientists, educators, entrepreneurs, engineers, healthcare professionals, and leaders who solve tomorrow's greatest challenges.

Curiosity is much more than wanting to know an answer. It is the desire to understand how the world works. Curious people look beyond the surface of a problem. They wonder why something happens, what causes it, and how it might be improved. Instead of accepting the first explanation they hear, they continue exploring until they develop a deeper understanding. This habit of asking questions encourages lifelong learning because every answer often leads to another interesting question.

Children naturally demonstrate curiosity from an early age. Young learners constantly ask questions about animals, weather, space, machines, and the people around them. They enjoy taking apart toys to see how they work, mixing colors to discover new shades, and experimenting with objects simply to observe what happens. Unfortunately, some people gradually stop asking questions because they worry about giving the wrong answer or appearing uninformed. One of the greatest goals of education is to protect and strengthen curiosity rather than allowing it to disappear. Schools should encourage students to investigate ideas confidently because every meaningful discovery begins with someone willing to ask, "Why?"

Artificial intelligence makes curiosity even more powerful. Imagine a student interested in marine biology. Instead of searching through dozens of books one at a time, AI can help organize research papers, explain scientific vocabulary, compare different species, summarize ocean conservation efforts, and identify recent discoveries. Within minutes, the student can explore information that once required weeks of research. However, AI does not replace the student's curiosity. The technology simply accelerates the learning process by making knowledge easier to explore. The student's questions remain the driving force behind every discovery.

Innovation grows from curiosity because questions often reveal problems that need solving. Consider transportation. People once traveled mainly on foot or by horseback. Curious inventors asked whether travel could become faster and safer. Their questions eventually led to bicycles, automobiles, trains, airplanes, and spacecraft. Medical researchers asked why certain diseases spread while others did not. Those questions helped scientists develop vaccines, antibiotics, improved surgical procedures, and modern medical equipment. Computer scientists wondered whether machines could process information more efficiently. Their curiosity eventually led to personal computers, smartphones, cloud computing, and artificial intelligence. Every major technological advancement began because someone refused to believe that existing methods were the only possibilities.

The AGI Generation has an opportunity to continue this tradition of innovation. Future students may discover cleaner energy sources, improve food production, design safer transportation systems, create new educational tools, develop advanced medical treatments, or protect endangered ecosystems using intelligent technologies. These achievements will not begin with machines working independently. They will begin with curious people who recognize challenges and believe solutions are possible. AI can become an extraordinary partner during this process, but human imagination remains the source of meaningful innovation.

Curiosity also strengthens critical thinking. Curious learners rarely accept information without asking additional questions. They compare evidence, examine different viewpoints, and seek reliable sources before reaching conclusions. This habit becomes especially important in the age of AI because intelligent systems can occasionally produce incomplete or inaccurate information. Responsible students understand that learning requires both curiosity and careful evaluation. They ask, "How do we know this is true?" "What evidence supports this conclusion?" and "Are there other explanations we should consider?" These questions help build informed, independent thinkers.

Innovation is not limited to science and technology. Artists innovate by creating new styles of painting, music, literature, architecture, and design. Teachers innovate by developing engaging lessons that inspire students to learn. Business owners innovate by creating products and services that improve people's lives. Community leaders innovate by finding better ways to solve local challenges. Parents innovate by discovering creative ways to encourage their children's growth and confidence. Innovation occurs whenever someone improves an existing idea or develops a new solution that benefits others.

Many people mistakenly believe innovation belongs only to individuals with exceptional intelligence. In reality, innovation often grows from persistence rather than perfection. Inventors rarely succeed on their first attempt. Scientists conduct experiments that fail before making important discoveries. Authors revise manuscripts repeatedly before publication. Engineers redesign products many times before they become reliable. Every setback provides valuable information that guides future improvements. Students who understand this process become more willing to experiment because they recognize that mistakes are part of learning rather than evidence of failure.

Schools play an important role in encouraging innovation. Classrooms should be places where students feel comfortable asking questions, sharing ideas, testing solutions, and learning from one another. Group projects encourage collaboration by allowing students with different strengths to work toward common goals. Science experiments help learners test predictions through observation. Engineering challenges encourage creative problem-solving. Classroom discussions expose students to different perspectives that broaden understanding. These experiences help students realize that learning is not simply about finding correct answers—it is about developing the confidence to investigate important questions.

Teachers serve as guides throughout this process. Great educators do not simply provide information; they encourage students to think independently. They ask open-ended questions, challenge assumptions, celebrate creative ideas, and support students when experiments do not produce expected results. A teacher who encourages curiosity often inspires students to continue exploring long after the lesson has ended. This influence may last a lifetime because curiosity becomes a habit rather than a classroom assignment.

Families also contribute to developing innovative thinkers. Parents and caregivers who encourage children to read, explore nature, build projects, ask questions, and discuss everyday experiences help strengthen curiosity outside the classroom. Visiting museums, libraries, science centers, historical landmarks, parks, and community events introduces children to new ideas that expand their understanding of the world. Simple conversations at home often inspire questions that eventually grow into lifelong interests.

One of the greatest opportunities for the AGI Generation is learning how to combine human curiosity with intelligent technology. AI can analyze information rapidly, simulate possible solutions, and organize complex data, but people continue providing purpose, imagination, values, and vision. This partnership allows students to investigate questions that previous generations may not have been able to explore as efficiently. The future will reward individuals who know how to ask meaningful questions, think creatively, collaborate respectfully, and use intelligent technology responsibly to improve society.

Innovation begins long before someone invents a new machine or discovers a scientific breakthrough. It begins the moment a curious student decides to ask one more question, explore one more idea, or imagine one more possibility. Every classroom contains future innovators whose greatest discoveries may still be waiting to be imagined. The AGI Generation has an extraordinary opportunity to continue humanity's long tradition of curiosity, discovery, and progress by asking questions that lead to solutions benefiting people around the world.

Chapter 7 – Part 2

Innovation Begins with Curiosity

Curiosity becomes even more powerful when it is combined with observation. Many of history's greatest discoveries did not happen because someone was searching for fame or recognition. They happened because someone noticed something unusual and decided to investigate further. A scientist might observe a surprising result during an experiment. An engineer might notice that a machine could operate more efficiently. A teacher may recognize that students understand a lesson better when it is explained in a different way. These observations often become the beginning of innovation because they encourage people to ask questions that others may have overlooked.

Observation teaches students an important lesson about learning. Answers do not always appear immediately. Sometimes understanding develops slowly as people gather information, compare evidence, and reflect on what they have learned. Artificial intelligence can organize enormous amounts of data in seconds, but people still need patience to study results carefully and recognize which discoveries are truly meaningful. Innovation is rarely the result of rushing. Instead, it grows through thoughtful investigation, careful testing, and a willingness to continue learning even when progress seems slow.

The AGI Generation will likely have access to research tools unlike anything previous generations experienced. Students may use intelligent assistants to analyze scientific information, compare historical events, organize research, create computer simulations, and explore ideas from many different fields of study. These tools can greatly expand learning opportunities, but they also require responsibility. Students should remember that technology provides information, while people provide purpose. A computer may generate hundreds of possible solutions to a problem, but human judgment determines which solution is practical, ethical, and beneficial to society.

One of the greatest strengths of curiosity is that it encourages students to explore subjects outside their comfort zones. A student who enjoys mathematics may become interested in music after discovering patterns in sound. A student fascinated by history may become curious about archaeology, architecture, or environmental science. Someone interested in computers may discover a passion for medicine after learning how artificial intelligence helps doctors diagnose diseases. Curiosity connects subjects that might initially seem unrelated, helping students understand that knowledge often grows stronger when different disciplines work together.

This ability to connect ideas is becoming increasingly valuable. Many of today's greatest challenges require knowledge from multiple fields. Improving renewable energy involves engineering, chemistry, environmental science, economics, and public policy. Developing safer transportation systems requires mathematics, computer science, psychology, and design. Protecting public health depends on biology, medicine, communication, statistics, and technology. Artificial intelligence supports this process by organizing information from different disciplines, but people continue making the creative connections that lead to meaningful breakthroughs.

Innovation also depends upon courage. New ideas are not always accepted immediately. Throughout history, inventors, scientists, educators, and entrepreneurs often faced criticism before their work became widely recognized. Some discoveries challenged traditional ways of thinking, while others required years of testing before people understood their value. Students should remember that responsible innovation sometimes requires the courage to continue exploring an idea even when success is not immediate. This does not mean ignoring evidence or refusing constructive feedback. Instead, it means believing that worthwhile goals often require persistence, patience, and determination.

The classroom provides an excellent place to practice innovative thinking because it allows students to experiment in a supportive environment. Group projects encourage learners to combine different perspectives while solving shared challenges. Science laboratories provide opportunities to test predictions and learn from unexpected results. Writing assignments encourage students to organize ideas creatively. Art classes help students express imagination visually. Robotics competitions challenge teams to design solutions under real-world constraints. Every classroom activity that encourages exploration strengthens the habits of innovation that students will use throughout adulthood.

Artificial intelligence can also become a creative partner during the innovation process. Students may use AI to brainstorm ideas, compare possible designs, organize research notes, or identify information that deserves further investigation. For example, a student designing a community garden might ask AI to suggest plants that grow well in a particular climate, estimate water needs, or recommend environmentally friendly irrigation methods. The student then evaluates these suggestions, considers local conditions, discusses ideas with teachers and classmates, and makes thoughtful decisions. The final project reflects both technological assistance and human creativity.

Innovation should always be guided by ethics. Every new invention affects people in some way. Before introducing a new technology, responsible innovators ask important questions. Will this improve people's lives? Could someone be harmed by the way it is used? Does it respect privacy and fairness? Can it be used responsibly by different communities? These questions help ensure that progress benefits society instead of creating unnecessary risks. The AGI Generation has an opportunity to become a generation of ethical innovators who understand that success is measured not only by what technology can accomplish but also by how wisely it is used.

Another valuable lesson is that innovation is not always about creating something completely new. Sometimes the greatest improvements come from making existing ideas better. A student might redesign a backpack to reduce strain on the shoulders. Another student might develop a better recycling program for the school. Someone else may create a mobile application that helps classmates organize homework more effectively. Small improvements can have significant impacts when they solve real problems experienced by many people. Students should never underestimate the importance of improving everyday life through thoughtful ideas.

Failure is often misunderstood in the innovation process. Many people see failure as the opposite of success, but innovators often view it differently. Every unsuccessful attempt provides information that helps improve the next attempt. Engineers test prototypes to discover weaknesses before products reach the public. Scientists analyze unsuccessful experiments to better understand natural processes. Entrepreneurs adjust business plans after learning from customer feedback. Students who adopt this mindset become more willing to take thoughtful risks because they recognize that every experience contributes to future growth. Curiosity encourages exploration, and exploration naturally includes moments when plans do not work exactly as expected.

The future will reward students who continue asking meaningful questions throughout their lives. Questions such as, "How can we make education more accessible?" "How can technology improve healthcare?" "How can communities protect the environment?" and "How can intelligent systems help people live healthier and safer lives?" may inspire tomorrow's greatest discoveries. Artificial intelligence will provide powerful research tools, but curiosity will continue providing the motivation to pursue answers.

Curiosity also encourages humility. The more people learn, the more they often realize there is still much left to discover. This understanding keeps learners open to new evidence, willing to reconsider ideas, and respectful of different perspectives. Humility strengthens innovation because it allows people to improve their thinking instead of assuming they already know everything. Great innovators remain lifelong learners who continue asking questions even after achieving success.

The AGI Generation has an extraordinary opportunity to become one of the most innovative generations in human history. Never before have students had access to so much knowledge, so many educational resources, and such powerful intelligent tools. Yet the most important ingredient for innovation has not changed. It is still the willingness to wonder, to explore, to imagine, and to ask questions that no one has asked before.

As you continue your educational journey, remember that every important discovery begins with curiosity. Every invention begins as an idea. Every breakthrough begins with someone refusing to stop asking questions. Whether your future leads you into science, medicine, education, engineering, business, agriculture, the arts, public service, or another profession, your curiosity will remain one of your greatest strengths.

The future will not simply be created by the most advanced machines. It will be created by curious people who use those machines wisely, think creatively, work collaboratively, act ethically, and dedicate themselves to improving the lives of others. That is the true power of innovation, and it begins with a single question.

Chapter 7 Summary

Innovation Begins with Curiosity

Curiosity is the foundation of innovation. Throughout history, nearly every important invention, scientific discovery, and technological breakthrough began because someone asked a meaningful question. Instead of accepting the world as it was, curious individuals explored new possibilities and searched for better solutions. The AGI Generation has the opportunity to continue this tradition by combining human curiosity with the powerful capabilities of artificial intelligence.

This chapter explained that curiosity is much more than wanting answers. It is the desire to understand how things work, why problems exist, and how they can be improved. Students learned that AI can help organize information, analyze data, and generate ideas, but people remain responsible for asking thoughtful questions, evaluating evidence, and deciding how technology should be used.

The chapter emphasized that innovation occurs in every field, not just science or engineering. Teachers, doctors, artists, entrepreneurs, farmers, engineers, business leaders, and community members all innovate when they improve existing ideas or create new solutions that benefit others. Students discovered that innovation often comes from persistence, observation, creativity, and collaboration rather than from natural talent alone.

Readers also learned that mistakes are an important part of the innovation process. Every unsuccessful experiment, prototype, or first draft provides valuable information that leads to improvement. Students were encouraged to view challenges as opportunities to learn instead of reasons to give up.

Finally, the chapter highlighted the importance of ethical innovation. Powerful technologies should always be guided by honesty, fairness, responsibility, and respect for human dignity. The AGI Generation has an opportunity to become a generation of responsible innovators who use curiosity, creativity, and intelligence to improve education, healthcare, the environment, communities, and the quality of life for people around the world.

Chapter 7 Reflection

Innovation Begins with Curiosity

Take time to think about the ideas presented in this chapter. Answer each question using complete sentences.

1. Why do you think curiosity is considered the beginning of innovation?
2. Describe a time when asking a question helped you understand something better.
3. How can AI support curiosity without replacing human imagination?
4. Why should students continue asking questions even after finding an answer?
5. Explain why failure is often an important part of innovation.
6. How can innovation improve your school or community?
7. Why should every innovation be guided by ethics?
8. What problem would you like to solve during your lifetime? Why is it important to you?

Personal Reflection

Imagine you are an inventor twenty years from now. Describe a problem you hope to solve, how AI could help you during the research process, and how your creativity, curiosity, and ethical decision-making would guide your work.

Chapter 7 Worksheet

Innovation Begins with Curiosity

Part A – Vocabulary

Define each term in your own words.

1. Curiosity
2. Innovation
3. Creativity
4. Observation
5. Collaboration
6. Critical Thinking
7. Ethical Innovation
8. Problem Solving
9. Artificial Intelligence
10. Persistence

Part B – Comprehension Questions

Answer each question using complete sentences.

1. Why is curiosity considered the starting point of innovation?
2. How does AI help students explore new ideas?
3. Why are observations important in the innovation process?
4. Explain how different school subjects work together to solve real-world problems.
5. Why should students learn from mistakes instead of fearing them?
6. How can teamwork strengthen innovation?
7. What does ethical innovation mean?
8. Why is lifelong curiosity important in the AGI era?

Part C – Critical Thinking

Answer each question in one or two paragraphs.

1. Imagine your school asks you to solve a real problem using AI. Describe the problem, your solution, and how your idea would benefit students.

2. Explain why innovation is not limited to scientists or engineers.
3. Discuss how curiosity, creativity, ethics, and artificial intelligence can work together to improve society.

Part D – Innovation Challenge

Create your own innovation plan.

Identify:

• One problem you would like to solve.

• Three questions you need to investigate.

• Three people or professions that could help you.

• Three ways AI could support your research.

• Three ethical responsibilities you must consider before sharing your solution.

Chapter 7 Quiz

Multiple Choice

Choose the best answer.

1. According to this chapter, innovation begins with:

A. Memorization

B. Curiosity

C. Luck

D. Competition

2. Artificial intelligence helps innovation by:

A. Replacing human imagination.

B. Organizing information and supporting research.

C. Eliminating creativity.

D. Preventing mistakes.

3. Which quality helps students continue learning after setbacks?

A. Persistence

B. Giving up

C. Avoiding challenges

D. Memorization

4. Ethical innovation means:

A. Building technology without considering people.

B. Using technology responsibly to benefit society.

C. Ignoring privacy.

D. Allowing AI to make every decision.

5. Which statement is true?

A. Innovation only happens in science laboratories.

B. Only adults can become innovators.

C. Innovation can happen in every profession.

D. AI eliminates the need for curiosity.

True or False

6. _____ Curiosity often leads to new discoveries.
7. _____ Mistakes can help people improve their ideas.
8. _____ AI replaces the need for human creativity.
9. _____ Responsible innovators consider how their work affects others.
10. _____ Students should continue asking questions throughout their lives.

Short Answer

11. Explain why curiosity is important for lifelong learning.
12. Describe one way AI can support innovation.
13. Why should students learn from failure?
14. Explain why ethics is important when creating new technologies.
15. In your own words, describe how curiosity and innovation work together.

Chapter 7 Answer Key

Multiple Choice

1. **B**
2. **B**
3. **A**
4. **B**
5. **C**

True or False

6. **True**
7. **True**
8. **False**
9. **True**
10. **True**

Short Answer (Sample Responses)

11. Curiosity encourages people to ask questions, explore new ideas, investigate problems, and continue learning throughout their lives. It motivates discovery and supports lifelong education.
12. AI can organize information, analyze large amounts of data, generate ideas, compare research, identify patterns, and help students explore possible solutions more efficiently.
13. Failure provides valuable feedback that helps people improve designs, strengthen understanding, discover better solutions, and develop resilience. Many successful innovations required multiple attempts before succeeding.

14. Ethics helps ensure that new technologies are safe, fair, responsible, respectful of privacy, and beneficial to individuals and society. Responsible innovators consider how their work affects other people before introducing new ideas.
15. Curiosity inspires people to ask meaningful questions, while innovation transforms those questions into practical solutions that improve lives. Together they drive discovery, creativity, and human progress.

Chapter 8 – Part 1

Ethics in an Intelligent World

Throughout history, every major technological advancement has brought both opportunities and responsibilities. The discovery of electricity transformed homes, schools, hospitals, and businesses, but people also learned that electricity must be used safely. The invention of the automobile made travel faster and connected communities, but traffic laws, driver's education, and safety standards became necessary to protect lives. The internet connected billions of people across the globe, yet it also introduced new concerns about privacy, cybercrime, misinformation, and online safety. Artificial intelligence is following a similar path. It offers extraordinary possibilities for improving education, healthcare, science, business, and everyday life, but it also requires thoughtful people who understand how to use it responsibly. This is where ethics becomes essential.

Ethics is the study of right and wrong choices. It helps people decide how their actions affect others and encourages decisions based on fairness, honesty, responsibility, respect, and compassion. Ethics is not limited to lawyers, judges, or government leaders. Every person makes ethical decisions every day. Students decide whether to complete assignments honestly. Friends choose whether to tell the truth. Business owners decide how to treat customers and employees. Scientists determine how research should be conducted responsibly. Engineers consider whether new technologies are safe before introducing them to the public. As artificial intelligence becomes more powerful, ethical decision-making will become one of the most valuable skills students can develop.

Artificial intelligence itself does not possess human values. An AI system analyzes information according to the data it receives and the instructions it is given. It does not naturally understand kindness, fairness, empathy, honesty, or compassion in the way people do. If an intelligent system produces harmful results, the responsibility belongs to the people who designed it, trained it, deployed it, or used it improperly. This is why human oversight remains essential. Technology reflects the choices of the people who create and use it.

Imagine a school using AI to help identify students who may need additional academic support. The goal is positive—to help students succeed before they fall behind. However, educators must also ask important ethical questions. Is the information accurate? Does the system treat every student fairly? Are students' personal records protected? Could incorrect information accidentally affect a student's educational opportunities? These questions demonstrate that good intentions alone are not enough. Responsible decision-making requires careful planning, testing, and continuous evaluation.

Privacy is one of the most important ethical topics in the age of AI. Every day, people create digital information by using smartphones, computers, websites, educational platforms, fitness devices, and countless other technologies. Some of this information helps improve services by making recommendations or personalizing experiences. At the same time, personal information deserves protection. Students should understand that names, addresses, passwords, financial information, medical records, and other personal details should be handled carefully. Responsible organizations develop policies to protect sensitive information, while responsible individuals learn safe digital habits such as creating strong passwords, recognizing online scams, and thinking carefully before sharing personal details.

Fairness is another essential ethical principle. Imagine two students applying for the same scholarship or two qualified candidates applying for the same job. If AI is used to help review applications, the system should evaluate everyone fairly according to appropriate criteria. If the data used to develop the system contains errors or reflects unfair historical patterns, the results may unintentionally disadvantage certain individuals. For this reason, organizations continually work to test AI systems, improve their accuracy, and reduce bias whenever possible. Students should understand that fairness requires ongoing attention rather than assuming technology automatically makes perfect decisions.

Honesty remains equally important in an intelligent world. Artificial intelligence can help students brainstorm ideas, organize information, summarize research, and explain difficult concepts. These are valuable educational tools. However, using AI to complete assignments dishonestly or presenting AI-generated work as entirely one's own weakens learning and undermines trust. Education is designed to help students develop their own knowledge, judgment, and confidence. AI should support learning, not replace personal effort. Honest work builds character while preparing students for future responsibilities where integrity is essential.

Transparency is another principle that guides ethical technology. Transparency means being open about how important decisions are made. When AI influences decisions affecting healthcare, education, employment, transportation, or public safety, people should understand how those decisions are reached whenever possible. Clear explanations build trust because individuals can ask questions, identify mistakes, and improve systems over time. Students should recognize that trustworthy technology is not only accurate but also understandable and accountable.

Responsibility accompanies every powerful tool. A hammer can build a house or damage property depending on how it is used. A computer can educate millions of people or spread harmful misinformation. Artificial intelligence follows the same principle. The technology itself is neither good nor bad. Its impact depends upon the decisions made by people. Responsible users think carefully before creating, sharing, or acting upon AI-generated information. They consider how their choices may affect classmates, families, coworkers, communities, and society as a whole.

Ethics also encourages respect for intellectual property. Writers, artists, musicians, photographers, scientists, software developers, and inventors invest significant time and effort creating original work. Students should learn to give proper credit when using someone else's ideas and understand why plagiarism undermines both learning and creativity. Artificial intelligence makes it easier to locate information, but it does not eliminate the importance of acknowledging original sources or producing thoughtful, original work. Respecting the work of others encourages innovation because creators know their efforts will be recognized and valued.

Another important ethical principle is accountability. Accountability means accepting responsibility for decisions and actions. If an AI-assisted recommendation leads to an unexpected result, people should not simply blame the computer. Instead, responsible individuals investigate what happened, correct mistakes, improve systems, and learn from the experience. Accountability builds trust because it demonstrates a commitment to continuous improvement rather than avoiding responsibility when challenges arise.

Students should also understand that ethical discussions often involve balancing different priorities. For example, AI may help emergency responders reach disaster areas more quickly by analyzing traffic patterns and weather conditions. This creates significant public benefits. At the same time, systems collecting location information must respect privacy and use data responsibly. Ethical decision-making rarely involves choosing between something completely good and something completely bad. More often, it requires thoughtful consideration of multiple benefits, possible risks, and the long-term impact of each decision.

Teachers play an important role in helping students develop ethical thinking. Classroom discussions encourage learners to examine different perspectives, support opinions with evidence, and respectfully consider ideas that differ from their own. These experiences prepare students to make thoughtful decisions throughout life. Instead of memorizing rules, students learn how to reason through complex situations where there may not be one simple answer. This ability becomes increasingly valuable as technology continues evolving.

Families also contribute to ethical development. Children learn honesty, kindness, responsibility, respect, and compassion long before they enter the workforce. Everyday conversations about fairness, helping others, keeping promises, and admitting mistakes build character that remains valuable throughout adulthood. As AI becomes more common at home and in school, families can continue discussing how technology should be used responsibly while reinforcing the values that guide good decision-making.

The AGI Generation will inherit some of the most advanced technologies humanity has ever created. With those opportunities comes an equally important responsibility. Students who combine technological knowledge with honesty, fairness, empathy, accountability, and respect will help ensure that artificial intelligence strengthens society instead of creating unnecessary harm. Ethics is not a barrier to innovation. It is the foundation that allows innovation to earn trust and improve people's lives.

Every generation is remembered not only for the technologies it develops but also for the values that guide those technologies. The AGI Generation has the opportunity to become a generation known for using intelligence wisely, acting responsibly, and ensuring that progress always serves humanity with fairness, compassion, and integrity.

Chapter 8 – Part 2

Ethics in an Intelligent World

As artificial intelligence becomes more capable, one of the greatest responsibilities facing society will be ensuring that people remain at the center of important decisions. AI can process information at incredible speed, identify patterns in large amounts of data, and recommend possible solutions to difficult problems. These abilities make intelligent systems valuable tools in education, healthcare, transportation, business, scientific research, and many other fields. However, there are moments when technology should support human decision-making rather than replace it. Decisions involving human lives, personal dignity, fairness, and public trust require thoughtful judgment that combines knowledge with compassion, experience, and ethical reasoning.

This idea is often called **human oversight**. Human oversight means that people continue reviewing important decisions made with the assistance of AI. For example, a doctor may use AI to analyze medical images, but the physician still examines the results, considers the patient's medical history, speaks directly with the patient, and determines the best course of treatment. A teacher may use AI to identify students who need additional academic support, but the teacher still understands each student's personality, motivation, learning style, and personal circumstances. Technology provides valuable information, but people remain responsible for making the final decisions.

Another important ethical topic is bias. Bias occurs when a decision unfairly favors or disadvantages certain people or groups. Bias can appear in many forms and is not limited to technology. Human beings can also make biased decisions based on incomplete information, assumptions, or personal experiences. AI systems learn from data, and if that data contains unfair patterns or historical inequalities, the technology may unintentionally produce biased results. Because of this possibility, researchers, engineers, educators, and organizations work continuously to improve AI systems by testing them carefully, reviewing results, correcting errors, and ensuring they serve people as fairly as possible. Students should understand that fairness requires continuous attention rather than assuming technology automatically makes perfect decisions.

The AGI Generation will likely become one of the first generations asked to participate in discussions about AI policies, ethical standards, and responsible innovation. These conversations will take place in classrooms, businesses, research laboratories, government agencies, hospitals, and communities around the world. Students should recognize that they do not need to become computer scientists to contribute meaningfully. Every profession benefits from ethical thinkers who understand how technology affects people. Teachers, doctors, nurses, engineers, artists, business owners, lawyers, scientists, journalists, and community leaders all help shape how intelligent systems are used within society.

Respect for human dignity must remain one of the guiding principles of every intelligent system. Human dignity means recognizing that every person deserves respect, fairness, privacy, and equal opportunity regardless of age, background, culture, language, or ability. Technology should strengthen these values rather than weaken them. For example, educational AI should help every student learn more effectively without unfairly limiting opportunities. Healthcare AI should improve patient care while respecting confidentiality. Workplace AI should assist employees rather than treating people as numbers or statistics. Responsible innovation always begins by asking how technology can improve the lives of real people.

Ethical leadership becomes especially important as intelligent systems grow more capable. Leaders of the future will not only make decisions about businesses, schools, hospitals, and governments—they will also make decisions about how AI is developed and applied. Ethical leaders ask questions before implementing new technology. Who benefits from this system? Could anyone be harmed? Are there safeguards to protect privacy? Can people understand how important decisions are made? What happens if the technology makes a mistake? Asking these questions demonstrates responsibility and builds public trust. Students who practice ethical thinking today will become leaders capable of guiding technology wisely tomorrow.

Trust is one of the most valuable qualities any society can develop. Communities function effectively because people trust teachers to educate students, doctors to provide healthcare, engineers to build safe bridges, pilots to fly airplanes, and public officials to make responsible decisions. Artificial intelligence must also earn trust through careful design, testing, transparency, and responsible use. Trust cannot be demanded; it must be earned through consistent honesty, reliability, and accountability. Students should remember that their own actions contribute to building trust every day. Completing assignments honestly, treating others respectfully, admitting mistakes, and keeping promises all strengthen personal character while preparing them to become trustworthy professionals.

Artificial intelligence also creates opportunities for global cooperation. Many challenges facing humanity affect people across national borders. Climate change, disease prevention, disaster response, food security, clean water, and environmental protection all require countries to work together. AI can help researchers share information more efficiently, analyze worldwide data, and identify solutions that benefit many communities. However, successful international cooperation depends upon mutual respect, open communication, and shared ethical principles.

Students of the AGI Generation may one day collaborate with people from many different countries to solve problems that no single nation can solve alone.

Another important responsibility involves recognizing the limits of technology. AI may become increasingly powerful, but it will never replace the importance of human compassion. A computer can analyze data, but it cannot comfort a frightened child the way a caring parent can. It cannot encourage a discouraged student with genuine understanding. It cannot celebrate personal achievements with heartfelt joy or provide wisdom developed through years of life experience. These uniquely human qualities remind us that technology should always strengthen relationships rather than replace them. Students should never underestimate the importance of kindness, empathy, patience, and encouragement in building a better world.

Education plays a central role in preparing ethical citizens. Schools do much more than teach mathematics, science, language arts, and history. They also help students develop honesty, responsibility, perseverance, respect, cooperation, and leadership. As AI becomes part of everyday learning, ethical education becomes even more important. Students should learn how to evaluate information carefully, recognize misinformation, respect intellectual property, protect privacy, and use technology in ways that strengthen learning rather than avoiding personal effort. These habits prepare students to become responsible users of intelligent systems throughout adulthood.

The AGI Generation has an opportunity unlike any previous generation. Today's students will likely witness remarkable advances in intelligent technology throughout their lives. They may contribute to scientific discoveries, improve educational systems, design safer transportation, develop life-saving medical innovations, protect natural resources, or create businesses that improve communities around the world. Yet the greatest contribution they can make may not be technological at all. It may be their commitment to ensuring that every technological advancement reflects the highest values of humanity.

Imagine a future where intelligent systems help doctors cure diseases more quickly, assist teachers in helping every student succeed, protect forests and oceans through environmental monitoring, improve disaster response, and make transportation safer for millions of people. This future is possible, but it depends on people choosing to use technology wisely. Every generation passes something valuable to the next generation. The AGI Generation has the opportunity to pass forward not only extraordinary technology but also a culture of responsibility, fairness, compassion, and ethical leadership.

Ethics should never be viewed as something that limits innovation. Instead, ethics provides the foundation that allows innovation to succeed. When people trust technology, they are more willing to embrace new ideas that improve society. Responsible innovation builds confidence because it demonstrates respect for people while encouraging scientific and technological progress. Ethics and innovation work best when they move forward together.

As you continue learning about artificial intelligence, remember that every decision you make helps shape the future. Whether you become a teacher, scientist, engineer, doctor, entrepreneur, artist, programmer, public servant, or community volunteer, your values will influence how technology affects other people. Knowledge gives you the ability to create. Ethics gives you the wisdom to create responsibly.

The AGI Generation will not simply inherit an intelligent world. It will help define what kind of intelligent world future generations will experience. By choosing honesty over deception, fairness over bias, responsibility over carelessness, and compassion over indifference, today's students can ensure that artificial intelligence becomes one of humanity's greatest tools for improving life while protecting the dignity and well-being of every person.

Chapter 8 Summary

Ethics in an Intelligent World

As artificial intelligence becomes more advanced, ethics becomes more important than ever. Ethics helps people make responsible decisions by guiding them with values such as honesty, fairness, respect, responsibility, compassion, integrity, and accountability. While AI can analyze information and complete many complex tasks, it does not naturally understand human values. People remain responsible for deciding how intelligent systems should be designed, used, and improved.

This chapter explained that AI should support human decision-making rather than replace it in situations involving people's lives, education, healthcare, privacy, or public safety. Students learned about **human oversight**, which means people continue reviewing important AI-assisted decisions to ensure they are fair, accurate, and responsible.

The chapter also introduced the concept of **bias**, explaining that AI systems can sometimes produce unfair results if they are trained using incomplete or unbalanced data. Responsible developers continuously test, improve, and monitor AI systems to reduce bias and increase fairness.

Students explored several important ethical principles, including privacy, transparency, accountability, intellectual property, honesty, fairness, and respect for human dignity. They learned that ethical leadership requires asking thoughtful questions before introducing new technologies and considering how those technologies may affect individuals and society.

The chapter emphasized that education plays a major role in preparing future ethical leaders. Schools and families help students develop good character by teaching honesty, responsibility, empathy, cooperation, and respect. These qualities remain valuable regardless of how advanced technology becomes.

Finally, the chapter reminded students that ethics and innovation are partners, not opposites. Responsible innovation allows society to trust new technologies while ensuring that scientific progress continues to improve the lives of people everywhere. The AGI Generation has the opportunity to build an intelligent world guided by wisdom, fairness, and compassion.

Chapter 8 Reflection

Ethics in an Intelligent World

Take time to think carefully about the ideas discussed in this chapter. Answer each question using complete sentences and your own thoughts.

1. Why do you believe ethics becomes more important as artificial intelligence becomes more powerful?
2. What does human oversight mean, and why should people remain involved in important AI-assisted decisions?
3. Why should students care about privacy when using technology?
4. Explain why fairness is important when AI helps make decisions.
5. Describe a situation where honesty is more important than convenience.
6. Why should innovation always be guided by ethical principles?
7. How can schools help students become responsible users of artificial intelligence?
8. What personal values do you hope will guide your decisions as technology continues to evolve?

Personal Reflection

Imagine you are leading a team developing an AI system that will help students learn. Describe the ethical rules you would require before allowing your system to be used in schools. Explain how those rules would protect students while encouraging learning and innovation.

Chapter 8 Worksheet

Ethics in an Intelligent World

Part A – Vocabulary

Define each term using your own words.

1. Ethics

2. Human Oversight
3. Bias
4. Privacy
5. Transparency
6. Accountability
7. Fairness
8. Human Dignity
9. Intellectual Property
10. Responsible Innovation

Part B – Comprehension Questions

Answer each question using complete sentences.

1. Why is ethics important when developing artificial intelligence?
2. Explain the meaning of human oversight.
3. Why should AI systems be tested for bias?
4. How can students protect their privacy online?
5. Why is honesty important when using AI for school assignments?
6. What does transparency mean in AI systems?
7. How do schools and families help students develop ethical values?
8. Why should technology always respect human dignity?

Part C – Critical Thinking

Write one or two paragraphs for each question.

1. Imagine your school begins using AI to help teachers monitor student progress. What ethical rules should be followed to protect students?
2. Describe a situation where AI could improve people's lives but also create ethical concerns. Explain how those concerns could be addressed.
3. Why do you believe ethics and innovation should always work together instead of being viewed as opposites?

Part D – Ethical Leadership Activity

Create your own "AI Ethics Code."

Include:

- Five ethical principles every AI developer should follow.
- Three ways students should use AI responsibly.
- Three actions schools should take to protect student privacy.
- Three responsibilities future AI leaders should always remember.
- One personal promise describing how you will use AI ethically throughout your life.

Chapter 8 Quiz

Multiple Choice

Choose the best answer.

1. Ethics helps people:

A. Build faster computers.

B. Make responsible and fair decisions.

C. Avoid learning.

D. Replace teachers with AI.

2. Human oversight means:

A. AI makes every decision independently.

B. People continue reviewing important AI-assisted decisions.

C. Computers replace human judgment.

D. Students stop asking questions.

3. Bias in AI refers to:

A. Faster computer processing.

B. Unfair or unbalanced results.

C. Better technology.

D. Higher internet speed.

4. Which principle helps protect personal information?

A. Privacy

B. Speed

C. Automation

D. Memorization

5. Responsible innovation means:

A. Building technology without rules.

B. Developing technology that benefits people while following ethical principles.

C. Ignoring safety concerns.

D. Allowing AI to replace all human decisions.

True or False

6. _____ AI should always be used responsibly.
7. _____ Human values remain important in an intelligent world.
8. _____ Transparency helps build trust in AI systems.
9. _____ Students should use AI honestly when completing schoolwork.
10. _____ Ethics slows progress and should be ignored.

Short Answer

11. Explain why human oversight is important.
12. Describe one way people can protect their digital privacy.
13. Why should AI systems be designed fairly?
14. What role does accountability play in ethical technology?
15. In your own words, explain why ethics is essential for the AGI Generation.

Chapter 8 Answer Key

Multiple Choice

1. **B**
2. **B**
3. **B**

4. **A**
5. **B**

True or False

6. **True**
7. **True**
8. **True**
9. **True**
10. **False**

Short Answer (Sample Responses)

11. Human oversight ensures that people continue reviewing important AI-assisted decisions, verify results, correct mistakes, consider ethical concerns, and remain responsible for decisions that affect others.
12. People can protect their privacy by using strong passwords, enabling multi-factor authentication, limiting the sharing of personal information, recognizing online scams, updating software, and carefully reviewing privacy settings.
13. Fair AI systems provide equal opportunities, reduce discrimination, increase public trust, and help ensure that technology benefits individuals from all backgrounds fairly and responsibly.
14. Accountability means accepting responsibility for decisions, correcting mistakes, improving systems, and ensuring that people—not machines alone—remain responsible for the outcomes of AI-assisted decisions.
15. Ethics is essential because it guides people to use artificial intelligence honestly, fairly, responsibly, and compassionately. Ethical principles help ensure that technological progress improves lives while protecting human dignity, privacy, safety, and trust.

Chapter 9 – Part 1

Building Trust with Intelligent Systems

Trust is one of the most valuable qualities in every successful relationship. People trust doctors to provide medical care, teachers to guide learning, engineers to design safe buildings, pilots to fly airplanes, and family members to provide love and support. Trust allows people to work together, solve problems, and build strong communities. As artificial intelligence becomes a larger part of everyday life, society must also learn when to trust intelligent systems, how to use them responsibly, and when human judgment should take priority. The AGI Generation will play an important role in building that trust.

Artificial intelligence is becoming increasingly capable of helping people perform many different tasks. AI can organize large amounts of information, translate languages, recommend educational resources, analyze scientific data, recognize patterns, and assist professionals in making informed decisions. These abilities make AI an extremely valuable tool, but they do not mean AI is perfect. Like every tool created by people, intelligent systems have strengths and limitations. Understanding both is essential for using AI wisely.

Imagine using a map while traveling to a place you have never visited before. A map provides valuable guidance, but it cannot tell you everything that may happen along the way. A road may be closed because of construction. Severe weather may require a different route. A bridge may temporarily be unavailable. Good travelers use maps while also paying attention to their surroundings and making thoughtful decisions when unexpected situations occur. Artificial intelligence works in a similar way. It provides useful guidance, but people must continue observing, thinking, and making responsible decisions based on the complete situation.

One of the first steps in building trust with intelligent systems is understanding where information comes from. AI systems learn by analyzing enormous collections of data that may include books, articles, scientific research, educational materials, public information, and many other sources. The quality of the information they produce depends greatly on the quality of the information they learn from. If information is incomplete, outdated, or inaccurate, the results may also contain mistakes. This is why responsible users always verify important information, especially when decisions affect health, education, finances, or public safety.

Verification is an important habit for every student. Instead of accepting every answer immediately, students should compare information from reliable sources, examine supporting evidence, and ask thoughtful questions. A science student researching climate change should compare findings from trusted scientific organizations. A history student should examine information from multiple historical sources. A health student should rely on qualified medical professionals and trusted health organizations. These habits strengthen critical thinking and help students become informed learners who understand how knowledge is developed.

Trust also grows through consistency. Imagine working with a classmate who always arrives prepared, completes assignments honestly, and contributes respectfully during group projects. Over time, classmates begin trusting that person's reliability because consistent actions build confidence. Intelligent systems must also demonstrate consistency. Organizations developing AI carefully test their systems to improve accuracy, identify weaknesses, and reduce errors before those systems are widely used. Even after deployment, many AI systems continue to be monitored and improved as new information becomes available. Continuous improvement helps strengthen trust because it shows a commitment to reliability and responsibility.

Transparency plays another important role in building trust. People generally feel more confident when they understand how important decisions are made. If AI helps recommend educational resources, identify medical concerns, or organize financial information, users should receive clear explanations whenever possible. Transparency encourages questions, allows mistakes to be corrected, and helps people understand both the strengths and limitations of intelligent technology. Students should remember that trustworthy systems do not hide from careful examination. They encourage responsible evaluation because openness builds confidence.

The AGI Generation will also need to recognize that confidence should never become overconfidence. It is possible to trust technology too much or too little. Someone who distrusts every technological tool may miss valuable opportunities to learn and solve problems. On the other hand, someone who blindly accepts every AI-generated answer without questioning it may make unnecessary mistakes. Responsible users seek balance. They appreciate the strengths of AI while continuing to exercise human judgment, common sense, and ethical reasoning.

Critical thinking becomes especially important when AI produces information that appears convincing. Sometimes an explanation may sound logical while still containing factual errors or incomplete reasoning. Students should ask questions such as: Does this information agree with other reliable sources? Is there evidence supporting these claims? Is the information current? Are important details missing? These habits help learners distinguish between information that is reliable and information that requires additional investigation. Trust grows stronger when it is supported by evidence rather than assumptions.

Communication also strengthens trust. Teachers who explain how AI is being used in the classroom help students understand its purpose. Doctors who discuss how AI assists with medical analysis help patients feel more comfortable with new technologies. Business leaders who communicate openly about AI-powered tools help employees understand how technology supports their work. Honest communication reduces fear because people understand what technology is doing and why it is being used. Students should develop the habit of asking respectful questions whenever they encounter unfamiliar technologies rather than making assumptions.

Trust is closely connected to responsibility. Every person using AI shares some responsibility for using it wisely. Students should use AI honestly when completing schoolwork. Researchers should carefully verify scientific findings. Business professionals should review important recommendations before making decisions. Healthcare providers should combine AI-assisted analysis with medical expertise and compassionate patient care. Technology supports people, but responsibility remains with the individuals who choose how technology will be applied.

Building trust also requires patience. Society did not immediately trust automobiles, airplanes, or the internet when those technologies first appeared. Over time, improvements in safety, education, regulations, and public understanding increased confidence. Artificial intelligence is following a similar path. As people learn more about how intelligent systems work, how they are tested, and how they are used responsibly, trust can continue growing through knowledge rather than uncertainty.

Perhaps the most important lesson for the AGI Generation is that trust is earned through actions. Intelligent systems become more trustworthy when they are accurate, transparent, fair, secure, and carefully monitored. People become more trustworthy when they use technology honestly, verify information carefully, respect others, and accept responsibility for their decisions.

Together, these qualities create partnerships where people and intelligent systems complement one another in positive and meaningful ways.

The future will not depend only on building more intelligent machines. It will also depend on building greater trust between people and the technologies they choose to use. Students who understand how trust is earned, maintained, and strengthened will be well prepared to lead responsibly in an increasingly intelligent world.

Chapter 9 – Part 2

Building Trust with Intelligent Systems

As artificial intelligence becomes part of everyday life, students will need to learn an important habit that has guided scientists, educators, engineers, and researchers for generations: never stop asking thoughtful questions. Trust does not mean accepting every answer without thinking. Instead, trust means understanding when a system has demonstrated reliability while still recognizing that mistakes are always possible. The most successful users of AI will be those who combine confidence with careful thinking. They will appreciate the value of intelligent systems while continuing to verify important information, evaluate evidence, and make responsible decisions.

One way students can build this habit is by practicing healthy skepticism. Healthy skepticism does not mean assuming that everything is wrong. It means carefully examining information before accepting it as true. For example, if an AI system provides a scientific explanation, students should compare it with trusted textbooks, educational resources, or information provided by their teachers. If AI summarizes a historical event, learners can compare multiple reliable sources to gain a more complete understanding. This process strengthens learning because students actively participate in evaluating information instead of becoming passive readers.

Another important part of trust is understanding confidence and uncertainty. Sometimes AI can provide highly reliable answers because the information is well established. At other times, especially when discussing future events, complex opinions, or incomplete research, uncertainty naturally exists. Responsible students learn that not every question has a simple answer. They become comfortable saying, "We need more evidence," or "Researchers are still studying this topic." Recognizing uncertainty is not a weakness. It is a sign of intellectual honesty and mature thinking.

The ability to recognize misinformation will also become an essential skill for the AGI Generation. Modern technology allows information to spread around the world within seconds. Unfortunately, inaccurate information can spread just as quickly as accurate information. Some false information is shared accidentally because people misunderstand the facts. Other misinformation is shared intentionally to confuse or mislead others. Artificial intelligence can sometimes make this challenge even more complicated because it can generate realistic-looking text, images, audio, and video. Students should learn to pause before believing or sharing information. Asking simple questions such as "Who created this?" "What evidence supports it?" and "Can I verify this through another trusted source?" helps reduce the spread of misinformation.

Digital literacy plays an important role in building trust. Digital literacy means understanding how technology works, how information is created, how online content is shared, and how to use digital tools responsibly. Students with strong digital literacy understand that search results, recommendations, and AI-generated responses should be evaluated thoughtfully. They know how to identify trustworthy organizations, recognize reliable evidence, and distinguish between facts, opinions, advertisements, and speculation. These skills prepare students to make informed decisions throughout their lives.

Cybersecurity is another important part of building trust. People are more willing to use intelligent technologies when they know their information is protected. Students should learn basic cybersecurity habits early in life. Creating strong passwords, enabling multi-factor authentication when available, avoiding suspicious links, keeping software updated, and protecting personal information all reduce digital risks. These simple habits help individuals become responsible technology users while strengthening confidence in digital systems.

Trust also grows when people understand the purpose of technology. AI should be viewed as a tool that helps people achieve meaningful goals rather than as a replacement for human intelligence. A calculator helps students perform calculations more efficiently, but it does not replace mathematical understanding. A navigation application suggests travel routes, but drivers remain responsible for operating their vehicles safely. In the same way, AI can organize information, identify patterns, and support decision-making, but people remain responsible for applying judgment, ethics, and common sense. Understanding this partnership prevents unrealistic expectations while encouraging responsible use.

The workplace of the future will depend heavily on trust between people and intelligent systems. Imagine an engineer designing a bridge with AI-assisted software. The software may analyze thousands of design possibilities in a short period of time, but the engineer still reviews safety requirements, considers environmental conditions, follows engineering standards, and approves the final design. Likewise, a healthcare professional may use AI to identify possible medical concerns, but compassionate patient care, communication, and treatment decisions remain human responsibilities. Trust grows because professionals understand both the strengths and the limits of intelligent technology.

Building trust also requires continuous learning. Artificial intelligence is evolving rapidly, and tomorrow's systems will likely be more capable than those available today. Students who remain curious and committed to lifelong learning will be better prepared to understand new developments. Instead of fearing change, they will have the confidence to learn about new technologies, ask informed questions, and evaluate how those technologies should be used responsibly. Lifelong learning helps people adapt while maintaining high standards of ethical decision-making.

Communities also play an important role in creating trustworthy technology. Schools teach responsible digital citizenship. Families encourage honesty and respect. Businesses develop ethical guidelines for AI use. Governments establish laws that protect privacy, safety, and fairness. Researchers continue improving AI systems while identifying potential risks. Every part of society contributes to building public confidence. Trust is not created by technology alone. It grows when people work together with shared values and a commitment to serving the common good.

Students should remember that trust takes time to build but can be lost quickly. A single dishonest action can damage relationships that required years to develop. The same principle applies to technology. Organizations that use AI responsibly, communicate openly, protect privacy, and correct mistakes strengthen public confidence over time. Those that ignore ethical responsibilities may lose the trust of the people they hope to serve. This lesson extends beyond technology into every part of life. Honesty, reliability, and accountability remain the foundation of lasting trust.

The AGI Generation has an opportunity to become one of the most informed and responsible generations in history. Rather than fearing intelligent systems or depending on them completely, students can learn to build thoughtful partnerships with technology. They can ask meaningful questions, verify information, communicate openly, respect privacy, protect security, and make decisions guided by ethics and evidence. These habits will help them become trusted professionals, responsible citizens, and confident leaders.

As artificial intelligence continues to advance, trust will remain one of humanity's greatest strengths. Intelligent machines may become faster, more accurate, and more capable, but they will achieve their greatest value only when guided by people who act with integrity, wisdom, compassion, and responsibility. The future belongs not simply to those who create powerful technologies, but to those who earn the confidence of others through honesty, fairness, and thoughtful leadership.

The AGI Generation has the opportunity to build more than intelligent systems. It has the opportunity to build a future where trust, knowledge, and human values work together, ensuring that technology remains a force for learning, innovation, cooperation, and hope for generations to come.

Chapter 9 Summary

Building Trust with Intelligent Systems

Trust is one of the most important foundations of successful relationships, strong communities, and responsible technology. As artificial intelligence becomes a larger part of everyday life, people must learn how to use intelligent systems wisely while continuing to rely on human judgment, ethical decision-making, and critical thinking.

This chapter explained that trust is earned through honesty, reliability, fairness, transparency, accountability, and responsible actions. Students learned that AI is a powerful tool that can organize information, analyze data, recognize patterns, and support decision-making, but it is not perfect. Intelligent systems can make mistakes, which is why people should always verify important information, especially when decisions involve education, healthcare, finances, or public safety.

The chapter introduced the importance of **human oversight**, reminding students that people remain responsible for reviewing AI-assisted decisions and making final judgments. Readers also learned about **healthy skepticism**, which encourages people to ask thoughtful questions, compare reliable sources, and evaluate evidence before accepting information as accurate.

Students explored the growing importance of digital literacy, cybersecurity, and recognizing misinformation in an AI-powered world. They learned that responsible technology users protect their personal information, think carefully before sharing content, and understand that trustworthy information should be verified using reliable sources.

The chapter also emphasized that trust depends upon continuous learning. As AI continues evolving, students should remain curious, adaptable, and committed to lifelong learning while developing the skills needed to evaluate new technologies responsibly.

Finally, the chapter concluded that the future of AI depends not only on intelligent machines but also on trustworthy people. By combining knowledge with integrity, responsibility, transparency, and ethical leadership, the AGI Generation can build a future where people and intelligent systems work together to improve society while protecting human values.

Chapter 9 Reflection

Building Trust with Intelligent Systems

Think carefully about the lessons from this chapter. Answer each question using complete sentences and your own ideas.

1. Why is trust important when people use artificial intelligence?
2. What does healthy skepticism mean, and why is it valuable?
3. Why should students verify AI-generated information before accepting it as true?
4. How can digital literacy help people become more responsible technology users?
5. Why is human oversight necessary when AI assists with important decisions?
6. Describe one way cybersecurity helps build trust in technology.
7. How can honesty strengthen trust between people and intelligent systems?
8. What personal habits will help you become someone others can trust in an AI-powered world?

Personal Reflection

Imagine you are leading a team responsible for introducing AI into your school district. Explain how you would build trust among students, teachers, parents, and the community. Describe the policies, communication, and ethical practices you would put in place to ensure that AI supports learning while protecting privacy, fairness, and human responsibility.

Chapter 9 Worksheet

Building Trust with Intelligent Systems

Part A – Vocabulary

Define each term using your own words.

1. Trust
2. Human Oversight
3. Transparency
4. Accountability
5. Digital Literacy
6. Cybersecurity
7. Healthy Skepticism
8. Verification
9. Misinformation
10. Reliability

Part B – Comprehension Questions

Answer each question using complete sentences.

1. Why is trust important when using AI?
2. Explain why AI should not replace human judgment.
3. What does it mean to verify information?
4. Why is transparency important in intelligent systems?
5. How does cybersecurity protect people?
6. What is healthy skepticism?
7. Why is lifelong learning important in an AI-powered world?
8. How can responsible technology users strengthen public trust?

Part C – Critical Thinking

Write one or two paragraphs for each question.

1. Imagine your school begins using AI to help students with homework. What rules should teachers create to ensure that students continue learning honestly while using AI responsibly?
2. Explain why trust is earned over time rather than created instantly. How does this idea apply to both people and AI systems?
3. Describe how families, schools, businesses, and governments can work together to build trustworthy AI systems that benefit society.

Part D – Building Trust Action Plan

Create your own "Responsible AI User Plan."

Include:

• Five habits that help build trust.

• Three ways to verify information before believing or sharing it.

• Three cybersecurity habits every student should practice.

• Three responsibilities you have when using AI.

• One personal commitment describing how you will earn the trust of others while using intelligent technology.

Chapter 9 Quiz

Multiple Choice

Choose the best answer.

1. According to this chapter, trust is built through:

A. Speed alone.

B. Honesty, reliability, transparency, and responsibility.

C. Artificial intelligence only.

D. Memorization.

2. Human oversight means:

A. AI makes every important decision independently.

B. People continue reviewing important AI-assisted decisions.

C. Computers replace teachers.

D. Technology eliminates responsibility.

3. Healthy skepticism encourages students to:

A. Believe everything immediately.

B. Ask questions and verify information.

C. Ignore evidence.

D. Avoid technology.

4. Digital literacy helps students:

A. Use technology responsibly.

B. Evaluate online information.

C. Recognize misinformation.

D. All of the above.

5. Cybersecurity helps protect:

A. Personal information and digital systems.

B. School lunch schedules only.

C. Paper notebooks.

D. Printed textbooks.

True or False

6. _____ AI should always be used with human judgment.
7. _____ Trust grows through consistent responsible behavior.
8. _____ Students should share online information without checking it first.
9. _____ Digital literacy is an important skill in the AGI era.
10. _____ Lifelong learning helps people adapt to new technologies.

Short Answer

11. Explain why verification is important when using AI.
12. Describe one example of healthy skepticism.
13. Why should students practice good cybersecurity habits?
14. How does transparency help build trust?
15. In your own words, explain what it means to build trust with intelligent systems.

Chapter 9 Answer Key

Multiple Choice

1. **B**
2. **B**
3. **B**
4. **D**
5. **A**

True or False

6. **True**
7. **True**
8. **False**
9. **True**
10. **True**

Short Answer (Sample Responses)

11. Verification helps ensure that AI-generated information is accurate, reliable, current, and supported by trustworthy evidence before important decisions are made.
12. Healthy skepticism means asking thoughtful questions, comparing multiple reliable sources, examining evidence, and avoiding the acceptance of information without careful evaluation.

13. Cybersecurity protects personal information, prevents unauthorized access, reduces online risks, and helps people use digital technology safely and responsibly.
14. Transparency allows people to understand how important AI-assisted decisions are made, encourages accountability, builds confidence, and makes it easier to identify and correct mistakes.
15. Building trust with intelligent systems means using AI responsibly, verifying important information, protecting privacy, practicing honesty, respecting others, maintaining human oversight, and combining technology with ethical judgment to benefit individuals and society.

Chapter 10 – Part 1

Lifelong Learning in the Age of AGI

For most of human history, education followed a fairly predictable path. Children attended school, learned the knowledge considered important at the time, graduated, and entered careers where many of those same skills remained useful for decades. Although people continued learning through experience, the pace of change was often slow enough that the education received during childhood could support an entire working life.

Today, that pattern is changing. Artificial intelligence, automation, robotics, biotechnology, advanced computing, and other rapidly developing technologies are transforming industries faster than ever before. New careers appear while existing jobs evolve. Scientific discoveries happen more quickly, and information spreads across the world in seconds. In this environment, education can no longer be viewed as something that ends with graduation. Instead, learning becomes a lifelong journey that continues throughout every stage of life.

The AGI Generation is growing up during one of the most significant technological transitions in history. These students will likely witness advances that previous generations could only imagine. Intelligent machines may help scientists develop new medicines, engineers build safer cities, educators personalize instruction, and environmental researchers protect natural resources. As these changes occur, the people who continue learning will be the ones best prepared to adapt, contribute, and lead.

Lifelong learning does not mean spending every day in a classroom. It means developing a mindset that welcomes new knowledge, new skills, and new experiences. A lifelong learner remains curious even after becoming an expert in a particular field. Instead of believing there is nothing left to discover, lifelong learners understand that every answer often leads to new questions. They recognize that learning is not a temporary activity but an ongoing habit that strengthens both personal growth and professional success.

Curiosity serves as the engine of lifelong learning. Curious people naturally explore topics beyond what is required. They read books, ask thoughtful questions, observe the world around them, conduct experiments, and seek conversations with people who have different experiences. Artificial intelligence can make this exploration easier by organizing information, explaining difficult concepts, and suggesting related topics for further study. However, AI cannot create genuine curiosity. That desire to learn begins within each individual.

One of the greatest advantages of lifelong learning is adaptability. As technology evolves, professionals who continue learning can confidently adjust to new tools, changing responsibilities, and emerging opportunities. Consider healthcare as an example. Doctors today use medical technologies that did not exist when many of them first entered medical school. Teachers now use digital learning platforms, interactive educational software, and AI-assisted instructional tools that were unavailable only a few years ago. Engineers regularly update their knowledge to work with new materials, improved design methods, and advanced computer systems. Lifelong learning allows professionals to remain effective as their careers evolve.

Students sometimes believe that successful people simply know more than everyone else. In reality, successful people often continue learning throughout their entire lives. They attend workshops, earn additional certifications, read professional journals, participate in conferences, collaborate with colleagues, and remain informed about new discoveries in their fields. They understand that knowledge grows continuously and that staying current requires ongoing effort.

Artificial intelligence can become an excellent learning partner throughout this process. Imagine a student interested in environmental science. AI can organize research about climate systems, explain scientific vocabulary, summarize recent studies, generate practice questions, and recommend additional resources for deeper learning. A future entrepreneur may use AI to analyze business trends, understand customer needs, or learn about financial planning. A future engineer might use intelligent tools to explore new construction materials or simulate design ideas. In every case, AI supports learning, but personal curiosity and determination remain the driving forces behind success.

Lifelong learning also strengthens confidence. Every time students master a new skill, solve a difficult problem, or understand a challenging concept, they prove to themselves that growth is possible. Confidence built through learning is different from confidence based only on natural ability. It comes from experience, persistence, and the knowledge that improvement is always possible through continued effort. Students who develop this mindset become less afraid of change because they trust their ability to learn whatever the future requires.

Another important benefit of lifelong learning is resilience. Technology will continue changing throughout the lives of today's students. Some skills that are valuable today may become less important tomorrow, while entirely new areas of expertise will emerge. Lifelong learners respond to these changes with flexibility rather than fear. Instead of asking, "What if my job changes?" they ask, "What new skills should I learn next?" This shift in thinking transforms uncertainty into opportunity.

Reading remains one of the most powerful tools for lifelong learning. Books introduce readers to new ideas, cultures, discoveries, and perspectives. Scientific articles explain recent research. Biographies teach lessons from the lives of remarkable individuals. Historical accounts help readers understand how past decisions continue influencing the present. Even in an age of advanced AI, reading develops concentration, vocabulary, comprehension, and critical thinking in ways that strengthen every other learning activity.

Equally important is the habit of reflection. Learning becomes more meaningful when students pause to think about what they have discovered. Reflection helps people connect new knowledge with previous experiences, recognize patterns, identify areas for improvement, and apply ideas to real-world situations. Journaling, discussing ideas with classmates, or simply taking time to think carefully after completing a project helps transform information into lasting understanding.

Teachers play an essential role in helping students become lifelong learners. Great educators do more than teach facts. They model curiosity by continuing to learn themselves. They encourage questions, celebrate improvement, and demonstrate that learning is an exciting adventure rather than a task to complete. When students see teachers enjoying discovery, they are more likely to develop the same attitude toward education.

Families also contribute to lifelong learning by encouraging reading, visiting museums, exploring nature, discussing current events, supporting hobbies, and celebrating curiosity. A simple family conversation about space exploration, local history, wildlife, or new technology may inspire interests that last a lifetime. Learning happens not only in classrooms but also in homes, libraries, parks, workplaces, and communities.

The AGI Generation has an extraordinary opportunity to become the most educated generation in history—not because students will memorize more information than previous generations, but because they will have unprecedented access to knowledge while developing the habits needed to keep learning throughout life. Their greatest advantage will not be what they already know, but their willingness to continue discovering what they do not yet know.

In a world where technology changes rapidly, the ability to learn may become the most valuable skill of all. Students who remain curious, adaptable, thoughtful, and committed to lifelong learning will be prepared not only to succeed in future careers but also to contribute meaningfully to their families, communities, and society. Lifelong learning is more than an educational strategy. It is a way of approaching life with hope, confidence, and the belief that every day offers another opportunity to grow.

Chapter 10 – Part 2

Lifelong Learning in the Age of AGI

One of the greatest changes brought about by artificial intelligence is not simply the speed at which information can be found. It is the way people learn. Previous generations often depended on schools, libraries, or workplace training as their primary sources of education. Today's students have access to online courses, educational videos, digital libraries, virtual classrooms, intelligent tutoring systems, interactive simulations, and AI learning assistants that are available almost anytime and almost anywhere. This abundance of learning opportunities means students have more responsibility than ever before for directing their own education.

Self-directed learning is the ability to take responsibility for personal growth. Instead of waiting for someone else to assign every lesson, self-directed learners ask questions, identify skills they want to develop, locate reliable learning resources, create study plans, and evaluate their own progress. This habit becomes especially valuable in the AGI era because knowledge continues expanding rapidly. Students who become independent learners will be better prepared to adapt as new discoveries and technologies emerge throughout their lives.

Artificial intelligence can become a valuable guide during this process. An AI learning assistant may recommend books, explain unfamiliar concepts, generate practice exercises, organize study schedules, or suggest new topics related to a student's interests. Imagine a student fascinated by renewable energy. AI might recommend learning about solar engineering, battery technology, environmental science, economics, and public policy. Instead of studying only one subject, the student gradually develops a broader understanding of how different fields work together to solve real-world problems. AI accelerates exploration, but the student's motivation continues driving the learning journey.

Learning should also become more personalized. Every student has unique strengths, interests, goals, and learning styles. Some people learn effectively by reading. Others prefer visual demonstrations, hands-on experiments, group discussions, or practical experience. Future educational technologies may adapt to these individual differences by presenting information in ways that help each learner understand concepts more effectively. Even with personalized instruction, however, students must remain actively engaged. No technology can replace the determination required to practice difficult skills, ask thoughtful questions, and continue improving through effort.

Another important aspect of lifelong learning is learning from failure. Many students become discouraged when they receive disappointing grades or struggle with difficult concepts. Yet failure often provides some of the most valuable learning opportunities. Scientists conduct experiments that do not produce expected results. Engineers redesign prototypes after identifying weaknesses. Writers revise manuscripts repeatedly before publication. Entrepreneurs improve business ideas after receiving customer feedback. Every challenge teaches valuable lessons that contribute to future success. Lifelong learners understand that temporary setbacks are part of the learning process rather than evidence of permanent inability.

Feedback also plays an important role in continuous improvement. Teachers provide feedback on assignments. Coaches help athletes improve techniques. Music instructors guide students toward stronger performances. Employers offer suggestions that help employees develop professionally. Artificial intelligence may also provide immediate feedback by identifying mistakes, explaining concepts, or recommending additional practice. However, successful learners understand that feedback should be welcomed rather than feared. Constructive feedback helps people recognize strengths while identifying opportunities for growth.

Mentorship becomes increasingly valuable as students prepare for future careers. A mentor is someone with experience who provides guidance, encouragement, and practical advice. Teachers, parents, coaches, business leaders, community volunteers, and experienced professionals often serve as mentors. AI can provide information, but mentors share wisdom gained through real-life experiences. They explain how to overcome obstacles, develop good habits, build professional relationships, and make thoughtful decisions. Students who seek mentors often gain confidence because they learn from individuals who have successfully faced similar challenges.

The AGI Generation will also benefit from learning communities. Education is no longer limited to a single classroom or school building. Students may collaborate with learners across different cities, states, or countries using intelligent communication tools. They may participate in international science competitions, engineering projects, environmental research, or cultural exchanges. These experiences expose students to new perspectives while strengthening communication, teamwork, and global understanding. Artificial intelligence helps organize these collaborations, but meaningful learning continues to depend upon respectful human interaction.

Creativity remains an essential part of lifelong learning. As AI becomes increasingly capable of generating information, students should focus on developing original ideas, asking creative questions, and exploring innovative solutions. Creativity allows learners to connect knowledge from different subjects, imagine possibilities that have never existed before, and solve problems in ways that improve society. Future careers will reward people who can think creatively while working responsibly alongside intelligent technologies.

Another important habit is setting personal learning goals. Successful learners rarely improve by accident. They identify specific objectives, develop plans, measure progress, and celebrate achievements along the way. A student may decide to improve public speaking, learn computer programming, strengthen mathematical reasoning, master another language, or study environmental science more deeply. Setting clear goals provides direction while helping students remain motivated during challenging periods. AI may assist by organizing study schedules or tracking progress, but commitment and persistence remain personal responsibilities.

Time management also becomes increasingly important. The digital world offers endless opportunities for learning, but it also presents many distractions. Social media, entertainment, games, and constant notifications compete for attention throughout the day. Lifelong learners develop habits that help them focus on meaningful priorities. They schedule study time, reduce unnecessary distractions, organize responsibilities, and balance learning with rest, exercise, family activities, and recreation. These habits support both academic success and personal well-being.

One of the greatest rewards of lifelong learning is confidence in facing change. Students cannot predict every technological breakthrough they will experience during adulthood. However, they can prepare themselves by developing confidence in their ability to continue learning. When new tools, careers, or discoveries appear, lifelong learners do not panic. Instead, they ask questions, explore reliable resources, practice new skills, and gradually become comfortable with unfamiliar ideas. This confidence allows them to adapt successfully throughout life.

The AGI Generation may become the first generation where learning truly has no boundaries. Intelligent technologies make education more accessible to people living in different countries, speaking different languages, and pursuing different careers. A student interested in astronomy can learn from scientists across the world. Someone interested in medicine can study the latest discoveries published by international researchers. Artists can collaborate with creators from different cultures. Entrepreneurs can learn business strategies from experienced professionals worldwide. Knowledge becomes more connected than ever before, allowing students to learn beyond the limits of traditional classrooms.

Yet even with these remarkable opportunities, the heart of lifelong learning remains unchanged. It still depends upon curiosity, perseverance, humility, discipline, and a willingness to improve. Technology can make learning faster and more convenient, but it cannot replace the satisfaction that comes from mastering a difficult skill, solving a challenging problem, or achieving a meaningful goal through personal effort.

As you continue preparing for your future, remember that your education does not end when you graduate from school. Every book you read, every conversation you have, every challenge you overcome, every question you ask, and every new skill you develop becomes part of your lifelong learning journey. The world will continue changing, and you will continue changing with it.

The AGI Generation has an extraordinary opportunity to become a generation of lifelong learners who embrace discovery, adapt confidently to new technologies, and use knowledge to improve the lives of others. Artificial intelligence may become one of the greatest educational tools ever created, but the true power of learning will always begin inside the human mind—with the decision to remain curious, keep growing, and never stop exploring the endless possibilities that knowledge can provide.

Chapter 10 Summary

Lifelong Learning in the Age of AGI

The world is changing faster than ever before because of advances in artificial intelligence, robotics, automation, and other emerging technologies. As careers, industries, and knowledge continue to evolve, education can no longer end with graduation. Lifelong learning has become one of the most valuable skills students can develop.

This chapter explained that lifelong learning is the continuous pursuit of knowledge, skills, and personal growth throughout a person's life. Lifelong learners remain curious, adaptable, and willing to explore new ideas. They understand that every new discovery creates opportunities to learn even more.

Students learned about the importance of self-directed learning, where individuals take responsibility for their own education by asking questions, setting goals, finding reliable resources, and evaluating their progress. Artificial intelligence can support this process by recommending learning materials, explaining concepts, generating practice activities, and organizing study plans, but personal motivation and curiosity remain essential.

The chapter also emphasized the importance of learning from failure. Mistakes should not be viewed as signs of weakness but as opportunities to improve understanding, develop resilience, and strengthen problem-solving skills. Feedback from teachers, mentors, coaches, and intelligent learning systems helps learners continue growing throughout their lives.

Readers explored the value of mentorship, global learning communities, creativity, goal setting, and time management. These habits prepare students to continue learning as technology, careers, and society evolve.

Finally, the chapter concluded that the AGI Generation has an opportunity to become one of the most educated and adaptable generations in history. Artificial intelligence may become an extraordinary learning partner, but lifelong curiosity, perseverance, discipline, and ethical responsibility will always remain the foundation of meaningful education.

Chapter 10 Reflection

Lifelong Learning in the Age of AGI

Think carefully about the lessons from this chapter. Answer each question using complete sentences.

1. Why is lifelong learning becoming more important in today's world?
2. What does it mean to become a self-directed learner?
3. How can AI help people continue learning throughout their lives?
4. Why should students view mistakes as opportunities instead of failures?
5. Describe a skill you hope to continue improving after graduating from school.
6. Why are mentors valuable throughout a person's life?
7. How can time management improve lifelong learning?
8. What personal habits do you want to develop that will help you remain curious throughout your life?

Personal Reflection

Imagine yourself twenty years from now. Describe how lifelong learning has helped you adapt to new technologies, improve your career, and make positive contributions to your family, community, and society. Explain how AI has supported your learning while your curiosity and determination continued guiding your personal growth.

Chapter 10 Worksheet

Lifelong Learning in the Age of AGI

Part A – Vocabulary

Define each term using your own words.

1. Lifelong Learning
2. Self-Directed Learning
3. Adaptability
4. Curiosity
5. Mentorship
6. Feedback
7. Resilience
8. Goal Setting
9. Time Management
10. Continuous Improvement

Part B – Comprehension Questions

Answer each question using complete sentences.

1. Why has lifelong learning become more important during the AGI era?
2. How does self-directed learning help students prepare for the future?
3. Name three ways AI can support lifelong learning.
4. Why is feedback valuable for personal growth?
5. Explain how resilience helps students continue learning.
6. Why should students establish personal learning goals?
7. How do mentors help lifelong learners succeed?
8. Why is curiosity considered the foundation of lifelong learning?

Part C – Critical Thinking

Write one or two paragraphs for each question.

1. Imagine you are preparing students for careers that do not yet exist. What learning habits would you encourage them to develop, and why?
2. Explain how lifelong learning can help people adapt to rapid technological changes while remaining confident and successful.
3. Describe how schools, families, communities, and AI can work together to encourage lifelong learning.

Part D – My Lifelong Learning Plan

Develop your own learning roadmap.

Include:

• Five skills you want to strengthen.

• Three new subjects you want to explore.

• Three habits that will help you become a lifelong learner.

• Three ways AI can support your education responsibly.

• One long-term learning goal you hope to accomplish during your lifetime.

Chapter 10 Worksheet

Lifelong Learning in the Age of AGI

Part A – Vocabulary

Define each term using your own words.

1. Lifelong Learning
2. Self-Directed Learning
3. Adaptability
4. Curiosity
5. Mentorship
6. Feedback
7. Resilience
8. Goal Setting
9. Time Management
10. Continuous Improvement

Part B – Comprehension Questions

Answer each question using complete sentences.

1. Why has lifelong learning become more important during the AGI era?
2. How does self-directed learning help students prepare for the future?

3. Name three ways AI can support lifelong learning.
4. Why is feedback valuable for personal growth?
5. Explain how resilience helps students continue learning.
6. Why should students establish personal learning goals?
7. How do mentors help lifelong learners succeed?
8. Why is curiosity considered the foundation of lifelong learning?

Part C – Critical Thinking

Write one or two paragraphs for each question.

1. Imagine you are preparing students for careers that do not yet exist. What learning habits would you encourage them to develop, and why?
2. Explain how lifelong learning can help people adapt to rapid technological changes while remaining confident and successful.
3. Describe how schools, families, communities, and AI can work together to encourage lifelong learning.

Part D – My Lifelong Learning Plan

Develop your own learning roadmap.

Include:

• Five skills you want to strengthen.

• Three new subjects you want to explore.

• Three habits that will help you become a lifelong learner.

• Three ways AI can support your education responsibly.

• One long-term learning goal you hope to accomplish during your lifetime.

Chapter 10 Quiz

Multiple Choice

Choose the best answer.

1. Lifelong learning means:

A. Learning ends after graduation.

B. Continuing to develop knowledge and skills throughout life.

C. Memorizing every textbook.

D. Learning only during school.

2. Self-directed learners:

A. Wait for others to teach them everything.

B. Take responsibility for their own learning.

C. Avoid asking questions.

D. Stop learning after finding a job.

3. AI can support lifelong learning by:

A. Organizing information.

B. Explaining difficult concepts.

C. Recommending learning resources.

D. All of the above.

4. Why is resilience important?

A. It helps learners recover from setbacks and continue improving.

B. It eliminates mistakes.

C. It replaces practice.

D. It guarantees success without effort.

5. Which habit supports lifelong learning?

A. Curiosity

B. Goal setting

C. Time management

D. All of the above.

True or False

6. _____ Lifelong learning helps people adapt to changing careers.
7. _____ AI replaces the need for personal motivation.
8. _____ Mentors can help people grow professionally and personally.
9. _____ Feedback can improve learning and performance.
10. _____ Curiosity encourages continuous learning throughout life.

Short Answer

11. Explain why lifelong learning is important in the AGI era.
12. Describe one benefit of self-directed learning.
13. How can AI become a learning partner?
14. Why should students welcome constructive feedback?
15. In your own words, explain how lifelong learning prepares people for the future.

Chapter 10 Answer Key

Multiple Choice

1. **B**
2. **B**
3. **D**
4. **A**
5. **D**

True or False

6. **True**
7. **False**
8. **True**
9. **True**
10. **True**

Short Answer (Sample Responses)

11. Lifelong learning helps people remain adaptable as technology, careers, and society continue changing. It allows individuals to develop new skills, stay informed, and contribute successfully throughout their lives.
12. Self-directed learning encourages students to take responsibility for their education by setting goals, asking questions, finding reliable resources, and continuing to improve independently.
13. AI can organize information, explain complex concepts, recommend educational resources, generate practice activities, provide feedback, and help learners explore new topics more efficiently.
14. Constructive feedback helps learners recognize strengths, identify areas for improvement, correct mistakes, and continue developing knowledge and skills throughout life.
15. Lifelong learning prepares people for the future by encouraging curiosity, adaptability, resilience, continuous skill development, and responsible use of technology. It enables individuals to respond confidently to new opportunities while contributing positively to their communities and professions.

Chapter 10 Answer Key

Multiple Choice

1. **B**
2. **B**
3. **D**
4. **A**
5. **D**

True or False

6. **True**
7. **False**
8. **True**
9. **True**
10. **True**

Short Answer (Sample Responses)

11. Lifelong learning helps people remain adaptable as technology, careers, and society continue changing. It allows individuals to develop new skills, stay informed, and contribute successfully throughout their lives.
12. Self-directed learning encourages students to take responsibility for their education by setting goals, asking questions, finding reliable resources, and continuing to improve independently.
13. AI can organize information, explain complex concepts, recommend educational resources, generate practice activities, provide feedback, and help learners explore new topics more efficiently.
14. Constructive feedback helps learners recognize strengths, identify areas for improvement, correct mistakes, and continue developing knowledge and skills throughout life.
15. Lifelong learning prepares people for the future by encouraging curiosity, adaptability, resilience, continuous skill development, and responsible use of technology. It enables individuals to respond confidently to new opportunities while contributing positively to their communities and professions.

Chapter 11 – Part 1

Leadership in the Age of Artificial General Intelligence

Every generation is remembered for the leaders it produces. Some leaders guide nations through difficult times. Others transform education, advance science, improve healthcare, build successful businesses, or strengthen local communities. Although their careers may be very different, effective leaders often share many of the same qualities. They communicate clearly, solve problems thoughtfully, treat people with respect, make responsible decisions, and inspire others to work toward meaningful goals. As Artificial General Intelligence (AGI) becomes part of everyday life, these qualities will become even more important.

Many people believe leadership belongs only to adults who hold important positions or manage large organizations. In reality, leadership begins much earlier. A student who helps a classmate understand a difficult lesson demonstrates leadership. A team captain who encourages teammates after a disappointing loss shows leadership. A volunteer who organizes a neighborhood cleanup becomes a leader by serving others. Leadership is not defined by a title. It is defined by actions that positively influence other people.

The AGI Generation will grow up in a world where intelligent systems assist with research, communication, planning, design, healthcare, transportation, manufacturing, and countless other activities. Some routine decisions may become faster because AI can organize and analyze information efficiently. However, the decisions that shape families, schools, businesses, and communities will still depend upon human leadership. People will continue deciding what goals are worth pursuing, how resources should be used, and how technology should serve society. These responsibilities require wisdom that goes far beyond technical knowledge.

One of the first qualities of strong leadership is vision. Vision is the ability to imagine a better future and inspire others to help achieve it. Every important improvement in history began because someone believed change was possible. Visionary leaders saw opportunities where others saw obstacles. They recognized problems that needed solutions and motivated people to work together toward meaningful progress. Artificial intelligence can analyze data about the present, but people create visions for the future by combining imagination, experience, values, and hope.

Communication is another essential leadership skill. Great ideas have little impact if they cannot be explained clearly. Leaders communicate with honesty, confidence, and respect. They listen carefully before speaking, ask thoughtful questions, and encourage others to share their perspectives. In the age of AGI, communication becomes even more valuable because leaders will often explain how intelligent technologies affect employees, students, patients, customers, or community members. People are more likely to accept change when they understand its purpose and feel included in the decision-making process.

Listening deserves special attention because it is one of the most overlooked leadership skills. Many people assume leaders spend most of their time giving instructions. Effective leaders often spend just as much time listening. They seek different opinions, consider concerns carefully, and remain open to new ideas. Listening builds trust because people feel respected when their voices are heard. It also leads to better decisions by allowing leaders to learn from the experiences and knowledge of others.

Trust is the foundation of leadership. Without trust, even the most advanced technology or carefully designed plans become difficult to implement. Trust develops through honesty, consistency, fairness, accountability, and integrity. Leaders earn trust by keeping promises, admitting mistakes, treating people respectfully, and making decisions that reflect ethical values. As AI becomes more common in schools and workplaces, leaders must also demonstrate that technology is being used responsibly, transparently, and fairly. People trust leaders who explain decisions openly and accept responsibility for the outcomes.

Decision-making is another responsibility that cannot be separated from leadership. Artificial intelligence may generate recommendations by analyzing large amounts of information, but leaders remain responsible for choosing among different options. Good decisions require careful evaluation of facts, ethical principles, long-term consequences, and the well-being of others. Sometimes there is no perfect solution. Leaders must balance competing priorities while remaining committed to fairness and responsibility. Students who practice thoughtful decision-making today are preparing themselves for future leadership roles.

Leadership also requires courage. Courage does not always involve dramatic actions. Often it means doing what is right even when it is difficult. A student who reports bullying, admits making a mistake, or stands up for someone being treated unfairly demonstrates courage. A business leader who refuses to sacrifice safety for higher profits demonstrates courage. A scientist who reports unexpected research results honestly demonstrates courage. Ethical leadership depends upon individuals who value integrity more than personal convenience.

Another important leadership quality is adaptability. Technology, economies, communities, and workplaces continue changing rapidly. Leaders cannot assume that yesterday's solutions will always solve tomorrow's problems. Instead, they remain flexible, continue learning, and adjust strategies when new information becomes available. Artificial intelligence can help leaders understand changing conditions more quickly, but people must still decide how organizations should respond. Adaptable leaders encourage innovation while remaining focused on long-term goals and human well-being.

Collaboration strengthens leadership because few meaningful achievements happen through individual effort alone. Schools depend upon teachers, students, families, administrators, and support staff working together. Hospitals rely on doctors, nurses, technicians, pharmacists, and many other professionals. Businesses succeed because employees contribute different skills toward shared goals. Artificial intelligence may help coordinate projects or analyze information, but successful collaboration depends upon mutual respect, communication, and shared responsibility. Effective leaders bring people together by helping every individual recognize the value of their contribution.

Leaders also understand the importance of continuous learning. They recognize that no one possesses every answer and that learning never truly ends. As AGI continues evolving, leaders who remain curious will be better prepared to guide organizations through technological change. They read, ask questions, seek advice, evaluate evidence, and encourage others to continue developing new skills. This willingness to learn creates organizations where improvement becomes part of everyday life rather than an occasional event.

Perhaps the most important lesson about leadership in the AGI era is that technology will never replace character. Intelligence helps people solve problems, but character determines how those solutions are used. Honesty, compassion, humility, responsibility, fairness, perseverance, and respect remain the qualities that inspire confidence in others. These values guide leaders when facing difficult decisions that affect real people.

The AGI Generation has an extraordinary opportunity to redefine leadership for an intelligent world. Tomorrow's leaders will understand advanced technology, but they will also understand people. They will know how to combine innovation with ethics, efficiency with compassion, and intelligence with wisdom. By strengthening these qualities today, students prepare themselves to become leaders who build stronger schools, healthier communities, more responsible businesses, and a future where technology serves humanity with integrity and purpose.

Chapter 11 – Part 2

Leadership in the Age of Artificial General Intelligence

One of the greatest misunderstandings about leadership is the belief that leaders exist to control other people. In reality, the most effective leaders see themselves as servants first. They understand that leadership is not about personal recognition, power, or status. It is about helping others succeed. This approach is often called **servant leadership**, and it has guided many respected leaders throughout history. Servant leaders ask an important question every day: "How can I help others reach their full potential?" Instead of focusing only on their own success, they invest time in encouraging, teaching, supporting, and developing the people around them.

Imagine a teacher preparing students for an important examination. A servant leader does not simply assign work and expect results. Instead, the teacher identifies students who need additional support, provides encouragement, answers questions patiently, and celebrates every improvement. The teacher understands that true success is measured by the growth of the students rather than by personal recognition. The same principle applies to business leaders who invest in employee development, coaches who encourage athletes after difficult losses, and community volunteers who dedicate their time to improving the lives of others. Leadership grows stronger when leaders place people before personal achievement.

The AGI Generation will also lead increasingly diverse teams. Future workplaces will bring together individuals from different cultures, languages, educational backgrounds, professional experiences, and areas of expertise. Artificial intelligence may help translate conversations, organize international projects, and coordinate global communication, but successful teamwork still depends on respect, empathy, and understanding. Great leaders recognize that different perspectives strengthen problem-solving because every person contributes unique knowledge and life experiences. Diversity becomes an advantage when leaders create environments where every individual feels valued and heard.

Conflict is another part of leadership that students should understand. Whenever people work together, disagreements naturally occur. Different opinions often lead to better ideas because they encourage careful thinking and healthy discussion. Effective leaders do not avoid conflict. Instead, they manage it respectfully. They listen carefully, encourage open communication, focus on solving problems rather than assigning blame, and search for solutions that benefit everyone whenever possible. Artificial intelligence may organize information or identify possible options, but resolving disagreements requires emotional intelligence, patience, fairness, and human understanding.

Emotional intelligence becomes one of the defining qualities of successful leaders. Leaders who understand emotions communicate more effectively, recognize stress within their teams, encourage cooperation, and build strong professional relationships. They notice when someone feels discouraged, celebrate achievements sincerely, and create environments where people feel safe sharing ideas. These abilities cannot be automated because they depend on genuine human connection. As intelligent systems continue improving technical efficiency, emotional intelligence will become even more valuable in distinguishing exceptional human leadership.

Leaders also inspire innovation by creating environments where people feel comfortable sharing new ideas. Many important discoveries begin with suggestions that initially seem unusual or uncertain. If people fear criticism or embarrassment, they may keep valuable ideas to themselves. Great leaders encourage curiosity by welcoming thoughtful questions, supporting creative thinking, and viewing mistakes as opportunities for improvement rather than reasons for punishment. This atmosphere allows innovation to flourish because people become confident enough to experiment responsibly and learn continuously.

Artificial intelligence can greatly assist innovative leaders. Imagine a research team developing cleaner energy technologies. AI may analyze scientific data, identify patterns, simulate possible designs, and recommend promising research directions. The human leader then brings the team together, evaluates different possibilities, considers ethical responsibilities, allocates resources wisely, and keeps everyone focused on the shared mission. Technology accelerates the research process, while leadership provides vision, purpose, and direction.

Decision-making often becomes more difficult during times of uncertainty. Future leaders will face situations where complete information may not be available. Economic conditions may change unexpectedly. New scientific discoveries may require updated policies. Natural disasters may require immediate action. AI can help analyze available information quickly, but leaders must still make thoughtful decisions based on evidence, ethics, and the needs of the people they serve. Good leaders remain calm during uncertainty because they understand that thoughtful decisions require careful evaluation rather than panic.

Accountability remains one of the strongest characteristics of trusted leaders. Accountability means accepting responsibility for decisions instead of blaming others when challenges occur. Every leader eventually makes mistakes because no one is perfect. What separates respected leaders from ineffective ones is how they respond. Responsible leaders admit errors honestly, correct problems quickly, learn from experience, and continue improving. This example encourages others to value honesty rather than perfection. Students who develop accountability early in life become adults whom others trust during difficult situations.

Leadership also requires resilience. Every meaningful goal includes obstacles. Businesses face competition. Schools encounter challenges. Communities experience change. Scientific research often requires years of experimentation before success. Leaders who remain optimistic during difficult times inspire confidence in others. They remind teams that setbacks are temporary and that perseverance often leads to future success. Resilience does not mean ignoring problems. It means believing that solutions can be found through cooperation, learning, and determination.

The AGI Generation will likely become one of the first generations to lead organizations where artificial intelligence is part of everyday operations. These leaders will need to understand both technology and humanity. They must know when AI can improve efficiency and when human judgment should remain the deciding factor. They must protect privacy, encourage fairness, communicate openly, and ensure that intelligent systems continue serving people rather than replacing meaningful human relationships. This balance will require wisdom as much as technical knowledge.

Another important leadership responsibility is mentoring future generations. Every experienced leader has an opportunity to guide someone who is just beginning. Teachers mentor students. Senior employees mentor new coworkers. Coaches mentor athletes. Parents mentor children. Community leaders mentor volunteers. Mentorship strengthens society because knowledge, experience, and wisdom continue passing from one generation to the next. Artificial intelligence can organize information, but mentorship provides encouragement, perspective, and personal guidance developed through real-life experiences.

One lesson every future leader should remember is that success is never achieved alone. Behind every accomplishment stands a team of people who contributed ideas, effort, encouragement, and support. Great leaders recognize these contributions and celebrate the achievements of others. They understand that giving credit builds trust, strengthens teamwork, and motivates people to continue working toward shared goals. Humility allows leaders to recognize that leadership is about helping others succeed rather than seeking personal attention.

The AGI Generation has the opportunity to redefine leadership for one of the most technologically advanced periods in human history. Yet the qualities that define great leadership remain remarkably consistent across generations. Honesty builds trust. Compassion strengthens relationships. Courage inspires action. Curiosity encourages discovery. Responsibility guides decisions. Integrity earns respect. These timeless values become even more important as technology grows increasingly powerful.

As you prepare for your future, remember that leadership does not begin when you receive a job title or manage an organization. Leadership begins every time you choose to help someone, solve a problem, encourage a teammate, admit a mistake, stand up for what is right, or continue learning despite challenges. These daily decisions gradually shape the kind of leader you will become.

Artificial intelligence will continue transforming the world, but people will continue shaping its direction. The AGI Generation has the opportunity to become a generation of leaders who combine advanced technology with ethical wisdom, lifelong learning, compassion, and service to others. Those leaders will not simply guide organizations. They will inspire people, strengthen communities, and help ensure that intelligence—both human and artificial—is always used to improve the lives of future generations.

Chapter 11 Summary

Leadership in the Age of Artificial General Intelligence

Leadership has always been important, but it will become even more valuable as Artificial General Intelligence (AGI) changes the way people live and work. While AI can analyze information, recognize patterns, and assist with decision-making, it cannot replace the human qualities that inspire trust, build relationships, and guide ethical decisions. Future leaders will need both technological knowledge and strong character.

This chapter explained that leadership is not determined by a job title or position of authority. Leadership begins whenever a person positively influences others through honesty, responsibility, service, communication, and good decision-making. Students learned that every person has opportunities to develop leadership skills through everyday actions at school, home, and in the community.

Readers explored several important leadership qualities, including vision, communication, listening, trust, courage, accountability, adaptability, collaboration, emotional intelligence, resilience, and lifelong learning. These qualities help leaders guide organizations, solve problems, support teams, and respond responsibly to change.

The chapter also introduced the idea of **servant leadership**, where leaders focus on helping others succeed rather than seeking personal recognition. Students learned that the strongest leaders encourage teamwork, celebrate the achievements of others, mentor future generations, and create environments where innovation and creativity can flourish.

Finally, the chapter emphasized that future leaders must understand how to work responsibly alongside AI. Human leaders remain responsible for ethical decision-making, protecting privacy, encouraging fairness, and ensuring that intelligent technology serves people rather than replacing human judgment. The AGI Generation has the opportunity to become a generation of leaders who combine advanced technology with wisdom, compassion, integrity, and service to others.

Chapter 11 Reflection

Leadership in the Age of Artificial General Intelligence

Answer each question thoughtfully using complete sentences.

1. What does leadership mean to you after reading this chapter?
2. Why is leadership about service rather than power?
3. Which leadership quality discussed in this chapter do you believe is your greatest strength? Explain why.
4. Which leadership skill would you most like to improve during the next year?
5. Why is emotional intelligence important for future leaders?
6. How can AI help leaders without replacing them?
7. Describe a leader you admire. What qualities make that person effective?
8. How can students begin developing leadership skills while they are still in school?

Personal Reflection

Imagine yourself leading an organization twenty years from now. Describe how you would use artificial intelligence responsibly while continuing to lead with honesty, compassion, fairness, accountability, and respect. Explain how your leadership would improve the lives of the people you serve.

Chapter 11 Worksheet

Leadership in the Age of Artificial General Intelligence

Part A – Vocabulary

Define each term using your own words.

1. Leadership
2. Vision
3. Accountability
4. Servant Leadership
5. Emotional Intelligence
6. Collaboration
7. Adaptability
8. Integrity
9. Resilience
10. Mentorship

Part B – Comprehension Questions

Answer each question using complete sentences.

1. Why is leadership important in the AGI era?
2. Explain the meaning of servant leadership.
3. Why is communication an important leadership skill?
4. How does emotional intelligence strengthen leadership?
5. Why must leaders continue learning throughout their lives?
6. How can AI support leadership without replacing human judgment?
7. Why is accountability important for trusted leaders?
8. How can mentors help develop future leaders?

Part C – Critical Thinking

Write one or two paragraphs for each question.

1. Imagine you are the principal of a school introducing AI into classrooms. Describe how you would lead teachers, students, and families through this transition while building trust and encouraging responsible technology use.
2. Explain why leadership is based on influence rather than authority. Include examples from school, sports, or community activities.

3. Discuss how future leaders can balance technological innovation with ethical responsibility.

Part D – My Leadership Development Plan

Create your own leadership roadmap.

Include:

• Five leadership qualities you want to strengthen.

• Three ways you can practice leadership at school.

• Three habits that build trust.

• Three ways AI could help you become a better leader.

• One personal leadership goal you hope to achieve before graduating.

Chapter 11 Quiz

Multiple Choice

Choose the best answer.

1. Leadership is best defined as:

A. Having the highest job title.

B. Positively influencing others toward meaningful goals.

C. Giving orders to people.

D. Controlling technology.

2. Servant leadership focuses on:

A. Personal recognition.

B. Helping others succeed.

C. Avoiding responsibility.

D. Competing against teammates.

3. Emotional intelligence helps leaders:

A. Understand and manage emotions.

B. Build stronger relationships.

C. Encourage teamwork.

D. All of the above.

4. Which leadership quality helps people adjust to change?

A. Adaptability

B. Memorization

C. Competition

D. Speed

5. AI should be used by leaders to:

A. Replace all human decisions.

B. Support informed decision-making while people remain responsible.

C. Eliminate communication.

D. Remove ethical responsibilities.

True or False

6. _____ Leadership begins long before someone receives a management position.
7. _____ Trust is earned through honesty and consistent actions.
8. _____ Future leaders should stop learning once they become successful.
9. _____ AI can support leadership, but human values remain essential.
10. _____ Mentorship helps prepare future generations of leaders.

Short Answer

11. Explain why communication is important for effective leadership.
12. Describe one characteristic of servant leadership.
13. Why is accountability important when leading others?
14. How can AI assist future leaders?
15. In your own words, explain what leadership in the AGI era means.

Chapter 11 Answer Key

Multiple Choice

1. **B**
2. **B**
3. **D**
4. **A**
5. **B**

True or False

6. **True**
7. **True**
8. **False**
9. **True**
10. **True**

Short Answer (Sample Responses)

11. Communication helps leaders explain ideas clearly, listen carefully, build trust, encourage teamwork, solve problems, and guide organizations through change.
12. Servant leadership focuses on helping others succeed by supporting, encouraging, mentoring, and developing the people being served rather than seeking personal recognition.
13. Accountability builds trust because leaders accept responsibility for their decisions, correct mistakes honestly, learn from experience, and demonstrate integrity during both success and failure.

14. AI can assist leaders by organizing information, analyzing data, identifying patterns, improving planning, supporting communication, and providing insights that help leaders make informed decisions while keeping humans responsible for final judgments.
15. Leadership in the AGI era means combining technology with human wisdom, integrity, empathy, ethical decision-making, communication, and service to others. Great leaders use AI as a tool while ensuring that people, fairness, and responsibility remain at the center of every important decision.

Chapter 12 – Part 1

Solving the World's Greatest Challenges with AGI

Every generation inherits a unique set of challenges. Some generations faced world wars, economic hardships, or devastating diseases. Others worked to expand education, improve civil rights, protect the environment, or develop new technologies that transformed society. Today's students are growing up during another important turning point in history. The challenges they will face are complex, global, and deeply connected. Climate change, healthcare, food security, clean water, natural disasters, cybersecurity, sustainable energy, and access to education are only a few of the issues that future generations must continue addressing. The encouraging news is that the AGI Generation will also have access to some of the most powerful tools humanity has ever created.

Artificial General Intelligence has the potential to become a remarkable partner in solving difficult problems. Unlike traditional computer programs that perform one specific task, future AGI systems may assist people across many different fields of knowledge. They may analyze scientific research, organize enormous amounts of information, identify hidden patterns, simulate possible solutions, and help experts work together more effectively. However, even with these extraordinary capabilities, the responsibility for choosing meaningful goals and making ethical decisions will remain with people. Technology may provide possibilities, but humanity decides which possibilities are worth pursuing.

One of the greatest global challenges is healthcare. Around the world, millions of people continue facing diseases that require better treatments, earlier diagnosis, and improved access to medical care. Doctors, nurses, researchers, pharmacists, engineers, and public health professionals already work together to improve health outcomes. Artificial intelligence is beginning to assist by analyzing medical images, identifying disease patterns, organizing patient information, and supporting medical research. Future AGI systems may help researchers study enormous collections of scientific data much more quickly than ever before, allowing promising treatments to be investigated sooner. Yet healthcare remains much more than science and technology. Patients need compassion, encouragement, trust, and human understanding. The future of medicine will likely combine advanced intelligence with the caring relationships that have always been at the heart of healing.

Another challenge facing humanity is protecting the environment. Forests, rivers, oceans, wildlife, and clean air support life across our planet. Scientists carefully study ecosystems to understand how pollution, climate, weather patterns, and human activity affect natural environments. AGI may help researchers analyze satellite images, predict environmental changes, monitor endangered species, and recommend strategies for protecting valuable natural resources. Students interested in environmental science may one day work alongside intelligent systems to restore ecosystems, improve recycling technologies, develop cleaner energy solutions, or design sustainable communities that protect the Earth for future generations.

Food security represents another important challenge. The world's population continues growing, increasing the need for reliable food production while protecting farmland and conserving natural resources. Farmers have always depended upon observation, experience, and careful planning. Today, advanced technologies help monitor soil conditions, weather forecasts, irrigation systems, and crop health. Future AGI systems may assist by predicting disease outbreaks in crops, improving harvest planning, reducing waste, and identifying efficient farming methods that produce healthy food while protecting the environment. Farmers will continue making important decisions based upon local knowledge, experience, and changing conditions, while intelligent technology provides valuable support.

Access to clean water remains essential for healthy communities. Water supports drinking, agriculture, sanitation, manufacturing, and countless daily activities. Scientists and engineers work continuously to improve water purification, conservation, and distribution systems. AGI may assist by monitoring water quality, identifying leaks in infrastructure, predicting drought conditions, and helping communities manage water resources more efficiently. Students who study engineering, environmental science, chemistry, or public policy may one day contribute to solutions that provide safe drinking water for millions of people around the world.

Education itself remains one of humanity's greatest opportunities. Every child deserves the opportunity to learn, develop talents, and prepare for a meaningful future. Unfortunately, educational resources are not equally available everywhere. Some communities lack qualified teachers, educational materials, reliable internet access, or safe learning environments. Artificial intelligence has the potential to expand educational opportunities by supporting teachers, translating lessons into different languages, providing personalized learning assistance, and making educational resources more accessible. Even so, education depends upon more than information. It depends upon teachers who inspire curiosity, families who encourage learning, and communities that believe every student deserves the opportunity to succeed.

Natural disasters also present ongoing challenges. Hurricanes, earthquakes, floods, wildfires, volcanic eruptions, and severe storms affect communities across the world. Emergency responders, scientists, engineers, healthcare professionals, and government agencies work together to protect lives before, during, and after these events. AGI may strengthen disaster preparedness by analyzing weather patterns, identifying high-risk areas, improving evacuation planning, and helping emergency teams coordinate resources more effectively. Quick access to accurate information can save lives, but courageous people remain at the center of every emergency response effort.

Cybersecurity is becoming increasingly important as societies depend more heavily on digital technology. Schools, hospitals, businesses, transportation systems, financial institutions, and governments all rely upon secure computer networks. Cybersecurity professionals work continuously to protect information from cyberattacks while ensuring that digital systems remain reliable and safe. Future AGI systems may help detect unusual network activity, identify potential security threats, and respond more quickly to cyber risks. However, cybersecurity also depends upon responsible human behavior. Strong passwords, careful online habits, ethical decision-making, and ongoing education remain essential parts of digital safety.

One lesson connects every one of these challenges: no single person can solve them alone. Scientists depend upon engineers. Doctors work alongside researchers. Educators collaborate with parents and community leaders. Environmental experts cooperate with government agencies, businesses, and nonprofit organizations. Artificial intelligence strengthens these partnerships by organizing knowledge and improving communication, but meaningful progress continues depending upon people working together with shared goals.

The AGI Generation should recognize that solving global challenges requires more than intelligence. It requires compassion, patience, creativity, resilience, and ethical leadership. Every important decision affects real people, real families, and real communities. Students preparing for the future should ask not only, "Can technology solve this problem?" but also, "How can technology improve people's lives while respecting human dignity, fairness, and the environment?" These questions encourage responsible innovation that benefits society as a whole.

Perhaps the greatest opportunity facing today's students is realizing that they are not simply preparing to observe the future. They are preparing to build it. Every subject studied in school—science, mathematics, language arts, history, engineering, technology, business, the arts, and civics—contributes knowledge that may someday help solve important global challenges. Learning today becomes the foundation for tomorrow's discoveries.

The AGI Generation will inherit remarkable technological tools, but the future will ultimately be shaped by the people who use those tools wisely. Students who combine knowledge with curiosity, compassion, collaboration, ethical leadership, and lifelong learning will be prepared to help solve some of humanity's greatest challenges. The world does not simply need more intelligent machines. It needs thoughtful people who know how to use intelligence—both human and artificial—to create healthier communities, stronger nations, and a brighter future for everyone.

Chapter 12 – Part 2

Solving the World's Greatest Challenges with AGI

As the world becomes more connected, solving global problems will require countries, organizations, scientists, educators, businesses, and communities to work together more closely than ever before. Artificial General Intelligence may become one of the most powerful tools for supporting this cooperation. Intelligent systems can help organize research from thousands of universities, translate information into many languages, compare scientific discoveries made in different countries, and allow experts to share knowledge much more quickly than in the past. While AGI may strengthen communication, people will continue building the partnerships that make meaningful progress possible.

Scientific discovery is one area where this cooperation can have an enormous impact. Every year, researchers publish millions of scientific papers covering medicine, engineering, chemistry, biology, environmental science, physics, agriculture, and many other fields. No single person can read and understand all of this information. Future AGI systems may help scientists organize research, identify important connections between different studies, and suggest new directions for investigation. This could reduce the time required to discover treatments for diseases, improve renewable energy technologies, or develop safer building materials. However, scientists will still perform experiments, verify results, question assumptions, and make careful conclusions based on evidence. Human curiosity and scientific integrity will continue guiding every important discovery.

Space exploration represents another exciting opportunity for the AGI Generation. Throughout history, people have looked toward the night sky with curiosity and wonder. Today, space agencies and private companies explore planets, study distant galaxies, launch satellites, and investigate the possibility of future human exploration beyond Earth. Artificial intelligence already assists with analyzing images from telescopes, planning spacecraft operations, and processing enormous amounts of astronomical data. Future AGI systems may help researchers identify interesting objects in space, improve spacecraft navigation, and support long-term missions. Yet every space mission begins with people asking questions about the universe and imagining what lies beyond the limits of current knowledge.

The exploration of space teaches an important lesson that also applies here on Earth. Solving difficult problems often requires patience. Some scientific discoveries require years or even decades of careful research before meaningful progress becomes visible. Students should understand that not every important achievement happens quickly. Persistence, careful planning, teamwork, and continuous learning are often more valuable than speed. The AGI Generation should be prepared to work steadily toward solutions that may benefit future generations as much as their own.

Reducing poverty is another challenge where intelligent technology may provide valuable assistance. Around the world, millions of people continue facing limited access to education, healthcare, employment, housing, and financial opportunities. Poverty is a complex issue influenced by many different factors, including economics, education, public health, infrastructure, and public policy. AGI may help governments and organizations analyze data, improve the distribution of resources, identify communities needing additional support, and evaluate which programs produce the strongest results. Even with advanced technology, lasting solutions will depend upon compassionate leadership, responsible planning, and cooperation among many different groups of people.

Transportation will also continue evolving as intelligent systems become more advanced. Cities around the world face challenges involving traffic congestion, road safety, pollution, and growing populations. Engineers and transportation planners already use data to improve traffic flow and public transportation systems. Future AGI may analyze millions of traffic patterns, weather conditions, construction projects, and transportation schedules simultaneously to recommend safer and more efficient solutions. Students interested in engineering, urban planning, computer science, or environmental studies may one day help design transportation systems that save lives, reduce pollution, and improve the quality of life for entire communities.

Communication itself will become an increasingly valuable tool for solving global challenges. Throughout history, misunderstandings between people, organizations, and nations have sometimes slowed progress. Intelligent translation technologies may help people communicate across many different languages, making international cooperation easier than ever before. Students may one day participate in research projects with classmates from other countries, exchange ideas with experts around the world, and work together to solve shared problems. These experiences will help build respect for different cultures while encouraging teamwork on a global scale.

One of the greatest strengths of the AGI Generation will be interdisciplinary thinking. This means combining knowledge from different subjects to solve complex problems. A student studying biology may also benefit from learning computer science. An engineer may improve designs by understanding environmental science and economics. A teacher may strengthen classroom instruction by learning about psychology, technology, and communication. Artificial intelligence supports this process by connecting information across many fields, but people continue making the creative connections that lead to innovative solutions.

Responsible innovation remains essential throughout this process. Every new technology should be evaluated not only for what it can accomplish but also for how it affects people. Students should continue asking important questions. Will this solution improve lives? Is it fair to everyone? Does it protect privacy? Is it environmentally responsible? Can it be used safely? These questions remind future innovators that technological progress should always serve humanity with integrity and compassion.

The future will also require resilient problem-solvers. Some challenges will not have immediate solutions. Climate patterns may continue changing. New diseases may appear. Technologies will evolve, creating both opportunities and new responsibilities. Students should not become discouraged when progress seems slow. Every important improvement in history has required dedication, cooperation, and perseverance. Each generation builds upon the work of those who came before it. The AGI Generation will continue that tradition by contributing its own knowledge, creativity, and determination.

Another lesson students should remember is that every individual can contribute to solving meaningful problems. Not everyone will become a scientist, engineer, physician, or software developer, but every profession has an important role. Teachers educate future innovators. Farmers provide food for growing populations. Electricians maintain critical infrastructure. Journalists communicate important information. Artists inspire creativity and cultural understanding. Entrepreneurs create jobs and develop new products. Community volunteers strengthen neighborhoods. Every person contributes something valuable when working toward a shared purpose.

Artificial intelligence should never reduce the importance of human values. In fact, as technology becomes more capable, qualities such as honesty, compassion, courage, humility, patience, and cooperation become even more important. Intelligent systems may calculate possibilities, but people continue deciding which possibilities best reflect the values of society. This partnership between advanced technology and strong character gives humanity its greatest opportunity for progress.

The AGI Generation has an extraordinary opportunity to become a generation of global problem-solvers. Students entering classrooms today may one day help cure diseases, protect endangered ecosystems, improve educational opportunities, develop sustainable energy, strengthen cybersecurity, explore distant planets, or design technologies that make daily life safer and healthier. These achievements will not happen because of technology alone. They will happen because curious, ethical, hardworking people choose to work together while using intelligent tools responsibly.

As you continue your educational journey, remember that every lesson you learn today may become part of a solution tomorrow. Every mathematics problem strengthens logical thinking. Every science experiment teaches investigation. Every history lesson provides perspective. Every writing assignment improves communication. Every act of teamwork develops collaboration. Education prepares you not simply to earn a career but to contribute to humanity's future.

The world's greatest challenges are also its greatest opportunities. With wisdom, integrity, curiosity, and responsible use of Artificial General Intelligence, the AGI Generation has the potential to improve lives on a scale never before possible. The future is waiting for students who are willing to learn, lead, serve, and work together to create solutions that benefit people everywhere.

Chapter 12 Summary

Solving the World's Greatest Challenges with AGI

The world faces many important challenges, including improving healthcare, protecting the environment, providing clean water, increasing food security, strengthening cybersecurity, responding to natural disasters, expanding educational opportunities, reducing poverty, and developing sustainable energy. The AGI Generation will inherit these challenges, but it will also have access to powerful intelligent technologies that can help create solutions.

This chapter explained that Artificial General Intelligence (AGI) can become an important partner by organizing information, analyzing large amounts of data, identifying patterns, supporting scientific research, and improving collaboration among experts from different fields. However, students learned that AGI should always assist human decision-making rather than replace it. People remain responsible for setting goals, making ethical decisions, and ensuring that technology benefits society.

Readers explored how AGI may improve healthcare by accelerating medical research, supporting disease diagnosis, and helping scientists develop better treatments. They also learned how intelligent systems can help protect the environment, improve farming, conserve water, strengthen cybersecurity, prepare for natural disasters, and make education more accessible around the world.

The chapter emphasized that solving global problems requires teamwork. Scientists, engineers, educators, healthcare professionals, governments, businesses, nonprofit organizations, and local communities all contribute different knowledge and skills. Artificial intelligence helps these groups work together more efficiently, but meaningful progress continues to depend on human cooperation, communication, and leadership.

Students also learned the importance of interdisciplinary thinking, which combines knowledge from many subjects to solve complex problems. Mathematics, science, engineering, history, communication, business, and the arts all contribute valuable perspectives when addressing real-world challenges.

Finally, the chapter reminded students that every individual can make a positive difference. Whether they become teachers, doctors, engineers, artists, entrepreneurs, scientists, or community leaders, members of the AGI Generation have the opportunity to improve the world by combining lifelong learning, ethical leadership, compassion, creativity, and responsible use of Artificial General Intelligence.

Chapter 12 Reflection

Solving the World's Greatest Challenges with AGI

Answer each question thoughtfully using complete sentences.

1. Which global challenge discussed in this chapter concerns you the most? Why?
2. How can Artificial General Intelligence help solve problems without replacing human responsibility?
3. Why is international cooperation important when solving worldwide challenges?
4. Explain why different professions must work together to solve complex problems.
5. How can education prepare students to become future problem-solvers?
6. Why should ethical thinking guide every technological advancement?
7. Describe one way you hope to improve your community during your lifetime.
8. What role do curiosity and lifelong learning play in solving future challenges?

Personal Reflection

Imagine you are a member of an international team working to solve one of the world's biggest problems. Describe the challenge, explain how AGI helps your team, and discuss how your knowledge, leadership, ethics, and teamwork contribute to creating a lasting solution that benefits people around the world.

Chapter 12 Worksheet

Solving the World's Greatest Challenges with AGI

Part A – Vocabulary

Define each term using your own words.

1. Artificial General Intelligence (AGI)
2. Collaboration
3. Sustainability
4. Food Security
5. Cybersecurity
6. Scientific Research
7. Interdisciplinary Thinking
8. Innovation
9. Global Cooperation
10. Problem Solving

Part B – Comprehension Questions

Answer each question using complete sentences.

1. Why can AGI become an important partner in solving global challenges?
2. How might AGI improve healthcare?
3. Describe two ways AGI can help protect the environment.
4. Why is cybersecurity becoming increasingly important?
5. Explain why solving global problems requires teamwork.
6. What is interdisciplinary thinking?
7. Why should technology always be guided by ethics?
8. How can today's students prepare to solve tomorrow's challenges?

Part C – Critical Thinking

Write one or two paragraphs for each question.

1. Choose one global challenge discussed in this chapter. Explain how education, science, technology, government, businesses, and local communities could work together to solve it.
2. Imagine you are designing an AGI system to improve education in underserved communities. Describe its features and explain how it would help students while protecting fairness, privacy, and human dignity.
3. Explain why the world's greatest challenges also create opportunities for innovation and leadership.

Part D – My Global Problem-Solving Plan

Create your own action plan.

Include:

• One global challenge you want to help solve.

• Five skills you need to develop.

• Three school subjects that will help prepare you.

• Three ways AGI could support your work.

• Three ethical principles you will always follow.

• One personal mission statement describing how you hope to improve the world.

Chapter 12 Quiz

Multiple Choice

Choose the best answer.

1. According to this chapter, AGI can best help solve global challenges by:

A. Replacing all human workers.

B. Supporting research, analysis, and collaboration.

C. Eliminating education.

D. Making all decisions independently.

2. Which global challenge was discussed in this chapter?

A. Healthcare

B. Environmental protection

C. Cybersecurity

D. All of the above

3. Interdisciplinary thinking means:

A. Studying only one subject.

B. Combining knowledge from different fields to solve problems.

C. Avoiding teamwork.

D. Memorizing information.

4. Responsible innovation requires:

A. Ignoring ethics.

B. Using technology without supervision.

C. Combining technology with ethical decision-making.

D. Avoiding scientific research.

5. The AGI Generation should become:

A. Passive users of technology.

B. Responsible global problem-solvers.

C. Dependent on machines.

D. Unwilling to learn.

True or False

6. _____ AGI can assist scientific research.
7. _____ Solving global problems requires cooperation among many professions.
8. _____ Technology alone can solve every world problem.
9. _____ Education prepares students to become future innovators.
10. _____ Ethics should guide technological progress.

Short Answer

11. Explain one way AGI may improve healthcare.
12. Why is teamwork important when solving global challenges?
13. Describe one benefit of interdisciplinary thinking.
14. Why should future innovators consider ethics before developing new technologies?
15. In your own words, explain how the AGI Generation can help solve the world's greatest challenges.

Chapter 12 Answer Key

Multiple Choice

1. **B**
2. **D**
3. **B**
4. **C**
5. **B**

True or False

6. **True**
7. **True**
8. **False**
9. **True**
10. **True**

Short Answer (Sample Responses)

11. AGI may improve healthcare by helping researchers analyze medical data, identify disease patterns, support earlier diagnoses, accelerate scientific research, and assist healthcare professionals in developing better treatments while human experts continue making final medical decisions.
12. Global challenges are complex and require expertise from many professions. Scientists, engineers, healthcare workers, educators, governments, businesses, and communities each contribute different knowledge and skills that work together to create effective, long-term solutions.
13. Interdisciplinary thinking allows people to combine ideas from different subjects—such as science, mathematics, engineering, communication, and environmental studies—to solve complex real-world problems more creatively and effectively.
14. Ethics ensures that new technologies are fair, safe, responsible, environmentally sustainable, respectful of privacy, and beneficial to individuals and society. Responsible innovation protects human dignity while encouraging scientific progress.
15. The AGI Generation can help solve the world's greatest challenges by continuing to learn, working collaboratively, thinking creatively, leading ethically, using AGI responsibly, and applying knowledge to improve healthcare, education, environmental protection, cybersecurity, and the overall quality of life for people everywhere.

Chapter 13 – Part 1

The Human Advantage in an AGI World

As technology continues advancing, many people ask an important question: **If Artificial General Intelligence becomes capable of performing many intellectual tasks, what role will humans continue to play?** This question appears in classrooms, businesses, research laboratories, government agencies, and homes around the world. Some people worry that intelligent machines may eventually perform many of the jobs people do today. Others believe AGI will create entirely new opportunities that have not yet been imagined. While no one can predict every detail of the future, one truth remains remarkably consistent throughout history. Every major technological advancement has changed the way people work, but it has also created new opportunities for those willing to learn, adapt, and grow.

The AGI Generation should not view this future as a competition between humans and intelligent machines. Instead, students should understand that the greatest successes will likely come from partnerships where people and intelligent systems work together. Artificial intelligence excels at processing enormous amounts of information, recognizing patterns, performing calculations, and completing repetitive tasks with remarkable speed. Human beings contribute qualities that remain deeply connected to life experience, relationships, creativity, ethical judgment, empathy, imagination, and purpose. These strengths complement one another rather than compete against each other.

One of humanity's greatest advantages is creativity. Creativity is the ability to imagine possibilities that do not yet exist. It allows artists to paint original works, musicians to compose new songs, architects to design inspiring buildings, scientists to develop new theories, entrepreneurs to create businesses, and engineers to invent technologies that improve everyday life. AI may generate ideas by analyzing existing information, but human creativity often begins with personal experiences, emotions, curiosity, dreams, and imagination. Creative people ask unusual questions, combine ideas from different fields, and envision futures that no machine can fully understand without human direction.

Another uniquely human strength is empathy. Empathy is the ability to understand and share the feelings of another person. When a teacher notices that a student seems discouraged, empathy guides the conversation. When a doctor comforts a worried patient, empathy builds trust. When a friend listens during a difficult time, empathy strengthens relationships. Artificial intelligence may recognize emotional patterns through language or facial expressions, but genuine compassion grows from human experience and authentic relationships. The AGI Generation should recognize that kindness, encouragement, patience, and understanding will remain among humanity's greatest strengths.

Ethical reasoning represents another important human advantage. Many decisions involve more than facts or calculations. They require thoughtful consideration of fairness, responsibility, dignity, privacy, cultural values, and long-term consequences. For example, a community deciding how to use AI in schools must consider student learning, teacher support, family concerns, privacy protection, and equal opportunities for every learner. These decisions involve human values that cannot be reduced to mathematical calculations alone. Future leaders will continue relying upon ethical reasoning when guiding society through technological change.

Imagination also gives people remarkable abilities. Imagination allows children to create stories, invent games, explore possibilities, and dream about future careers. Scientists imagine new experiments before conducting them. Engineers imagine designs before constructing them. Writers imagine characters and worlds before putting words on paper. Entrepreneurs imagine products that customers have never seen before. Every important innovation begins with someone's imagination. Artificial intelligence can assist with organizing ideas, but imagination gives those ideas purpose and direction.

Human curiosity remains equally valuable. Curiosity motivates exploration beyond what is already known. It inspires students to ask questions, investigate mysteries, study nature, explore space, and search for better solutions to difficult problems. Curiosity cannot be forced. It grows naturally when people become fascinated by learning. Throughout history, curiosity has driven exploration across oceans, discoveries in medicine, advances in science, and technological innovation. Artificial intelligence helps answer questions more efficiently, but people continue asking the questions that move civilization forward.

Communication represents another uniquely human strength. Language involves much more than exchanging information. People communicate emotions, humor, encouragement, cultural traditions, personal stories, hopes, and shared experiences. Great communicators know how to inspire confidence, resolve disagreements, build friendships, and unite communities around common goals. Future workplaces will continue depending upon people who communicate clearly, listen respectfully, and collaborate effectively with others. Artificial intelligence may translate languages and summarize conversations, but meaningful relationships continue growing through authentic human interaction.

Another human advantage is adaptability. Throughout history, people have repeatedly demonstrated the ability to adjust to changing circumstances. Farmers adapted to new agricultural methods. Factory workers learned to operate modern machinery. Teachers incorporated computers into classrooms. Businesses adopted the internet to reach customers around the world. Each technological advancement required learning new skills rather than abandoning human potential. The AGI Generation will continue this tradition by adapting to intelligent technologies while developing new careers and opportunities that emerge over time.

Resilience also distinguishes human beings. Every person experiences disappointment, setbacks, unexpected challenges, and moments of uncertainty. What allows individuals to continue growing is resilience—the determination to learn from difficulties and keep moving forward. Students who struggle with mathematics may eventually become excellent engineers through persistence. Athletes recover from losses by continuing to practice. Entrepreneurs improve businesses after unsuccessful attempts. Scientists repeat experiments until discoveries emerge. Resilience transforms obstacles into opportunities for learning and growth.

Collaboration strengthens every human achievement. No single person built modern civilization. Every advancement depends upon cooperation among individuals with different talents, experiences, and perspectives. Hospitals require doctors, nurses, technicians, pharmacists, administrators, and many other professionals. Schools depend upon teachers, families, counselors, administrators, and community members. Scientific discoveries often involve international research teams working together over many years. Artificial intelligence may coordinate information more efficiently, but people continue building the relationships that make successful collaboration possible.

One lesson the AGI Generation should always remember is that intelligence alone does not guarantee wisdom. A person may possess extraordinary knowledge yet make poor decisions if honesty, humility, compassion, and responsibility are absent. Wisdom develops through experience, reflection, ethical thinking, and concern for the well-being of others. Future societies will need wise leaders who know how to combine technological knowledge with human values. Artificial intelligence may increase access to information, but wisdom remains one of humanity's greatest achievements.

Perhaps the greatest human advantage is purpose. Machines perform tasks because they are instructed to do so. Human beings ask why those tasks matter. Purpose gives meaning to education, careers, families, friendships, communities, and lifelong goals. People dedicate themselves to helping others because they believe their work has value. Teachers educate because they want students to succeed. Healthcare professionals care for patients because human life matters. Scientists pursue discoveries because they hope to improve society. Purpose inspires perseverance even when challenges become difficult.

The AGI Generation has every reason to look toward the future with confidence. Rather than fearing intelligent systems, students can prepare to become the partners that technology needs most—creative thinkers, compassionate leaders, ethical decision-makers, lifelong learners, and responsible citizens. As artificial intelligence continues advancing, the qualities that make us uniquely human will become even more valuable. Those qualities will help ensure that technology remains focused on improving lives while strengthening the relationships, values, and aspirations that define humanity itself.

Chapter 13 – Part 2

The Human Advantage in an AGI World

As Artificial General Intelligence becomes more capable, the skills that make people uniquely human will become even more valuable. Many routine tasks may become faster and more efficient through intelligent technology, allowing people to spend more time solving meaningful problems, developing relationships, creating new ideas, and serving others. Instead of asking what jobs AI might replace, students should begin asking a more important question: **What human abilities will become even more valuable because AI exists?** The answer to that question will help define the future of the AGI Generation.

One of those abilities is wisdom. Knowledge and wisdom are not the same. Knowledge involves collecting facts, understanding concepts, and remembering information. Wisdom involves knowing how to apply that knowledge responsibly in real-life situations. A person may understand how a powerful technology works, but wisdom helps determine whether it should be used, when it should be used, and how it should be used responsibly. Wisdom develops through experience, reflection, ethical thinking, and learning from both successes and failures. Future leaders will rely on wisdom whenever they face decisions that affect families, communities, schools, businesses, or entire nations.

Another human advantage is moral courage. Throughout history, progress has depended upon individuals who were willing to stand for what was right even when doing so was difficult. Moral courage may involve protecting someone being treated unfairly, reporting dishonest behavior, defending truth, or making ethical decisions despite personal pressure. Artificial intelligence may provide information about possible choices, but only people can choose to act with integrity. The AGI Generation will need individuals whose character remains strong regardless of changing technologies.

The future will also reward curiosity that crosses traditional boundaries. Many of tomorrow's greatest discoveries will likely occur where different subjects come together. Medicine may combine biology with artificial intelligence. Agriculture may combine environmental science with robotics. Education may combine psychology, communication, and intelligent tutoring systems. Engineers may collaborate with artists to design technology that is both functional and inspiring. Students who enjoy learning across many different subjects will often discover creative solutions that specialists working alone may overlook.

One skill that will become increasingly important is asking excellent questions. Artificial intelligence can answer questions remarkably quickly, but people still decide which questions deserve attention. Consider the difference between asking, "How can we build a faster computer?" and asking, "How can we use computing to improve healthcare for children?" The second question introduces purpose, compassion, and human values. Great innovators are often remembered not because they had all the answers but because they asked questions that changed the direction of human thinking.

The AGI Generation will also benefit from developing strong decision-making skills. Every important decision requires balancing facts, values, risks, opportunities, and long-term consequences. Leaders often make decisions without having complete information because real life rarely provides perfect certainty. Students who practice evaluating evidence, considering different viewpoints, listening carefully, and thinking critically will become confident decision-makers prepared for the challenges of adulthood. Artificial intelligence can organize information, but responsible decisions remain a human responsibility.

Another advantage people possess is the ability to inspire one another. Throughout history, great leaders, teachers, coaches, parents, artists, and community members have motivated others through encouragement, vision, and personal example. A teacher who believes in a struggling student may completely change that student's future. A coach who encourages perseverance may inspire an athlete to overcome disappointment. A parent who models kindness teaches lessons that last a lifetime. Inspiration spreads from person to person in ways that technology alone cannot reproduce. Human encouragement gives people confidence to accomplish goals they once believed were impossible.

Communities will continue depending upon cooperation. Artificial intelligence may help organize projects and improve communication, but communities become stronger when people volunteer, mentor young learners, care for neighbors, and work together during difficult times. Human relationships create belonging, trust, and shared purpose. These qualities cannot be measured simply by data because they are built through everyday acts of kindness, respect, and service. Students should remember that some of the greatest contributions they make during their lives may involve helping other people succeed.

Another important human strength is cultural understanding. Every community has traditions, languages, histories, beliefs, and experiences that shape its identity. Intelligent systems may translate words between languages, but understanding another culture requires respect, curiosity, listening, and meaningful interaction. The AGI Generation will likely work with people from many different countries throughout their careers. Appreciating cultural diversity will strengthen teamwork while encouraging creative ideas that reflect many different perspectives.

Humility is another characteristic that future leaders should develop. Humility does not mean lacking confidence. Instead, it means recognizing that every person has something valuable to learn from others. Humble individuals welcome feedback, admit mistakes, ask questions, and remain open to new ideas. These qualities strengthen learning because they encourage continuous improvement rather than assuming that one person already possesses every answer.

As technology continues evolving, humility will help people adapt by remaining curious throughout life.

Service to others may become one of the defining characteristics of the AGI Generation. Throughout history, the greatest leaders have often measured success by the positive difference they made in other people's lives. Doctors serve patients. Teachers serve students. Engineers serve communities by designing safe infrastructure. Scientists serve humanity through research. Business owners serve customers by creating useful products and meaningful employment opportunities. Artificial intelligence can increase efficiency, but service gives work lasting meaning because it focuses on improving the lives of others.

Students should also remember that happiness and success are not determined only by intelligence or financial achievement. Meaningful friendships, healthy families, personal integrity, community involvement, lifelong learning, and purposeful work contribute greatly to a fulfilling life. Artificial intelligence may assist people in many areas, but it cannot replace the satisfaction that comes from helping someone, solving a difficult problem, achieving a meaningful goal, or making a positive contribution to society. These experiences remind us why education exists—to prepare individuals not only for careers but also for lives of purpose and responsibility.

The AGI Generation will have opportunities unlike any previous generation. Intelligent technologies may eliminate many routine tasks, allowing people to devote more time to creativity, innovation, discovery, education, healthcare, environmental protection, scientific research, entrepreneurship, and community service. This future should inspire hope rather than fear because it offers the possibility of solving problems that have challenged humanity for generations. However, success will depend upon people choosing to use these powerful tools responsibly.

As you continue preparing for your future, remember that your greatest strengths are already beginning to develop. Every time you practice kindness, strengthen your character, solve a problem, encourage a classmate, complete an honest assignment, ask a thoughtful question, or continue learning after making a mistake, you are strengthening qualities that will remain valuable throughout your entire life. These habits build the human advantage that no technology can replace.

Artificial General Intelligence may become one of the most remarkable achievements in human history, but humanity itself remains the greatest source of purpose, creativity, compassion, wisdom, and hope. The future belongs not simply to those who understand intelligent machines, but to those who understand people. The AGI Generation has the opportunity to become a generation that combines extraordinary technology with extraordinary character, ensuring that intelligence always serves humanity with dignity, integrity, and compassion.

The greatest achievement of the future will never be measured only by how intelligent our machines become. It will be measured by how wisely, ethically, and compassionately people choose to use them. That is the true human advantage, and it will remain one of humanity's greatest strengths for generations to come.

Chapter 13 Summary

The Human Advantage in an AGI World

As Artificial General Intelligence becomes more capable, many people wonder what role humans will continue to play. This chapter explained that the future should not be viewed as a competition between humans and intelligent machines. Instead, the greatest success will come from partnerships where people and AGI work together, each contributing unique strengths.

Students learned that while AGI can process enormous amounts of information, recognize patterns, perform calculations, and assist with complex tasks, human beings possess qualities that technology cannot replace. These include creativity, imagination, empathy, ethical reasoning, wisdom, curiosity, communication, resilience, adaptability, cultural understanding, moral courage, humility, and purpose.

The chapter emphasized that creativity allows people to imagine ideas that have never existed before, while empathy helps build relationships based on compassion and understanding. Ethical reasoning guides responsible decision-making by considering fairness, dignity, and the well-being of others. Wisdom enables people to apply knowledge responsibly, and purpose gives meaning to education, careers, service, and lifelong goals.

Readers also discovered that future leaders must ask meaningful questions, communicate effectively, inspire others, and work collaboratively across cultures and professions. Human values remain the foundation for solving complex problems and ensuring that intelligent technologies are used responsibly.

Finally, the chapter reminded students that their greatest advantage will not be competing with AI but developing the qualities that make them uniquely human. The AGI Generation has the opportunity to combine advanced technology with strong character, compassion, lifelong learning, and ethical leadership to build a future that benefits all of humanity.

Chapter 13 Reflection

The Human Advantage in an AGI World

Answer each question thoughtfully using complete sentences.

1. Which human quality discussed in this chapter do you believe is the most important? Explain your answer.
2. Why is creativity still valuable even if AGI becomes extremely intelligent?
3. How does empathy strengthen relationships that technology cannot replace?
4. Explain the difference between knowledge and wisdom.
5. Why is purpose important in a person's life and career?

6. How can curiosity help students prepare for careers that may not yet exist?
7. Why should future leaders develop humility along with confidence?
8. How can your personal strengths make a positive difference in your family, school, or community?

Personal Reflection

Imagine yourself twenty-five years in the future working alongside advanced AGI systems. Describe how your creativity, compassion, wisdom, ethics, communication, and leadership help solve important problems while ensuring that technology continues serving humanity responsibly.

Chapter 13 Worksheet

The Human Advantage in an AGI World

Part A – Vocabulary

Define each term using your own words.

1. Creativity
2. Empathy
3. Ethical Reasoning
4. Wisdom
5. Curiosity
6. Moral Courage
7. Adaptability
8. Humility
9. Purpose
10. Resilience

Part B – Comprehension Questions

Answer each question using complete sentences.

1. Why should humans view AGI as a partner instead of a competitor?
2. Explain how creativity differs from information processing.
3. Why is empathy important in leadership and everyday life?
4. What is the difference between knowledge and wisdom?
5. Why is asking thoughtful questions an important human skill?
6. How can cultural understanding improve teamwork?

7. Why is purpose considered one of humanity's greatest strengths?
8. How can students strengthen their human advantages during school?

Part C – Critical Thinking

Write one or two paragraphs for each question.

1. Imagine a future workplace where people and AGI work together every day. Describe how human strengths and AGI strengths complement each other.
2. Explain why character may become even more valuable as technology becomes more advanced.
3. Discuss how schools can help students develop creativity, empathy, ethical reasoning, and leadership alongside technological skills.

Part D – My Human Advantage Plan

Develop your personal growth plan.

Include:

• Five human strengths you want to improve.

• Three habits that strengthen your character.

• Three ways you can practice empathy every day.

• Three ways AI can support your learning without replacing your thinking.

• One personal mission statement describing how you hope to use your talents to improve the lives of others.

Chapter 13 Quiz

Multiple Choice

Choose the best answer.

1. According to this chapter, the future relationship between humans and AGI should be:

A. A competition.

B. A partnership.

C. A replacement.

D. A conflict.

2. Which quality is considered uniquely human?

A. Empathy

B. Ethical reasoning

C. Purpose

D. All of the above

3. Wisdom is best described as:

A. Memorizing facts.

B. Applying knowledge responsibly.

C. Processing information quickly.

D. Solving math problems.

4. Moral courage means:

A. Avoiding difficult decisions.

B. Doing what is right even when it is difficult.

C. Following others without question.

D. Ignoring ethical concerns.

5. Human purpose gives people:

A. Direction and meaning.

B. Faster computers.

C. More internet access.

D. Better calculators.

True or False

6. _____ AGI can replace every human quality.
7. _____ Creativity remains valuable in the AGI era.
8. _____ Wisdom and knowledge have the same meaning.
9. _____ Purpose helps people contribute to society.
10. _____ Human values should continue guiding technological progress.

Short Answer

11. Explain one reason creativity remains important in the AGI era.
12. Describe how empathy helps build stronger relationships.
13. Why should future leaders develop wisdom?
14. How can curiosity prepare students for the future?
15. In your own words, explain what the "human advantage" means.

Chapter 13 Answer Key

Multiple Choice

1. **B**
2. **D**
3. **B**
4. **B**
5. **A**

True or False

6. **False**
7. **True**
8. **False**
9. **True**
10. **True**

Short Answer (Sample Responses)

Chapter 14 – Part 1

Preparing for Careers That Do Not Yet Exist

Imagine walking into a classroom one hundred years ago and asking students whether they wanted to become a cybersecurity analyst, artificial intelligence engineer, drone systems operator, cloud architect, robotics technician, or machine learning specialist. Most of those careers did not exist because the technology that created them had not yet been invented. The students of that time prepared for the future using the knowledge available to them, but they could not fully imagine the careers that later generations would experience.

Today, the AGI Generation stands in a similar position. Many of the careers that today's students will have as adults have not yet been created. Some jobs will evolve into entirely new professions, while others will combine skills from several different fields. Artificial General Intelligence will likely accelerate this transformation by helping industries solve problems more efficiently, automate repetitive tasks, and create opportunities that have never existed before. Rather than fearing these changes, students should recognize that they are preparing for an exciting future filled with possibilities.

Throughout history, technological progress has consistently changed the nature of work. The invention of the printing press created new opportunities for publishing, education, and communication. The Industrial Revolution transformed manufacturing while creating new engineering professions. Computers gave rise to software development, information technology, digital design, and internet-based businesses. Smartphones created careers involving mobile applications, digital marketing, content creation, and online commerce. Each generation adapted by learning new skills while continuing to build upon the strengths developed by previous generations. The AGI Generation will continue this pattern by preparing for careers that combine human creativity with intelligent technology.

One of the most important lessons students should understand is that careers are built on skills rather than job titles. Job titles may change as technology evolves, but valuable skills continue serving people throughout many different professions. Communication, problem-solving, teamwork, ethical decision-making, creativity, adaptability, leadership, critical thinking, and lifelong learning remain valuable regardless of how technology changes. Students who strengthen these abilities will be prepared for careers that may not even have names yet.

Artificial intelligence will likely reduce the amount of time people spend performing repetitive tasks. Instead of replacing human potential, this shift may allow professionals to focus more on creative thinking, innovation, relationship building, strategic planning, and solving complex challenges. Imagine a teacher who spends less time grading routine assignments because AI provides immediate feedback, allowing more time for mentoring students and designing engaging lessons. Imagine a physician who receives AI-assisted analysis of medical images, creating more time to speak with patients and explain treatment options. Imagine an engineer who uses AGI to test thousands of design possibilities before selecting the safest and most efficient solution. Technology increases efficiency while people continue providing judgment, leadership, and purpose.

Many future careers will require knowledge from more than one subject. A healthcare professional may need to understand biology, artificial intelligence, ethics, communication, and data analysis. An environmental engineer may combine chemistry, computer science, mathematics, public policy, and sustainability. A business leader may rely upon economics, psychology, technology, marketing, and leadership. This interdisciplinary approach allows professionals to understand problems from multiple perspectives and develop more effective solutions. Students should avoid thinking that subjects learned in school exist independently. In reality, mathematics supports science, language arts strengthens communication, history provides perspective, and technology connects knowledge across many different disciplines.

Entrepreneurship will also become increasingly important in the AGI era. Entrepreneurs identify problems that need solving and create products or services that improve people's lives. Artificial intelligence may help entrepreneurs analyze markets, understand customer needs, organize financial information, and develop business strategies. However, successful businesses still depend on vision, honesty, creativity, customer service, and responsible leadership. Students who develop entrepreneurial thinking learn to recognize opportunities, solve problems creatively, and adapt when circumstances change.

Another important career skill is digital literacy. Digital literacy goes beyond knowing how to operate computers or use mobile devices. It includes understanding how digital information is created, how AI systems work, how to evaluate online sources, how to protect personal information, and how to use technology responsibly. Every profession—from healthcare and education to construction, agriculture, finance, manufacturing, and public service—is becoming increasingly connected to digital tools. Students who become confident technology users while maintaining strong ethical standards will have significant advantages throughout their careers.

Communication continues to distinguish outstanding professionals in every field. Intelligent systems may organize reports, summarize information, or translate languages, but people remain responsible for building relationships, explaining ideas clearly, negotiating agreements, inspiring teams, and resolving misunderstandings. Employers consistently value individuals who communicate effectively because strong communication strengthens teamwork, improves customer service, reduces mistakes, and builds trust. Students should continue developing speaking, writing, listening, and presentation skills because these abilities remain valuable regardless of technological change.

Problem-solving may become one of the defining skills of future careers. Many routine tasks can be automated, but complex challenges often require creativity, collaboration, ethical reasoning, and adaptability. Future professionals may face questions involving climate resilience, cybersecurity, healthcare innovation, sustainable energy, intelligent transportation, educational equity, or space exploration. Solving these challenges requires people who ask thoughtful questions, evaluate evidence carefully, and remain committed to improving society through responsible innovation.

Adaptability will continue separating successful professionals from those who struggle with change. Technology evolves quickly, meaning employees will likely learn new tools throughout their careers. Students should become comfortable learning continuously rather than expecting education to end after graduation. Those who enjoy learning, welcome constructive feedback, and remain curious will find it easier to adapt to new opportunities as industries evolve.

Another essential career skill is collaboration. Modern challenges rarely belong to one profession alone. Engineers work with environmental scientists. Healthcare professionals collaborate with software developers. Educators cooperate with psychologists and technology specialists. Business leaders work alongside designers, accountants, marketers, and data analysts. Artificial intelligence helps coordinate projects, but successful collaboration depends upon respect, communication, shared goals, and appreciation for the strengths of every team member.

Character remains one of the most valuable qualifications any employer can seek. Technical knowledge opens doors, but honesty, responsibility, dependability, integrity, and professionalism build long-term success. Employers trust individuals who arrive prepared, complete responsibilities carefully, communicate respectfully, admit mistakes honestly, and continue learning. These qualities cannot be replaced by technology because they reflect personal values rather than technical ability.

Perhaps the greatest opportunity for the AGI Generation is recognizing that education prepares students not only for today's careers but also for tomorrow's possibilities. Every mathematics lesson strengthens logical thinking. Every science experiment develops investigation skills. Every writing assignment improves communication. Every group project builds teamwork. Every ethical discussion prepares students to make responsible decisions. These experiences create a foundation that remains valuable even as careers continue evolving.

The future job market may look very different from today's, but the qualities that lead to success remain remarkably consistent. Students who combine curiosity, adaptability, creativity, integrity, communication, collaboration, and lifelong learning will be prepared not only to enter new careers but also to create entirely new opportunities that improve the lives of others. The AGI Generation is not simply preparing for jobs that already exist. It is preparing to build the professions, industries, and innovations that will define the future.

Chapter 14 – Part 2

Preparing for Careers That Do Not Yet Exist

One of the most exciting aspects of the future is that today's students have the opportunity to help invent entirely new careers. Every major technological breakthrough has created professions that previous generations could never have imagined. Before airplanes existed, there were no airline pilots. Before computers became common, there were no software developers or cybersecurity specialists. Before smartphones connected billions of people, there were no mobile application designers or social media managers. In the same way, Artificial General Intelligence will likely create occupations that do not yet have names. Some students reading this book may become pioneers in professions that future textbooks will describe for generations to come.

Future careers will likely emphasize solving problems rather than performing repetitive tasks. As intelligent systems automate routine work, human professionals will focus more on innovation, leadership, creativity, strategic planning, ethical decision-making, communication, and relationship building. Employers will increasingly seek individuals who can think independently, work effectively with diverse teams, adapt to changing technologies, and develop original solutions to complex challenges. These abilities remain valuable because they depend upon human judgment and experience rather than automation alone.

The AGI Generation should also recognize that learning new skills will become a normal part of every career. In previous generations, employees often remained in the same profession for decades while using similar methods throughout much of their working lives. Tomorrow's professionals may update their knowledge regularly as technologies evolve. A teacher may learn new AI-powered instructional tools every few years. A physician may adopt improved diagnostic technologies throughout an entire career. Engineers may continually learn about advanced materials, robotics, and intelligent design systems. Lifelong learning becomes a professional responsibility rather than an optional activity.

Students should also understand that flexibility creates opportunity. Sometimes people become discouraged when career paths change unexpectedly. However, history shows that change often creates new possibilities. A person who develops adaptable skills can move between industries, continue learning, and discover rewarding opportunities that were previously unavailable. Instead of fearing uncertainty, successful professionals learn to view change as an invitation to grow. This mindset allows people to respond confidently as new careers emerge.

Another important career skill is systems thinking. Systems thinking means understanding how different parts of a larger system work together. Consider a hospital. Excellent healthcare depends not only on doctors but also on nurses, pharmacists, laboratory technicians, information technology specialists, administrators, maintenance workers, emergency responders, medical researchers, and many others. Artificial intelligence may assist many of these professionals, but understanding how each role contributes to the entire healthcare system leads to better decisions. Similar systems exist in education, transportation, agriculture, manufacturing, business, and government. Students who understand how different parts work together become stronger problem-solvers because they recognize the connections between people, technology, and organizations.

Financial literacy will also become increasingly valuable. Regardless of career choice, students benefit from understanding budgeting, saving, investing, responsible borrowing, entrepreneurship, and long-term financial planning. Artificial intelligence may assist people by organizing financial information, identifying spending patterns, and supporting informed decisions, but individuals remain responsible for managing their finances wisely. Financial responsibility creates stability while allowing people to pursue educational opportunities, career development, and personal goals with greater confidence.

The future workplace will also reward emotional intelligence. Employees who communicate respectfully, resolve conflicts professionally, encourage teamwork, and demonstrate empathy often become trusted leaders. Technical expertise remains important, but organizations also depend on individuals who build positive relationships, mentor others, and create healthy work environments. Artificial intelligence can process information efficiently, but emotional intelligence helps people understand one another, strengthen collaboration, and develop lasting professional partnerships.

Innovation will continue driving economic growth throughout the AGI era. Students should remember that innovation is not limited to inventing completely new technologies. Improving existing processes, increasing efficiency, reducing waste, strengthening customer experiences, or solving local community problems all represent valuable forms of innovation. A student who develops a better recycling program, designs an educational application, improves accessibility for people with disabilities, or creates environmentally friendly products contributes meaningfully to society. Innovation begins with observing problems and believing they can be solved.

Global collaboration will become increasingly common as communication technologies continue improving. Future professionals may work with colleagues living on different continents while contributing to the same project. Engineers may collaborate internationally to develop sustainable energy systems. Medical researchers may share discoveries that improve healthcare worldwide. Educators may exchange teaching strategies across cultures. Artificial intelligence may help translate conversations and organize international projects, but successful collaboration still depends upon respect, patience, cultural understanding, and effective communication.

Ethics will remain essential in every profession. As intelligent technologies become more powerful, professionals will face important decisions involving privacy, fairness, transparency, environmental responsibility, cybersecurity, and human well-being. Future employers will value individuals who demonstrate honesty, accountability, and integrity because trust remains the foundation of every successful organization. Technical ability creates opportunities, but ethical character sustains long-term success.

Another valuable lesson for students is that careers should provide both personal satisfaction and opportunities to serve others. While earning a living is important, meaningful work often includes improving people's lives. Teachers educate future generations. Engineers design safer infrastructure. Scientists pursue discoveries that benefit society. Healthcare professionals care for patients. Entrepreneurs create jobs while solving customer problems. Artists inspire creativity and cultural appreciation. Every profession contributes something valuable when approached with purpose and responsibility.

Mentorship will continue helping students prepare for future careers. Teachers, parents, community leaders, experienced professionals, and business owners can share practical advice developed through years of experience. Mentors often help students discover strengths they may not recognize in themselves while providing encouragement during difficult moments. Artificial intelligence can organize information and answer questions, but mentors provide wisdom, perspective, and personal guidance that grows through genuine human relationships.

The AGI Generation should never underestimate the importance of character. Employers consistently value individuals who are dependable, respectful, honest, punctual, responsible, cooperative, and willing to learn. These qualities build trust with coworkers, customers, and community members. As technology continues changing, character remains remarkably stable because it reflects personal values rather than technical knowledge. A person known for integrity often earns opportunities because others trust that individual to make responsible decisions.

Students should also remember that success is rarely defined by one achievement alone. Successful careers are built gradually through thousands of daily decisions. Completing assignments carefully, arriving prepared, treating others respectfully, asking thoughtful questions, practicing new skills, learning from mistakes, and continuing to improve each day all contribute to long-term professional growth. Great careers are not created overnight. They are built through consistent habits developed over many years.

As you prepare for the future, remember that your education is giving you far more than information. Every lesson strengthens your ability to think, communicate, solve problems, collaborate, and lead. These abilities will remain valuable regardless of how technology changes because they reflect your capacity to continue learning and adapting throughout life.

The AGI Generation has an extraordinary opportunity to shape the future of work. Rather than waiting for new careers to appear, today's students may become the people who create them. Through curiosity, innovation, ethical leadership, lifelong learning, and responsible use of Artificial General Intelligence, this generation can build professions that improve healthcare, strengthen education, protect the environment, expand scientific discovery, support economic growth, and improve the quality of life for people around the world.

The careers of tomorrow are not waiting to be discovered. They are waiting to be created by students who are willing to imagine new possibilities, continue learning throughout life, and use their talents to solve meaningful problems. The future belongs to those who prepare today, embrace change with confidence, and combine human potential with the remarkable capabilities of intelligent technology.

Chapter 14 Summary

Preparing for Careers That Do Not Yet Exist

The future of work is changing rapidly because of Artificial General Intelligence, automation, robotics, and other emerging technologies. Many careers that today's students will have during adulthood have not yet been created. Instead of preparing only for today's jobs, students should develop skills that will help them succeed in careers that continue evolving throughout their lives.

This chapter explained that successful careers are built on transferable skills rather than job titles. Communication, creativity, critical thinking, collaboration, ethical decision-making, leadership, adaptability, digital literacy, emotional intelligence, and lifelong learning will remain valuable regardless of technological change.

Students learned that AGI will likely automate many repetitive tasks while allowing people to focus more on innovation, problem-solving, leadership, relationship building, and creative thinking. Human professionals will continue making ethical decisions, setting goals, serving communities, and guiding technology responsibly.

The chapter introduced several important career preparation concepts, including interdisciplinary learning, entrepreneurship, financial literacy, systems thinking, mentorship, and global collaboration. Students discovered that future careers will often combine knowledge from multiple subjects and require cooperation with people from many different professions and cultures.

Readers also learned that character remains one of the most valuable career qualifications. Honesty, integrity, responsibility, dependability, and professionalism build trust that technology cannot replace. Employers continue valuing individuals who communicate respectfully, work well with others, and demonstrate strong ethical principles.

Finally, the chapter emphasized that today's students may become the creators of tomorrow's professions. The AGI Generation has an extraordinary opportunity to shape the future by combining lifelong learning, innovation, ethical leadership, and responsible use of Artificial General Intelligence to improve the lives of people around the world.

Chapter 14 Reflection

Preparing for Careers That Do Not Yet Exist

Answer each question thoughtfully using complete sentences.

1. Why do you think many future careers have not yet been invented?
2. Which career skill discussed in this chapter do you believe will be most valuable during your lifetime? Explain your answer.
3. How can lifelong learning prepare people for careers that continue changing?
4. Why is adaptability an important quality in the AGI era?
5. How can AI improve future careers without replacing human purpose?
6. Why do employers continue valuing character along with technical knowledge?
7. If you could invent a completely new career that helps society, what would it be? Describe its purpose.
8. What habits can you begin developing today that will prepare you for tomorrow's careers?

Personal Reflection

Imagine yourself thirty years from now working in a career that does not yet exist today. Describe your daily responsibilities, explain how AGI supports your work, and discuss how your creativity, ethics, leadership, communication, and problem-solving skills make a positive difference in the lives of others.

Chapter 14 Worksheet

Preparing for Careers That Do Not Yet Exist

Part A – Vocabulary

Define each term using your own words.

1. Adaptability
2. Entrepreneurship
3. Digital Literacy
4. Systems Thinking
5. Financial Literacy
6. Collaboration
7. Innovation
8. Emotional Intelligence
9. Professionalism
10. Lifelong Learning

Part B – Comprehension Questions

Answer each question using complete sentences.

1. Why are transferable skills more valuable than specific job titles?
2. How can AGI change the future workplace?
3. Explain the meaning of systems thinking.
4. Why is financial literacy important regardless of career choice?
5. How does emotional intelligence strengthen teamwork?
6. Why should students continue learning throughout their careers?
7. What role do mentors play in career development?
8. Why is character considered one of the most important career qualifications?

Part C – Critical Thinking

Write one or two paragraphs for each question.

1. Design a future career that could exist twenty years from now. Describe its responsibilities, required skills, and how AGI helps professionals perform their work responsibly.
2. Explain why schools should teach communication, ethics, leadership, and problem-solving alongside science and technology.
3. Discuss how future careers may require knowledge from many different academic subjects instead of only one specialty.

Part D – My Future Career Plan

Create your own career preparation roadmap.

Include:

• Five career skills you want to strengthen.

• Three school subjects that will help prepare you.

• Three ways AGI could assist you in your future profession.

• Three ethical values you want to demonstrate throughout your career.

• One personal career mission statement describing how you hope to improve society through your work.

Chapter 14 Quiz

Multiple Choice

Choose the best answer.

1. According to this chapter, many future careers:

A. Already exist.

B. Have not yet been created.

C. Will eliminate education.

D. Require no new skills.

2. Which career skill remains valuable regardless of technological change?

A. Communication

B. Adaptability

C. Leadership

D. All of the above

3. Systems thinking helps people:

A. Understand how different parts work together.

B. Memorize information faster.

C. Avoid teamwork.

D. Eliminate technology.

4. Emotional intelligence improves:

A. Relationships and teamwork.

B. Computer speed.

C. Internet connections.

D. Calculator performance.

5. Employers continue valuing:

A. Character and integrity.

B. Responsibility.

C. Professionalism.

D. All of the above.

True or False

6. ______ AGI will likely automate some repetitive tasks.
7. ______ Lifelong learning prepares people for changing careers.
8. ______ Technical knowledge is more important than character.
9. ______ Future careers may combine many different academic subjects.
10. ______ Students may create careers that do not yet exist today.

Short Answer

11. Explain why adaptability is important for future careers.
12. Describe one benefit of digital literacy.
13. Why is lifelong learning essential in the AGI era?
14. How can AGI support professionals without replacing them?
15. In your own words, explain why today's students are preparing for careers that have not yet been invented.

Chapter 14 Answer Key

Multiple Choice

1. **B**
2. **D**
3. **A**
4. **A**
5. **D**

True or False

6. **True**
7. **True**
8. **False**
9. **True**
10. **True**

Short Answer (Sample Responses)

11. Adaptability allows people to learn new skills, adjust to changing technologies, respond confidently to workplace changes, and remain successful as careers continue evolving throughout their lives.
12. Digital literacy helps individuals understand technology, evaluate online information, protect personal data, use AI responsibly, and communicate effectively in modern workplaces.
13. Lifelong learning enables professionals to continue developing knowledge and skills as industries, technologies, and careers change. It prepares individuals to adapt successfully while remaining valuable contributors throughout their working lives.
14. AGI can support professionals by analyzing information, organizing data, automating routine tasks, identifying patterns, improving efficiency, and assisting decision-making while people continue providing leadership, ethics, creativity, communication, and final judgment.
15. Today's students are preparing for careers that have not yet been invented because technology continues creating new industries, new opportunities, and new professional roles. By developing transferable skills such as communication, creativity, leadership, adaptability, ethics, and lifelong learning, students will be prepared to succeed in whatever careers the future brings.

Chapter 15 – Part 1

Becoming a Responsible Citizen in the AGI Era

Every generation has a responsibility to leave the world better than it found it. Some generations built schools, hospitals, roads, and communication systems. Others expanded scientific knowledge, protected civil rights, explored space, or developed technologies that transformed everyday life. Today's students are entering a world where Artificial General Intelligence may become one of the most influential technologies in human history. Along with its opportunities comes an important responsibility. The AGI Generation must learn not only how to use intelligent technology but also how to become responsible citizens who ensure that technology serves humanity wisely, fairly, and ethically.

Citizenship is often associated with legal rights and responsibilities within a country, but responsible citizenship reaches much further. It involves contributing positively to families, schools, neighborhoods, workplaces, and communities. Responsible citizens obey laws, respect others, participate in civic life, protect public resources, help solve community problems, and contribute to the common good. As intelligent technologies become part of everyday life, digital citizenship and responsible technology use become essential parts of modern citizenship.

A responsible citizen understands that every action can affect other people. This principle applies whether someone is speaking face-to-face, posting online, sharing information through social media, or using artificial intelligence. Students should remember that technology makes communication faster, but it does not eliminate personal responsibility. Words shared online can influence opinions, spread helpful information, or unfortunately contribute to misunderstanding if they are not used carefully. Responsible digital citizens think before they post, verify information before sharing it, and communicate with honesty and respect.

Artificial intelligence increases the importance of media literacy. Every day, enormous amounts of information are created and shared across the internet. Some information is carefully researched and accurate. Other information may be misleading, incomplete, outdated, or intentionally false. Future AGI systems may generate articles, videos, images, voices, and other digital content that appears highly realistic. Students must therefore develop the habit of asking important questions before accepting information as true. Who created this information? What evidence supports it? Can it be verified through trusted sources? These habits strengthen responsible citizenship because informed citizens make better decisions.

Participation is another important characteristic of responsible citizenship. Healthy communities depend upon people who become involved rather than remaining passive observers. Students may participate by volunteering, helping classmates, joining school organizations, supporting local events, protecting the environment, or contributing ideas that improve their schools and neighborhoods. As adults, they may vote, serve on community boards, mentor young people, or support charitable organizations. Technology can help people communicate and organize community efforts more efficiently, but meaningful participation continues depending upon individuals who care enough to become involved.

Respect for different perspectives also strengthens responsible citizenship. Communities include people from many different backgrounds, cultures, beliefs, professions, and life experiences. Artificial intelligence may help people communicate across languages and share information globally, but respectful conversations still depend upon human attitudes. Responsible citizens listen carefully, disagree respectfully, seek common ground, and recognize that thoughtful discussions often produce stronger solutions than arguments based on anger or misinformation. Students who practice respectful communication today prepare themselves to become effective leaders tomorrow.

Environmental responsibility is another important part of citizenship. Every generation shares responsibility for protecting the natural world. Students should understand how daily decisions affect energy use, water conservation, recycling, waste reduction, and environmental sustainability. Artificial intelligence may help communities monitor pollution, improve recycling systems, conserve natural resources, and design cleaner technologies. However, lasting environmental progress depends upon people making responsible choices every day. Small actions performed consistently by millions of individuals often produce significant long-term improvements.

Responsible citizenship also includes protecting privacy. As technology becomes more connected, personal information travels through countless digital systems. Students should understand the importance of protecting passwords, respecting other people's information, recognizing online scams, and carefully deciding what personal details should remain private. Organizations using AI also have responsibilities to protect sensitive information and explain clearly how data is collected and used. Privacy builds trust because people feel more confident using technology when they know their information is handled responsibly.

Another essential quality is accountability. Responsible citizens accept responsibility for their actions instead of blaming others when mistakes occur. If misinformation is shared accidentally, responsible individuals correct it. If technology is used improperly, responsible users learn from the experience and improve their behavior. Accountability builds trust because it demonstrates honesty and a willingness to grow. Artificial intelligence may assist with many tasks, but accountability always remains a human responsibility.

The AGI Generation will also have opportunities to contribute to public discussions about technology. Future citizens may help shape laws, educational policies, workplace standards, environmental regulations, and ethical guidelines involving artificial intelligence. These conversations require informed individuals who understand both technological possibilities and human values. Students should recognize that civic participation includes asking thoughtful questions about how technology affects education, healthcare, employment, privacy, and public safety. Responsible citizens remain informed because good decisions depend upon accurate knowledge.

Communities also become stronger when citizens help one another. During natural disasters, economic hardships, or personal emergencies, neighbors often provide assistance that no technology can replace. Volunteers distribute food, emergency responders protect lives, healthcare professionals provide treatment, teachers support students, and families care for one another. Artificial intelligence may improve coordination and communication during these situations, but compassion and service remain deeply human qualities that strengthen society.

Responsible citizenship requires balancing rights with responsibilities. Every individual deserves opportunities to learn, express ideas respectfully, and participate in society. At the same time, every person shares responsibility for respecting others, protecting public resources, following ethical principles, and contributing positively to community life. This balance creates healthy societies where freedom exists alongside mutual respect and shared responsibility.

Perhaps the most important lesson students can learn is that citizenship begins long before adulthood. Every classroom discussion, group project, volunteer activity, and everyday decision provides opportunities to practice honesty, responsibility, cooperation, and leadership. Students become responsible citizens gradually by developing habits that reflect integrity and concern for others. These habits remain valuable throughout life regardless of how technology continues evolving.

The AGI Generation has the opportunity to become one of the most informed and connected generations in history. With access to extraordinary knowledge and intelligent tools comes the responsibility to use those resources wisely. Responsible citizens understand that technology achieves its greatest value when it strengthens communities, protects human dignity, encourages lifelong learning, and improves the quality of life for everyone. By developing these habits today, students prepare themselves not only to succeed personally but also to contribute meaningfully to a more ethical, compassionate, and intelligent world.

Chapter 15 – Part 2

Becoming a Responsible Citizen in the AGI Era

As Artificial General Intelligence becomes part of everyday life, responsible citizenship will extend beyond local communities and national borders. Students growing up today will live in a world where communication happens instantly across continents, businesses operate internationally, and global challenges require cooperation among many nations. The AGI Generation will become part of a worldwide community connected through technology, education, science, and shared human goals. This global connection creates new opportunities as well as new responsibilities.

One of the greatest responsibilities of future citizens will be protecting truth. Throughout history, societies have depended upon accurate information to make wise decisions. Communities cannot solve problems effectively if they rely on false information or misunderstand important facts. As AGI becomes capable of creating realistic text, images, audio, and video, students must become skilled at verifying information before believing it or sharing it with others. Responsible citizens do not spread rumors simply because they appear convincing. They pause, investigate, compare reliable sources, and think critically before acting. Protecting truth strengthens democracy, education, science, and public trust.

The AGI Generation will also play an important role in encouraging respectful online behavior. Digital communication allows people to share ideas with audiences around the world, but it also creates opportunities for misunderstanding, cyberbullying, harassment, and harmful behavior. Responsible digital citizens understand that every person deserves dignity and respect, whether communication happens face-to-face or through a computer screen. Kindness should not disappear simply because technology creates distance between people. Students should remember that behind every online message is another human being deserving of respect and consideration.

Another important responsibility involves reducing digital inequality. Around the world, many communities still lack reliable internet access, modern technology, educational resources, or opportunities to develop digital skills. Future leaders should work toward expanding educational opportunities so that technology benefits as many people as possible rather than increasing existing inequalities. Artificial intelligence has enormous potential to improve education, healthcare, and economic opportunity, but these benefits become most meaningful when they are accessible to diverse communities rather than only a small portion of society.

Responsible citizens also understand the importance of lifelong civic learning. Laws, technologies, environmental challenges, healthcare systems, and economic conditions continue changing throughout life. People who remain informed become better prepared to participate in community discussions, vote responsibly, evaluate public policies, and contribute thoughtful ideas. Artificial intelligence may summarize information quickly, but citizens must continue asking questions, verifying facts, and considering multiple perspectives before reaching conclusions.

One area where responsible citizenship and AGI intersect is public policy. Governments around the world continue discussing how intelligent technologies should be developed, tested, and used responsibly. These discussions involve topics such as privacy protection, cybersecurity, education, healthcare, employment, transparency, and fairness. Students may someday become lawmakers, educators, engineers, researchers, business leaders, or community advocates helping shape these important decisions. Their understanding of ethics and responsible technology use will influence policies affecting future generations.

The AGI Generation should also recognize the importance of protecting democratic values. Healthy democracies depend upon informed citizens who participate respectfully, evaluate evidence carefully, and remain willing to listen to different viewpoints. Technology can strengthen civic participation by improving communication and access to information, but it can also create challenges when misinformation spreads rapidly. Responsible citizens help protect democratic institutions by promoting respectful dialogue, encouraging fact-based discussions, and participating thoughtfully in civic life.

Volunteerism remains another important expression of responsible citizenship. Every community benefits when individuals freely contribute their time and talents to help others. Volunteers tutor children, assist senior citizens, protect natural habitats, support food banks, organize neighborhood improvement projects, coach youth sports, and respond during emergencies. Artificial intelligence may help organize volunteer efforts more efficiently, but compassion continues motivating people to serve others. Students who volunteer learn valuable lessons about leadership, teamwork, empathy, and social responsibility.

Future citizens must also understand the importance of balancing innovation with responsibility. Every technological advancement creates both opportunities and new questions. Should every capability be used simply because it exists? How should privacy be protected? How can fairness be ensured? What safeguards should exist before new technologies are widely adopted? Responsible citizens understand that progress should never ignore ethics. Instead, innovation and responsibility must advance together so that technology continues serving humanity rather than creating unnecessary harm.

Economic responsibility also becomes part of good citizenship. Every society depends upon individuals who contribute through honest work, responsible financial decisions, entrepreneurship, innovation, and support for community development. Future professionals using AGI will help create businesses, products, educational opportunities, scientific discoveries, and public services that strengthen local and global economies. Students should understand that productive work benefits not only individuals but also families, neighborhoods, and entire nations.

One of the greatest strengths of responsible citizens is hope. History demonstrates that humanity has repeatedly overcome difficult challenges through cooperation, determination, scientific discovery, and compassionate leadership. Diseases have been treated. Educational opportunities have expanded. Living conditions have improved. New technologies have solved problems that once seemed impossible. Every generation has contributed something valuable to human progress. The AGI Generation now has an opportunity to continue this tradition by approaching future challenges with confidence rather than fear.

Students should also recognize that citizenship is demonstrated through ordinary daily choices rather than extraordinary moments alone. Returning a lost item, helping a classmate understand a difficult assignment, recycling waste responsibly, telling the truth even when it is difficult, respecting school rules, thanking those who serve the community, and treating others with kindness all strengthen society. These everyday actions develop habits that later influence leadership, careers, families, and community life.

Character remains the foundation of responsible citizenship. Honesty builds trust. Compassion strengthens relationships. Integrity encourages ethical decisions. Respect promotes cooperation. Responsibility creates accountability. Courage inspires positive change. Humility encourages lifelong learning. These qualities remain valuable regardless of how advanced technology becomes because they define the kind of people society depends upon during both ordinary times and periods of great change.

As you prepare for adulthood, remember that becoming a responsible citizen is not a destination reached at a particular age. It is a lifelong commitment to serving others, protecting truth, respecting human dignity, caring for the environment, strengthening communities, and using knowledge wisely. Every lesson you learn, every decision you make, and every opportunity you accept contributes to the citizen you are becoming.

The AGI Generation has an extraordinary opportunity to become one of the most responsible generations in history. With access to powerful intelligent technologies comes the responsibility to ensure those technologies improve lives while protecting fairness, freedom, privacy, safety, and human dignity. Future citizens will not be remembered simply because they lived during the age of Artificial General Intelligence. They will be remembered because they chose to use intelligence with wisdom, compassion, integrity, and service.

The future of society will not depend only on the intelligence of its machines. It will depend on the character of its citizens. The AGI Generation has the opportunity to build communities where technology supports education, healthcare, opportunity, innovation, and cooperation while people continue leading with honesty, responsibility, courage, and hope. That is the true meaning of responsible citizenship in the age of Artificial General Intelligence.

Chapter 15 Summary

Becoming a Responsible Citizen in the AGI Era

Artificial General Intelligence will become one of the most influential technologies in human history, but technology alone cannot build strong communities or create a better future. Responsible citizens play the most important role by using technology ethically, respecting others, protecting truth, and contributing positively to society.

This chapter explained that citizenship extends far beyond legal rights and responsibilities. Responsible citizens strengthen their families, schools, neighborhoods, workplaces, and communities through honesty, service, accountability, cooperation, and respect. In the AGI era, digital citizenship becomes equally important because people communicate, learn, and make decisions through increasingly advanced technologies.

Students learned that media literacy and critical thinking are essential skills for evaluating online information. As AGI becomes capable of creating realistic digital content, responsible citizens must verify information, recognize misinformation, and think carefully before sharing anything online.

The chapter also explored environmental responsibility, privacy protection, civic participation, volunteerism, and global cooperation. Students discovered that communities become stronger when people contribute their time, talents, and knowledge to improve the lives of others. Artificial intelligence can organize information and improve efficiency, but compassion, integrity, and service remain uniquely human responsibilities.

Readers also learned that responsible citizens help shape the future by participating in public discussions about technology, supporting ethical innovation, protecting democratic values, and encouraging respectful communication across cultures and communities.

Finally, the chapter concluded that the future of society depends not only on intelligent machines but also on the character of its citizens. The AGI Generation has an opportunity to become one of the most responsible generations in history by combining advanced technology with honesty, fairness, compassion, courage, lifelong learning, and a commitment to serving others.

Chapter 15 Reflection

Becoming a Responsible Citizen in the AGI Era

Answer each question thoughtfully using complete sentences.

1. What does responsible citizenship mean to you after reading this chapter?
2. Why is digital citizenship becoming more important in the AGI era?
3. How can students help reduce the spread of misinformation?
4. Why is volunteer service valuable for both individuals and communities?
5. How can responsible citizens help ensure that AGI benefits society fairly?
6. Why is protecting privacy an important responsibility?

7. Which character quality discussed in this chapter do you most want to strengthen? Explain why.
8. How can your daily decisions make your school or community a better place?

Personal Reflection

Imagine you are an adult community leader living in an AGI-powered society. Describe how you would encourage honesty, respect, responsible technology use, environmental stewardship, civic participation, and community service while helping people use Artificial General Intelligence ethically and responsibly.

Chapter 15 Worksheet

Becoming a Responsible Citizen in the AGI Era

Part A – Vocabulary

Define each term using your own words.

1. Citizenship
2. Digital Citizenship
3. Media Literacy
4. Accountability
5. Civic Participation
6. Privacy
7. Volunteerism
8. Global Cooperation
9. Ethical Innovation
10. Community Service

Part B – Comprehension Questions

Answer each question using complete sentences.

1. Why is responsible citizenship important in the AGI era?
2. Explain the meaning of digital citizenship.
3. Why should people verify information before sharing it online?
4. How can AGI support communities without replacing human responsibility?
5. Why is volunteerism important for strong communities?
6. Explain why protecting privacy builds trust.
7. How can citizens contribute to ethical discussions about AI?
8. Why does character remain important regardless of technological progress?

Part C – Critical Thinking

Write one or two paragraphs for each question.

1. Imagine your city is introducing AGI into schools, hospitals, and public services. Describe the responsibilities citizens should have to ensure these technologies are used fairly, safely, and ethically.
2. Explain why protecting truth may become one of the most important responsibilities of citizens during the AGI era.
3. Discuss how families, schools, governments, businesses, and community organizations can work together to develop responsible digital citizens.

Part D – My Responsible Citizenship Plan

Develop your personal citizenship action plan.

Include:

• Five habits that demonstrate responsible citizenship.

• Three ways you can improve your school or community.

• Three ways you will use AI responsibly.

• Three habits that help protect truth and reduce misinformation.

• One personal citizenship mission statement describing the kind of citizen you hope to become throughout your life.

Chapter 15 Quiz

Multiple Choice

Choose the best answer.

1. Responsible citizenship includes:

A. Serving the community.

B. Respecting others.

C. Using technology responsibly.

D. All of the above.

2. Digital citizenship means:

A. Owning a computer.

B. Using technology ethically, safely, and responsibly.

C. Playing online games.

D. Creating social media accounts.

3. Media literacy helps people:

A. Recognize reliable information.

B. Identify misinformation.

C. Evaluate evidence before sharing information.

D. All of the above.

4. Volunteerism strengthens communities by:

A. Encouraging people to serve others.

B. Building teamwork.

C. Improving local communities.

D. All of the above.

5. Responsible citizens should use AGI to:

A. Benefit society while protecting ethics and human dignity.

B. Replace all human decision-making.

C. Ignore privacy concerns.

D. Spread information without verification.

True or False

6. _____ Responsible citizenship begins long before adulthood.
7. _____ AI removes the need for human responsibility.

8. _____ Protecting privacy helps build public trust.
9. _____ Respectful communication strengthens communities.
10. _____ Character remains important regardless of technological progress.

Short Answer

11. Explain why media literacy is important in the AGI era.
12. Describe one responsibility of digital citizens.
13. Why should communities encourage volunteer service?
14. How can responsible citizens help guide the ethical use of AGI?
15. In your own words, explain what responsible citizenship means in an AI-powered world.

Chapter 15 Answer Key

Multiple Choice

1. **D**
2. **B**
3. **D**
4. **D**
5. **A**

True or False

6. **True**
7. **False**
8. **True**
9. **True**
10. **True**

Short Answer (Sample Responses)

11. Media literacy helps people evaluate information carefully, recognize misinformation, verify sources, distinguish facts from opinions, and make informed decisions before believing or sharing digital content created by humans or AI.

12. A responsible digital citizen communicates respectfully, protects personal and private information, verifies information before sharing it, follows ethical online behavior, and uses technology to contribute positively to society.
13. Volunteer service strengthens communities by helping people in need, building teamwork, encouraging compassion, solving local problems, developing leadership skills, and creating stronger relationships among community members.
14. Responsible citizens help guide the ethical use of AGI by participating in public discussions, supporting fair policies, protecting privacy, promoting transparency, encouraging accountability, and ensuring that intelligent technology serves people with dignity and respect.
15. Responsible citizenship in an AI-powered world means using technology wisely, protecting truth, respecting others, serving the community, safeguarding privacy, participating in civic life, and combining technological knowledge with honesty, compassion, integrity, and ethical decision-making to improve society for everyone.

Chapter 16 – Part 1

The Generation That Will Shape the Future

Every generation inherits the world left behind by those who came before it. Each generation also leaves its own mark on history by solving problems, creating new ideas, building stronger communities, and preparing opportunities for the people who follow. Some generations witnessed the invention of electricity. Others experienced the birth of airplanes, computers, the internet, smartphones, or space exploration. The students reading this book belong to a generation that will experience something equally extraordinary—the emergence of Artificial General Intelligence.

History often remembers technological inventions, but history is truly shaped by the people who choose how those inventions are used. A hammer can build a home or damage one. Electricity can power hospitals or create dangerous situations if used carelessly. The internet can connect billions of people through education and communication, or it can spread misinformation when used irresponsibly. Artificial General Intelligence will follow the same pattern. The technology itself is powerful, but its greatest impact will depend upon the character, wisdom, and decisions of the people who guide it. That responsibility now belongs to the AGI Generation.

Many students wonder whether they will truly have the ability to influence the future. The answer is yes. Every major improvement in history began with ordinary people who chose to do extraordinary things. Teachers inspired future scientists. Engineers designed safer bridges and cleaner transportation. Physicians developed life-saving treatments. Entrepreneurs created businesses that improved daily life. Community volunteers strengthened neighborhoods through acts of service. Researchers asked questions that changed scientific understanding. None of these individuals began their journeys knowing exactly how history would remember them. They simply continued learning, working, and serving others one day at a time.

The AGI Generation has opportunities unlike any previous generation because knowledge has become more accessible than ever before. Students today can explore scientific discoveries from around the world, communicate with people from different cultures, participate in online learning communities, conduct research using intelligent tools, and develop skills that once required access to specialized institutions. Education is no longer limited to one classroom or one textbook. Learning can happen anywhere curiosity exists.

With greater opportunity comes greater responsibility. Information alone does not improve the world. People improve the world by applying knowledge with integrity, compassion, wisdom, and purpose. Throughout this book, you have learned about artificial intelligence, ethical leadership, lifelong learning, responsible citizenship, human creativity, collaboration, and the many ways AGI may transform society. These topics all point toward one central truth: technology becomes most valuable when guided by people who care about improving the lives of others.

The future will require problem-solvers rather than passive observers. Many of tomorrow's challenges have not yet appeared. New diseases may emerge. Environmental conditions may change. Scientific discoveries may raise new ethical questions. Industries may continue evolving in unexpected directions. Rather than fearing uncertainty, students should prepare themselves to become adaptable learners who welcome opportunities to solve problems through knowledge, teamwork, and innovation. Every challenge also contains the possibility of meaningful progress.

Throughout history, education has provided hope during times of change. When new technologies transformed agriculture, education prepared farmers to adopt better methods. When industries expanded, education trained engineers, technicians, and skilled workers. When computers entered schools and workplaces, education helped people learn digital skills. Artificial General Intelligence will create another period of transformation, and once again education will become one of society's greatest strengths. Students who continue learning will be prepared not only to adapt to change but also to lead it.

One of the greatest lessons students should remember is that success is measured by more than personal achievement. A successful life includes helping others succeed as well. Teachers celebrate when students learn. Doctors celebrate when patients recover. Engineers celebrate when communities become safer. Parents celebrate when children grow into responsible adults. Entrepreneurs celebrate when businesses create opportunities for employees and customers. Meaningful success often comes from improving the lives of other people rather than focusing only on personal accomplishments.

Artificial intelligence will likely become one of the greatest educational tools ever created. Intelligent tutoring systems may personalize instruction for individual learners. Scientific research may become faster. Medical discoveries may accelerate. Businesses may solve problems more efficiently. Governments may improve public services. Communities may organize resources more effectively. Yet every one of these advancements depends upon individuals who ask thoughtful questions, evaluate evidence carefully, and make ethical decisions. Human responsibility remains at the center of every technological achievement.

The AGI Generation should also remember that learning never truly ends. Graduation is not the conclusion of education but the beginning of a lifetime of discovery. Every experience, conversation, challenge, book, project, and opportunity becomes another lesson that contributes to personal growth. Lifelong learners remain curious because they understand that the future belongs to those who continue expanding their knowledge and adapting to new opportunities.

Another important lesson is that no one succeeds entirely alone. Families provide encouragement. Teachers inspire learning. Friends offer support. Communities create opportunities. Mentors share wisdom. Colleagues contribute ideas. Artificial intelligence may assist people in remarkable ways, but human relationships continue providing encouragement, trust, and shared purpose. Success grows strongest when people help one another reach meaningful goals.

Students should also remember that courage is often quiet rather than dramatic. Courage may involve asking a difficult question, admitting a mistake, standing up for fairness, trying something new, continuing after failure, or helping someone in need. These everyday acts of courage shape character over time. The AGI Generation will need courageous individuals who choose honesty over convenience, service over selfishness, and integrity over short-term success.

Perhaps the most exciting reality is that the future has not yet been written. Every student reading this book has the opportunity to contribute something unique to humanity. Some will become scientists making remarkable discoveries. Others will educate future generations, develop businesses, create works of art, protect natural resources, improve healthcare, design intelligent technologies, strengthen communities, or simply become compassionate neighbors who improve the lives of the people around them. Every contribution matters because progress depends upon millions of people working together toward shared goals.

The AGI Generation is not defined simply by the technology it will inherit. It is defined by the choices it will make. Those choices begin today—in classrooms, homes, neighborhoods, libraries, laboratories, and communities where students are learning to think critically, communicate honestly, solve problems creatively, and serve others responsibly. These habits will shape not only individual futures but also the future of humanity itself.

Chapter 16 – Part 2

The Generation That Will Shape the Future

As you reach the end of this book, take a moment to think about how much the world has already changed during your lifetime. New technologies appear almost every year. Devices become more powerful. Scientific discoveries happen more quickly. Communication connects people across the globe in seconds. Artificial intelligence has already become part of classrooms, businesses, hospitals, transportation systems, scientific research, and everyday life. Yet this is only the beginning. The coming decades will likely bring changes greater than anything humanity has experienced before.

Many people describe the future as uncertain. While that is true, uncertainty should not create fear. Instead, it should create opportunity. Every generation enters a future that cannot be fully predicted. The students who graduated before the invention of the internet could not imagine online classrooms, smartphones, or video calls with people across the world. The scientists who first built early computers could not fully imagine today's intelligent systems. In the same way, no one can completely predict the world that today's students will inherit. What can be predicted, however, is that people who continue learning, adapting, and serving others will always remain valuable.

The AGI Generation has something extraordinary that previous generations did not possess. You have the opportunity to grow alongside intelligent technology from the very beginning of your education. Instead of learning about AGI after it has already transformed society, you are preparing while these technologies are still developing. This gives you a unique advantage. You can help shape how artificial intelligence is designed, how it is used, how it is governed, and how it benefits humanity.

As technology becomes more capable, the importance of human character becomes even greater. Intelligence without honesty can become dangerous. Innovation without ethics can create harm. Efficiency without compassion can ignore human needs. Knowledge without wisdom can lead to poor decisions. Throughout this book, one message has appeared repeatedly because it remains true regardless of how technology changes: human values must always guide intelligent technology.

The future will reward people who combine technical knowledge with strong character. Employers will seek individuals who communicate well, solve problems creatively, demonstrate integrity, work respectfully with others, and continue learning throughout life. Communities will depend upon citizens who protect truth, respect different perspectives, volunteer their time, and use technology responsibly. Nations will need leaders who understand both advanced technology and the importance of protecting human dignity, privacy, fairness, and freedom.

One of the greatest gifts you can give yourself is the habit of asking meaningful questions. Every important discovery begins with curiosity. Why does this problem exist? How can we improve people's lives? What have we overlooked? What can we learn from others? Artificial intelligence may provide impressive answers, but thoughtful questions will continue guiding humanity toward meaningful progress. Never lose your curiosity because it will become one of your greatest lifelong strengths.

Remember that learning is not measured only by grades or test scores. True learning changes the way you think. It teaches you to evaluate evidence carefully, communicate respectfully, solve problems responsibly, and understand perspectives different from your own. Every book you read, every teacher who inspires you, every challenge you overcome, and every mistake you learn from helps prepare you for opportunities that may not yet exist. Education is one of the few investments that continues growing throughout your entire life.

Do not underestimate the influence of small daily decisions. Great leaders are not created in a single moment. Scientists do not make discoveries overnight. Successful businesses are not built in one day. Character develops through ordinary choices repeated consistently over time. Choosing honesty when no one is watching. Helping someone who needs encouragement. Completing your work carefully. Treating people with kindness. Continuing after disappointment. Listening before speaking. These habits gradually shape the person you become.

The AGI Generation will also have an opportunity to redefine success. Success should never be measured only by income, popularity, or personal recognition. A meaningful life includes improving the lives of others. A teacher who inspires students, a nurse who comforts patients, an engineer who designs safer bridges, a scientist who develops life-saving medicine, an entrepreneur who creates meaningful jobs, or a volunteer who strengthens a neighborhood all contribute to society in valuable ways. Success becomes most meaningful when personal achievement is combined with service to others.

As Artificial General Intelligence continues evolving, people may sometimes focus only on what machines can accomplish. This book has encouraged you to remember something even more important: what people can accomplish together. Human creativity has built civilizations. Human compassion has cared for the sick. Human courage has defended freedom. Human curiosity has explored the oceans, climbed mountains, and reached the moon. Human cooperation has solved problems that once seemed impossible. Artificial intelligence becomes most powerful when it strengthens these human qualities rather than replacing them.

The future will belong to those who continue asking questions, seeking knowledge, embracing change, and acting with integrity. Some of you may become scientists discovering new medical treatments. Others may become engineers designing sustainable cities, teachers inspiring future generations, entrepreneurs creating innovative businesses, artists expanding human imagination, or public servants improving communities. Whatever path you choose, remember that your greatest contribution will not simply be what you accomplish, but how your work improves the lives of others.

One day, future generations may look back on this period as the beginning of a new chapter in human history. They may study how artificial intelligence transformed education, medicine, transportation, communication, science, business, and countless other fields. More importantly, they may study how the AGI Generation chose to guide those changes with wisdom, fairness, compassion, and responsibility. History will not remember only the technology that was created. It will remember the people who decided how that technology would serve humanity.

You have spent this book learning about the opportunities, responsibilities, and possibilities of living in the age of Artificial General Intelligence. You have explored ethics, leadership, creativity, lifelong learning, responsible citizenship, careers of the future, global problem-solving, and the unique qualities that make human beings extraordinary. These lessons are not simply ideas to remember for a test. They are principles that can guide your decisions throughout your entire life.

As you close this book, remember one final truth: **the future is not something that happens to you—it is something you help create.** Every question you ask, every lesson you learn, every challenge you overcome, every person you encourage, every ethical decision you make, and every opportunity you pursue becomes part of the future that your generation is building.

The AGI Generation has the opportunity to become one of the most educated, compassionate, innovative, and responsible generations in history. With Artificial General Intelligence as a powerful partner and human values as a trusted guide, your generation can solve problems that once seemed impossible, create opportunities that previous generations could only imagine, and build a world where technology strengthens education, expands opportunity, protects human dignity, and improves the quality of life for people everywhere.

The future is waiting.

The next great discoveries are waiting.

The next generation of leaders is waiting.

And that generation is **you**.

Learn AI. Understand AI. Shape the Future.

— Susie Hala
IntelliGloss Press

Chapter 16 Summary

The Generation That Will Shape the Future

This final chapter reminds students that every generation has the opportunity to shape history. The AGI Generation will grow up during one of the most important technological transitions in human civilization as Artificial General Intelligence becomes part of education, healthcare, science, business, government, and everyday life. However, technology alone will never determine humanity's future. The people who use it wisely will.

Students learned that AGI should be viewed as a powerful partner rather than a replacement for human potential. While intelligent systems can analyze information, recognize patterns, and solve complex problems, people continue providing creativity, compassion, wisdom, ethical leadership, purpose, and responsibility. These uniquely human qualities ensure that technology serves humanity rather than the other way around.

The chapter emphasized the importance of lifelong learning, adaptability, courage, integrity, curiosity, communication, and service to others. Students discovered that the future belongs to individuals who continue asking thoughtful questions, developing new skills, solving meaningful problems, and helping improve the lives of others.

Readers also learned that success should be measured not only by personal achievements but also by positive contributions to families, schools, communities, and society. Every profession has the potential to make a difference when guided by honesty, compassion, and a desire to serve.

The chapter concluded with an encouraging message that the future has not yet been written. Today's students have the opportunity to become scientists, teachers, engineers, healthcare professionals, entrepreneurs, artists, public servants, and community leaders who use Artificial General Intelligence responsibly while protecting human dignity, fairness, freedom, and hope.

The AGI Generation is not simply preparing to live in the future—it is preparing to build it.

Chapter 16 Reflection

The Generation That Will Shape the Future

Answer each question thoughtfully using complete sentences.

1. After reading this book, how has your understanding of Artificial General Intelligence changed?
2. Which lesson from this book do you believe will help you the most during your lifetime? Explain why.
3. Why is character just as important as intelligence in the AGI era?
4. How can lifelong learning help you succeed in a rapidly changing world?
5. In what ways can you use your talents to improve the lives of others?
6. Why should future leaders combine technology with ethics and compassion?
7. What kind of legacy do you hope your generation will leave behind?
8. How do you plan to continue learning about AI and future technologies after finishing this book?

Final Personal Reflection

Imagine yourself fifty years from now looking back on your life. Write a letter to today's students describing how your generation used Artificial General Intelligence to improve education, healthcare, science, business, environmental protection, and communities around the world. Explain the values that guided your decisions and the lessons future generations should never forget.

Chapter 16 Worksheet

The Generation That Will Shape the Future

Part A – Vocabulary Review

Define each term using your own words.

1. Artificial General Intelligence (AGI)
2. Lifelong Learning
3. Leadership
4. Innovation
5. Ethical Decision-Making
6. Human Dignity
7. Collaboration
8. Responsibility
9. Integrity
10. Purpose

Part B – Comprehension Questions

Answer each question using complete sentences.

1. Why is the AGI Generation unique in history?
2. Why should students view AGI as a partner rather than a competitor?
3. Explain why human values remain essential even as technology advances.
4. Why is curiosity important throughout life?
5. How can education prepare students for an uncertain future?
6. Why does meaningful success include helping others?
7. What role does lifelong learning play in future careers?
8. How can every student contribute to building a better future?

Part C – Critical Thinking

Write one or two paragraphs for each question.

1. Imagine your community twenty-five years from now. Describe how people and AGI work together to improve education, healthcare, transportation, environmental protection, and public safety while protecting ethics and human dignity.
2. Explain why history remembers people who use technology wisely rather than simply remembering the technology itself.
3. Describe the qualities you believe the AGI Generation should demonstrate to become one of the greatest generations in history.

Part D – My Future Commitment

Write your own personal commitment.

Include:

• Five values you promise to live by.

• Five lifelong learning goals.

• Three ways you will use AI responsibly.

• Three ways you will serve your community.

• Three leadership qualities you will continue developing.

• A personal mission statement describing the future you hope to help create for the next generation.

Chapter 16 Quiz

Multiple Choice

Choose the best answer.

1. According to this chapter, the future will primarily be shaped by:

A. Machines alone.

B. Human decisions and responsible use of technology.

C. Computers replacing people.

D. Automation only.

2. Which human quality remains essential in the AGI era?

A. Integrity

B. Compassion

C. Wisdom

D. All of the above

3. Lifelong learning helps people:

A. Adapt to change.

B. Continue developing new skills.

C. Prepare for future opportunities.

D. All of the above.

4. Meaningful success includes:

A. Helping improve the lives of others.

B. Learning continuously.

C. Leading responsibly.

D. All of the above.

5. The AGI Generation should become:

A. Passive users of technology.

B. Responsible builders of the future.

C. Dependent on intelligent machines.

D. Fearful of technological change.

True or False

6. _____ Human values should continue guiding Artificial General Intelligence.
7. _____ Curiosity encourages lifelong learning.
8. _____ Character becomes less important as technology improves.
9. _____ Every student has the opportunity to make a positive difference.
10. _____ The future is created by the choices people make today.

Short Answer

11. Explain why AGI should be considered a partner rather than a replacement for people.
12. Describe two qualities that make humans uniquely valuable in an AGI-powered world.
13. Why is lifelong learning important for future generations?
14. How can students begin shaping the future while they are still in school?
15. In your own words, explain the meaning of the statement: **"The future is not something that happens to you—it is something you help create."**

Chapter 16 Answer Key

Multiple Choice

1. **B**
2. **D**
3. **D**
4. **D**
5. **B**

True or False

6. **True**
7. **True**
8. **False**
9. **True**
10. **True**

Short Answer (Sample Responses)

11. AGI should be viewed as a partner because it can analyze information, automate routine tasks, and support problem-solving, while humans continue providing creativity, ethics, leadership, compassion, wisdom, and responsibility. Together, people and AGI can accomplish more than either could alone.
12. Human qualities such as creativity, empathy, ethical reasoning, integrity, curiosity, communication, resilience, and purpose allow people to make responsible decisions and build meaningful relationships that intelligent systems cannot replace.
13. Lifelong learning prepares people to adapt to changing technologies, develop new skills, respond to future opportunities, solve emerging problems, and continue growing throughout their personal and professional lives.
14. Students begin shaping the future by learning diligently, asking thoughtful questions, helping others, practicing honesty, developing leadership skills, respecting different perspectives, using technology responsibly, and contributing positively to their schools and communities.
15. The statement means that every decision, habit, lesson, and action contributes to building tomorrow's world. Rather than waiting for the future to arrive, individuals actively shape it through learning, ethical leadership, responsible technology use, service to others, and continuous personal growth.

GLOSSARY

Letter A

1. Access Time

The amount of time it takes for an AI system or computer to locate and retrieve data from memory or storage. Access time affects how quickly megabytes of data can be used during AI processing.

2. Activation Data

Intermediate data generated inside an AI model while it is running. Activation data is stored temporarily in memory and often measured in megabytes during model execution.

3. Adaptive Storage

A storage approach that automatically adjusts how data is stored or moved based on usage patterns. In AI systems, adaptive storage helps manage large volumes of megabytes efficiently.

4. Algorithmic Data Size

The total amount of data an algorithm needs to operate effectively. In AI, this size is often measured in megabytes or larger units, depending on model complexity.

5. Allocation (Memory Allocation)

The process of assigning a specific number of megabytes in memory or storage for an AI task, model, or dataset.

6. Analytics Dataset

A structured collection of data used for analysis or AI training. The size of an analytics dataset is commonly measured in megabytes, gigabytes, or more.

7. Annotation Storage

The space required to store labels, tags, or explanations added to AI training data. These annotations contribute additional megabytes to total dataset size.

8. Artificial Neural Network (ANN) Size

The total memory footprint of a neural network, including weights, biases, and parameters. ANN size is often described in megabytes when discussing model efficiency.

9. Asset Compression

The process of reducing the number of megabytes required to store AI-related files such as models, images, or datasets without losing essential information.

10. Available Memory

The amount of free memory, measured in megabytes, that an AI system can still use to load data, run models, or perform computations.

ANI (Artificial Narrow Intelligence)

Artificial Narrow Intelligence refers to AI systems designed to perform **one specific task or a narrow set of tasks** rather than general intelligence. ANI systems rely on data stored and processed in memory and storage measured in **megabytes, gigabytes, or more**. Examples include image recognition, speech-to-text, recommendation systems, and chatbots. ANI does not understand beyond its training scope, but it can process large amounts of data efficiently within its defined function.

Letter B

1. Bandwidth

The amount of data that can be transferred between systems in a given time. In AI systems, bandwidth determines how quickly megabytes of data can move between storage, memory, and processors.

2. Batch Processing

A method where AI systems process large groups of data all at once instead of one item at a time. Batch processing often involves handling many megabytes of data in a single operation.

3. Binary Encoding

The process of representing information using binary values (0s and 1s). All megabytes of AI data are ultimately stored and transmitted using binary encoding.**4. Bit Depth**

The number of bits used to represent a single piece of data, such as a pixel or audio sample. Higher bit depth increases data quality but also increases the number of megabytes required.

5. Bitmap Data

A type of image data where each pixel is stored as a set of bits. Bitmap images can quickly grow in size, consuming large numbers of megabytes in AI vision systems.

6. Buffer Memory

Temporary memory used to hold data while it is being transferred or processed. Buffers store data in chunks measured in megabytes to keep AI systems running smoothly.

7. Bulk Data Storage

Large-scale storage designed to hold massive datasets used for AI training or analysis. Bulk storage capacity is measured in megabytes, gigabytes, or larger units.

8. Byte Stream

A continuous flow of bytes transmitted or processed by a system. AI applications often analyze byte streams that accumulate into megabytes of data.

9. Bytecode

An intermediate form of program code that is easier for machines to execute than human-written code. Bytecode files occupy storage space measured in megabytes.

10. Byzantine Fault Tolerance (BFT)

A system property that allows AI or distributed systems to continue functioning even when some components fail or act unpredictably. Implementing BFT requires additional data handling and storage overhead measured in megabytes.

Letter C

1. Cache Memory

A small, high-speed memory area that stores frequently used data so the processor can access it faster. Cache helps reduce the time needed to move megabytes of data from main memory or storage.

2. Capacity Planning

The process of estimating how much memory and storage an AI system will need. Capacity planning ensures there are enough megabytes available to handle data, models, and future growth.

3. Checkpoint File

A saved snapshot of an AI model during training. Checkpoint files are stored in memory or storage and often consume many megabytes so training can resume without starting over.

4. Chunking

The practice of breaking large datasets into smaller pieces. Chunking helps AI systems process megabytes of data more efficiently by handling them in manageable parts.

5. Cloud Storage

A method of storing data on remote servers accessed through the internet. Cloud storage manages files measured in megabytes and allows AI systems to scale beyond local hardware limits.

6. Compression

The process of reducing the size of data so it uses fewer megabytes. Compression helps AI systems store, transfer, and process data more efficiently.

7. Compute Load

The amount of processing work required to run an AI task. Compute load often increases as the number of megabytes being processed grows.

8. Context Window

The amount of data an AI model can consider at one time. Context windows consume memory measured in megabytes, especially in language and vision models.

9. Corpus

A large collection of text or data used to train AI models. A corpus is usually measured in megabytes or larger units depending on its size.

10. CUDA Memory

Specialized memory used by GPUs to accelerate AI computations. CUDA memory holds model data and intermediate results measured in megabytes during processing.

Letter D

1. Data Allocation

The process of assigning a specific amount of memory or storage for data use. In AI systems, data allocation determines how many megabytes are reserved for datasets, models, or tasks.

2. Data Buffer

A temporary storage area that holds data while it is being transferred or processed. Data buffers manage megabytes of information to keep AI systems running smoothly.

3. Data Compression

A technique used to reduce the size of data so it consumes fewer megabytes. AI systems use data compression to save storage space and speed up data transfer.

4. Data Footprint

The total amount of data an AI system uses, including datasets, models, and temporary files. A data footprint is measured in megabytes, gigabytes, or more.

5. Data Loader

A software component that loads data into memory for AI training or inference. Data loaders handle batches of data measured in megabytes.

6. Data Migration

The process of moving data from one storage system to another. During AI system upgrades, data migration may involve transferring large numbers of megabytes.

7. Data Throughput

The rate at which data is processed or transferred by a system. Higher throughput allows AI systems to move more megabytes efficiently.

8. Dataset Size

The total amount of data in a dataset used for AI training or testing. Dataset size is commonly measured in megabytes or larger units.

9. Deep Learning Model Size

The amount of memory required to store a deep learning model, including its parameters and weights. Model size is often described in megabytes to assess efficiency.

10. Disk Storage

Long-term storage used to save files, datasets, and AI models. Disk storage capacity and usage are measured in megabytes, gigabytes, or terabytes.

Letter E

1. Edge Computing

A computing approach where data is processed closer to where it is generated rather than sent to a central server. Edge computing reduces how many megabytes must be transferred over networks.

2. Embedding Size

The amount of memory required to store vector representations used by AI models. Embedding size is often measured in megabytes and affects model performance and storage needs.

3. Encoded Data

Data that has been converted into a specific format for storage or transmission. Encoded data occupies megabytes depending on the encoding method used.

4. Encoding Scheme

A rule set that defines how data is represented digitally, such as text or images. Different encoding schemes can increase or reduce the number of megabytes required.

5. Encrypted Storage

Storage that protects data by converting it into a secure format. Encryption may slightly increase the number of megabytes used due to added security information.

6. End-to-End Data Pipeline

The full path data takes from collection to processing and storage. Each stage of the pipeline manages data volumes measured in megabytes.

7. Energy Efficiency (AI Systems)

A measure of how much energy an AI system uses to process data. Systems that move and store fewer megabytes are often more energy efficient.

8. Execution Memory

The memory required while a program or AI model is running. Execution memory usage is tracked in megabytes during runtime.

9. External Storage

Storage devices located outside a computer, such as USB drives or external hard drives. External storage capacity is measured in megabytes and larger units.

10. Extracted Features

Important data patterns identified by AI models during processing. Extracted features are stored temporarily or permanently in memory measured in megabytes.

Letter F

1. Feature Map

A structured output produced by AI models, especially in image and signal processing. Feature maps are stored in memory and can consume significant megabytes during computation.

2. Feature Scaling

The process of adjusting data values to a consistent range before training an AI model. Feature scaling affects how efficiently megabytes of data are processed and stored.

3. File Allocation Table (FAT)

A file system structure that tracks where files are stored on a disk. FAT helps manage how megabytes are organized and retrieved from storage.

4. File Compression Format

A standardized way to reduce file size so it uses fewer megabytes. Compression formats help AI systems store and transfer data efficiently.

5. File System Cache

A temporary memory area that stores frequently accessed files. File system caches reduce repeated access to storage and manage megabytes more efficiently.

6. Floating-Point Data

Numerical data that includes decimal values and is commonly used in AI calculations. Floating-point data requires more bits per value, increasing memory usage measured in megabytes.

7. Frame Buffer

A region of memory that stores image or video frames before they are displayed or processed. Frame buffers often consume large numbers of megabytes in AI vision systems.

8. Fragmentation

A condition where data is stored in scattered locations instead of one continuous block. Fragmentation can reduce storage efficiency even when megabytes appear available.

9. Free Memory

The amount of unused memory available for programs or AI tasks. Free memory is measured in megabytes and determines how much additional data can be loaded.

10. Full Dataset Load

The act of loading an entire dataset into memory at once. This approach can require large amounts of megabytes and is common in AI training scenarios.

Letter G

1. Garbage Collection

An automatic memory-management process that frees memory no longer in use. Garbage collection helps reclaim megabytes so AI programs can continue running efficiently.

2. Generalization Data

Data used to test how well an AI model performs on new, unseen inputs. Storing and evaluating generalization data requires additional megabytes beyond training data.

3. Gigabyte (GB)

A larger unit of data measurement equal to 1,024 megabytes (or commonly approximated as 1,000 MB). Gigabytes are used when datasets or models grow beyond megabyte scale.

4. Graph Data Structure

A way of organizing data using nodes and connections. Graph-based AI systems store graph data in memory and storage measured in megabytes.

5. GPU Memory

Specialized memory used by graphics processing units to accelerate AI workloads. GPU memory holds model parameters and data batches measured in megabytes.

6. Gradient Data

Numerical values calculated during AI training to update model parameters. Gradient data is stored temporarily in memory and contributes to overall megabyte usage.

7. Granularity

The level of detail at which data is stored or processed. Finer granularity often increases the number of megabytes required.

8. Greedy Algorithm

An algorithm that makes the best immediate choice at each step. Greedy algorithms may reduce memory usage by limiting how many megabytes of data must be stored at once.

9. Ground Truth Data

Correct, labeled data used to train or evaluate AI systems. Ground truth datasets are stored in files measured in megabytes or larger units.

10. Growth Rate (Data)

The speed at which data size increases over time. In AI systems, a high data growth rate means storage needs measured in megabytes can expand quickly.

Letter H

1. Hard Disk Capacity

The total amount of data a hard disk can store. Capacity is measured in megabytes and larger units.

2. Hardware Acceleration

The use of specialized hardware to speed up AI processing. Acceleration often reduces how long megabytes of data stay in memory.

3. Hash Table

A data structure that stores information for fast lookup. Hash tables occupy memory measured in megabytes in large AI systems.

4. Hierarchical Storage

A storage design that uses multiple layers such as RAM, disk, and cloud. Each layer manages data measured in megabytes.

5. High-Dimensional Data

Data with many features or variables. High-dimensional datasets often require large numbers of megabytes.

6. Host Memory

Main system memory used by the CPU. Host memory stores AI data and models measured in megabytes.

7. Hybrid Storage

A combination of different storage types working together. Hybrid storage systems manage megabytes across multiple devices.

8. Hyperparameter Storage

Memory used to store configuration values for AI models. These settings are saved in files measured in megabytes.

9. Hyperscale Data

Extremely large datasets used by major AI systems. Hyperscale data is tracked from megabytes up to much larger units.

10. Heuristic Data

Information used by AI systems to guide decision-making. Heuristic data contributes to the overall data size in megabytes.

Letter I

1. Image Dataset Size

The total amount of storage required for image data. Size is measured in megabytes or more.

2. Inference Memory

The memory used when an AI model is making predictions. Inference memory usage is tracked in megabytes.

3. Input Buffer

A temporary area where incoming data is stored. Input buffers hold megabytes before processing begins.

4. Intermediate Data

Data produced during processing steps. Intermediate data can significantly increase memory usage in megabytes.

5. Index File

A file that helps locate data quickly. Index files use additional megabytes to improve performance.

6. Information Density

The amount of useful data stored within a given size. Higher density means more information per megabyte.

7. Initialization Data

Data loaded when an AI system starts. Initialization data occupies memory measured in megabytes.

8. In-Memory Processing

Processing data directly in RAM instead of storage. This approach uses large amounts of memory measured in megabytes.

9. Input Feature Size

The amount of data required to represent input features. Feature size affects how many megabytes are needed.

10. Instruction Cache

A small memory area that stores frequently used instructions. Instruction caches manage small but critical megabytes.

Letter J

1. Job Queue

A list of tasks waiting to be processed. Job queues may store task data measured in megabytes.

2. Joint Dataset

A dataset created by combining multiple sources. Joint datasets often increase total size in megabytes.

3. JSON Data Size

The amount of storage required for data stored in JSON format. JSON files can grow quickly in megabytes.

4. Jitter Buffer

A temporary storage area that smooths data flow. Jitter buffers store megabytes during real-time processing.

5. Job Scheduler

A system that decides when tasks run. Schedulers manage memory and data measured in megabytes.

6. Just-in-Time Processing

Processing data only when needed. This approach can reduce how many megabytes are stored at once.

7. Joint Memory Allocation

Memory shared across multiple AI tasks. Joint allocation must carefully manage available megabytes.

8. Java Bytecode Size

The storage size of compiled Java programs. Bytecode files occupy megabytes on disk.

9. Job Metadata

Information describing AI tasks. Metadata adds additional megabytes to total system storage.

10. Junction Storage Point

A logical link between storage locations. Junctions help organize data measured in megabytes.

Letter K

1. Kernel Memory

Memory reserved for core system operations. Kernel memory usage is tracked in megabytes.

2. Key-Value Store

A data storage method that pairs keys with values. Large key-value stores consume many megabytes.

3. Knowledge Base Size

The total amount of stored knowledge in an AI system. Size is measured in megabytes or larger units.

4. K-Means Dataset Size

The amount of data used in clustering algorithms. Dataset size affects memory usage in megabytes.

5. Keras Model Size

The storage required for AI models built with Keras. Model size is measured in megabytes.

6. Keyframe Data

Important frames selected from video data. Keyframe storage contributes to total megabyte usage.

7. Kernel Cache

A cache used by the operating system kernel. Kernel caches store frequently used data in megabytes.

8. Knowledge Graph Storage

Memory used to store relationships between data points. Knowledge graphs require significant megabytes.

9. Kinetic Data Stream

Continuously changing data from sensors or systems. These streams generate growing megabytes over time.

10. K-Nearest Neighbor Memory Usage

The memory required by nearest-neighbor algorithms. Memory use increases as datasets grow in megabytes.

Letter L

1. **Latency**
   The delay between requesting data and receiving it. Latency affects how quickly megabytes move through AI systems.
2. **Layer Output Size**
   The amount of data produced by a neural network layer. Output size is measured in megabytes during processing.
3. **Load Balancing**
   Distributing work across systems so no single device is overloaded. Balancing helps manage megabytes efficiently.
4. **Local Storage**
   Data stored on a device rather than the cloud. Local storage capacity is measured in megabytes.
5. **Log File Size**
   The amount of storage used by system logs. Logs can accumulate many megabytes over time.
6. **Loss History Data**
   Stored values showing how model error changes during training. Loss history consumes megabytes.
7. **Low-Precision Data**
   Data stored using fewer bits per value. Low-precision formats reduce megabyte usage.
8. **Labeled Dataset**
   Data that includes tags or labels for AI training. Labels increase total dataset size in megabytes.
9. **Linear Model Size**
   The storage required for a linear AI model. Size is measured in megabytes.
10. **Load Time**
    The time required to bring data or models into memory. Load time depends on megabytes involved.

Letter M

1. **Memory Allocation**
   Assigning a specific amount of memory for tasks. Allocation is tracked in megabytes.
2. **Memory Footprint**
   The total memory an AI program uses. Footprint is measured in megabytes.

3. **Metadata Size**
   The storage used by descriptive information about data. Metadata adds extra megabytes.
4. **Mini-Batch Size**
   The amount of data processed at once during training. Batch size affects megabyte usage.
5. **Model Checkpoint Size**
   The storage required for saved training states. Checkpoints often consume many megabytes.
6. **Model Compression**
   Reducing model size while preserving performance. Compression lowers megabytes required.
7. **Model Parameters**
   Values learned by an AI model. Parameter storage contributes to total megabytes.
8. **Memory Bandwidth**
   The rate at which memory transfers data. Bandwidth affects how fast megabytes move.
9. **Multimodal Dataset**
   Data combining text, images, audio, or video. Multimodal data uses large megabytes.
10. **Mutable Data**
    Data that changes during processing. Mutable data can increase temporary megabyte usage.

Letter N

1. **Network Bandwidth**
   The capacity of a network connection. Bandwidth controls how many megabytes can be transferred.
2. **Neural Network Size**
   The total storage required for a neural network. Size is measured in megabytes.
3. **Node Memory**
   Memory available on a computing node. Node memory limits megabytes per task.
4. **Normalization Data**
   Values used to scale data consistently. Normalization adds to dataset megabytes.
5. **Non-Volatile Memory**
   Memory that retains data without power. Capacity is measured in megabytes.
6. **Numerical Precision**
   The detail level of stored numbers. Higher precision increases megabytes.
7. **Noise Data**
   Unwanted or random information in datasets. Noise increases data size in megabytes.
8. **Neural Activation Size**
   Memory used to store neuron outputs. Activation size is measured in megabytes.
9. **Network Transfer Size**
   The amount of data sent across a network. Transfer size is tracked in megabytes.
10. **Node Cache**
    Temporary storage on a node for faster access. Cache size uses megabytes.

Letter O

1. **Object Storage**
   A storage method that manages data as objects. Capacity is measured in megabytes.
2. **Offline Dataset**
   Data stored locally rather than streamed. Offline datasets occupy megabytes.
3. **On-Device Storage**
   Storage located on the AI device itself. On-device capacity is measured in megabytes.
4. **Operational Memory**
   Memory used during active AI operations. Usage is tracked in megabytes.
5. **Optimization Data**
   Information used to improve model performance. Optimization data uses megabytes.
6. **Output Buffer**
   Temporary storage for results before delivery. Buffers hold megabytes.
7. **Overhead Data**
   Extra data required for system operation. Overhead increases total megabytes.
8. **Object Detection Output Size**
   The amount of data produced by detection models. Output size is measured in megabytes.
9. **Online Storage**
   Storage accessible via the internet. Online storage limits are measured in megabytes.
10. **Open Dataset Size**
    The storage footprint of publicly available datasets. Size is measured in megabytes.

Letter P

1. **Parameter Count**
   The total number of model values. Count correlates with megabytes required.
2. **Persistent Storage**
   Long-term storage that retains data. Capacity is measured in megabytes.
3. **Pipeline Buffer**
   Temporary storage between processing stages. Buffers manage megabytes in motion.
4. **Preprocessing Data**
   Data created while preparing datasets. Preprocessing adds megabytes.
5. **Precision Reduction**
   Lowering numeric detail to save space. Reduction decreases megabyte usage.
6. **Prediction Output Size**
   The amount of data produced by model predictions. Size is measured in megabytes.
7. **Primary Memory**
   Main system memory used for processing. Capacity is measured in megabytes.
8. **Processing Overhead**
   Extra resources needed during computation. Overhead increases megabyte usage.

9. **Profiling Data**
   Information collected to analyze performance. Profiling data uses megabytes.
10. **Paged Memory**
    Memory divided into fixed-size blocks. Paging manages megabytes efficiently.

Letter Q

1. **Quantization**
   A technique that reduces numerical precision to lower memory usage. Quantization helps AI models use fewer megabytes.
2. **Query Cache**
   Stored results from previous searches or requests. Query caches save megabytes by avoiding repeated computation.
3. **Query Latency**
   The time it takes to retrieve data after a request. Latency depends on how many megabytes must be accessed.
4. **Queue Buffer**
   A temporary holding area for data waiting to be processed. Buffers store megabytes in order.
5. **Quick Access Memory**
   Memory designed for fast retrieval. It handles megabytes needed immediately by AI tasks.
6. **Quantitative Dataset**
   Data made up of numerical values. These datasets are stored and measured in megabytes.
7. **Query Result Size**
   The amount of data returned from a query. Result size is measured in megabytes.
8. **Quorum Storage**
   A distributed storage method requiring agreement across systems. Data is replicated in megabytes.
9. **Quality Metrics Data**
   Information used to measure model performance. Metrics consume storage in megabytes.
10. **Quantized Model Size**
    The reduced size of an AI model after quantization. Size is typically measured in megabytes.

Letter R

1. **RAM Usage**
   The amount of active memory in use. RAM usage is tracked in megabytes.
2. **Read Throughput**
   The speed at which data is read from storage. Throughput affects how fast megabytes are accessed.

3. **Real-Time Processing**
   Processing data immediately as it arrives. Real-time systems manage megabytes continuously.
4. **Recursive Memory Use**
   Memory consumption during repeated function calls. Usage accumulates in megabytes.
5. **Redundant Storage**
   Extra copies of data kept for reliability. Redundancy increases total megabytes stored.
6. **Resource Allocation**
   Assigning system resources like memory and storage. Allocation is measured in megabytes.
7. **Runtime Memory**
   Memory required while a program is running. Runtime memory usage is tracked in megabytes.
8. **Raw Dataset Size**
   The size of unprocessed data. Raw datasets often require many megabytes.
9. **Read-Only Memory Footprint**
   The storage space used by non-modifiable data. Footprint is measured in megabytes.
10. **Retrieval Speed**
    How quickly stored data can be accessed. Speed depends on the number of megabytes involved.

Letter S

1. **Sample Size**
   The number of data examples used in AI training. Larger samples increase megabytes.
2. **Scalable Storage**
   Storage that grows with demand. Scalability supports increasing megabytes.
3. **Serialized Data Size**
   The storage size of data converted into a transferable format. Size is measured in megabytes.
4. **Shared Memory**
   Memory accessible by multiple processes. Shared memory usage is tracked in megabytes.
5. **Snapshot Size**
   The storage required for saved system states. Snapshots consume megabytes.
6. **Sparse Data Representation**
   A storage method that saves space when data contains many empty values. Sparsity reduces megabytes.
7. **Storage Capacity**
   The total amount of data a system can store. Capacity is measured in megabytes or more.
8. **Streaming Data Buffer**
   Temporary storage for incoming data streams. Buffers handle megabytes in motion.
9. **System Cache**
   Memory that stores frequently used data. Caches manage megabytes for faster access.

10. **Synchronization Data**
    Information used to keep systems aligned. Sync data adds to total megabytes.

Letter T

1. **Temporary Storage**
   Short-term storage used during processing. Temporary storage holds megabytes briefly.
2. **Tensor Size**
   The memory required to store multidimensional data structures. Tensor size is measured in megabytes.
3. **Throughput Rate**
   The amount of data processed per unit time. Rate is often described in megabytes per second.
4. **Training Dataset Size**
   The total amount of data used to train AI models. Size is measured in megabytes.
5. **Transfer Buffer**
   Temporary memory used during data movement. Buffers hold megabytes during transfer.
6. **Transactional Storage**
   Storage that ensures data consistency. Transactions add overhead measured in megabytes.
7. **Thread Memory Usage**
   Memory consumed by execution threads. Usage is tracked in megabytes.
8. **Token Storage Size**
   The memory required to store processed tokens. Token data uses megabytes.
9. **Time-Series Data Size**
   The storage footprint of data collected over time. Size increases in megabytes.
10. **Training Checkpoint Size**
    The storage required for saved training states. Checkpoints are measured in megabytes.

Letter U

1. **Unified Memory**
   A memory system shared between CPU and GPU. Unified memory manages data in megabytes efficiently across processors.
2. **Upload Size**
   The amount of data sent to storage or the cloud. Upload size is measured in megabytes.
3. **User Data Storage**
   Storage allocated for user-generated files. Capacity is tracked in megabytes.
4. **Utilization Rate**
   The percentage of memory or storage currently in use. Utilization reflects how many megabytes are occupied.
5. **Uncompressed Data Size**
   The size of data before compression. Uncompressed data often uses more megabytes.

6. **Update Payload**
   Data sent during software or model updates. Payload size is measured in megabytes.
7. **Uptime Storage Logs**
   Logs recorded while systems run continuously. Logs accumulate megabytes over time.
8. **Unified Dataset**
   A dataset combined from multiple sources. Size is measured in megabytes.
9. **User Session Memory**
   Memory allocated for active users. Session memory uses megabytes dynamically.
10. **Usage Quota**
    A storage limit set for users or systems. Quotas are defined in megabytes or larger units.

Letter V

1. **Validation Dataset Size**
   The amount of data used to evaluate AI models. Size is measured in megabytes.
2. **Vector Embedding Size**
   The memory required to store numerical representations of data. Size is measured in megabytes.
3. **Virtual Memory**
   A system that extends RAM using disk storage. Virtual memory is managed in megabytes.
4. **Volatile Memory**
   Memory that loses data when power is off. Capacity is measured in megabytes.
5. **Video Dataset Size**
   The storage required for video data. Video datasets consume many megabytes.
6. **Versioned Storage**
   Storage that keeps multiple file versions. Versioning increases megabyte usage.
7. **Vision Model Size**
   The memory footprint of computer vision models. Size is measured in megabytes.
8. **Vector Database Storage**
   Storage used for similarity search data. Vector databases consume large megabytes.
9. **Virtualized Storage**
   Storage abstracted from physical hardware. Capacity is tracked in megabytes.
10. **Volume Capacity**
    The total size of a storage volume. Capacity is measured in megabytes or more.

Letter W

1. **Weight Parameters**
   Learned values in AI models. Weight storage contributes to megabytes used.

2. **Working Memory**
   Memory actively used during processing. Working memory usage is measured in megabytes.
3. **Write Throughput**
   The speed at which data is written to storage. Throughput affects megabytes per second.
4. **Warm Cache**
   Cached data that is already loaded. Warm caches reduce repeated megabyte transfers.
5. **Workflow Data Size**
   The total data used across an AI workflow. Size is measured in megabytes.
6. **Web Dataset Size**
   The storage required for web-based data. Size is tracked in megabytes.
7. **Weight Compression**
   Reducing model weight size to save memory. Compression lowers megabytes used.
8. **Window Size (AI Context)**
   The amount of data processed at once. Window size affects memory megabytes.
9. **Writable Storage**
   Storage that allows data modification. Capacity is measured in megabytes.
10. **Workload Memory Demand**
    The memory required for tasks. Demand is expressed in megabytes.

Letter X

1. **X-Axis Data Size**
   Data stored along one dimension of a dataset. Size contributes to megabytes used.
2. **XML Data Size**
   The storage footprint of XML-formatted data. XML files often use many megabytes.
3. **XOR Encoding**
   A binary operation used in data processing. Encoded data occupies megabytes.
4. **Execution Context Size**
   Memory required during task execution. Size is measured in megabytes.
5. **External Dataset Size**
   The size of data sourced externally. External datasets add megabytes.
6. **Expanded Memory Use**
   Memory growth during processing. Expansion increases megabytes consumed.
7. **Experimental Dataset**
   Data used for testing AI models. Size is measured in megabytes.
8. **Extraction Buffer**
   Temporary storage during data extraction. Buffers store megabytes briefly.
9. **Extended Storage Capacity**
   Additional storage added to a system. Capacity is measured in megabytes.
10. **Explainability Data Size**
    Data used to explain AI decisions. Explainability outputs consume megabytes.

Letter Y

1. **Yield Data Size**
   The amount of useful output data produced. Yield is measured in megabytes.
2. **Yearly Data Growth**
   Annual increase in stored data. Growth is tracked in megabytes.
3. **YAML File Size**
   The storage footprint of YAML configuration files. Size is measured in megabytes.
4. **Y-Axis Feature Size**
   Feature data along a dataset dimension. Size contributes to megabytes.
5. **Young Generation Memory**
   Memory area for newly created data. Usage is measured in megabytes.
6. **Yield Optimization Data**
   Data used to improve output efficiency. Stored in megabytes.
7. **YourAIStudyBuddy Dataset Size**
   The total data used by AI study tools. Size is measured in megabytes.
8. **Yottabyte Reference Scale**
   A conceptual upper scale of data measurement. Used for comparison beyond megabytes.
9. **Yield Metrics Storage**
   Storage used for performance metrics. Metrics consume megabytes.
10. **Yoked Memory Allocation**
    Linked memory regions used together. Allocation is measured in megabytes.

Letter Z

1. **Zero-Copy Memory**
   A method that avoids duplicating data. Zero-copy reduces megabytes in motion.
2. **Zipped Dataset Size**
   The storage size after compression. Zipped files use fewer megabytes.
3. **Zettabyte Scale (Reference)**
   A large-scale data concept. Used to compare growth beyond megabytes.
4. **Zone-Based Storage**
   Storage divided into regions. Zones manage megabytes efficiently.
5. **Z-Score Normalization Data**
   Statistical values used in preprocessing. Data adds megabytes.
6. **Zero Padding**
   Adding placeholder data to inputs. Padding increases memory megabytes.
7. **Zoomed Feature Maps**
   Scaled representations in vision models. Stored in megabytes.
8. **Zonal Cache**
   Cache divided by region. Cache size is measured in megabytes.
9. **Zero-Day Model Update Size**
   The storage required for emergency updates. Size is measured in megabytes.

10. **Zipped Model Archive**
    Compressed AI model files. Archives reduce megabytes required.

Teacher's Overview and Instructional Guide

The AGI Generation

Preparing Today's Students to Build Tomorrow's Intelligent World

By Susie Hala
IntelliGloss AI Education Series
Module 2: Artificial General Intelligence (AGI)

Welcome, Educators

Thank you for choosing **The AGI Generation** as part of your classroom instruction. This book is designed to introduce students to one of the most important technological developments of the twenty-first century—**Artificial General Intelligence (AGI)**—using language that is clear, age-appropriate, engaging, and easy to understand.

Artificial intelligence is rapidly becoming part of education, healthcare, business, engineering, agriculture, science, transportation, and nearly every other profession. Today's students are growing up in a world where intelligent technologies will become everyday tools throughout their education and future careers. This book prepares students not simply to use these technologies, but to understand them, think critically about them, and use them responsibly.

Unlike many books that focus primarily on technical concepts, **The AGI Generation** emphasizes the human side of intelligent technology. Students will discover that while AI can process information, recognize patterns, and assist with decision-making, people continue to provide creativity, ethical judgment, compassion, leadership, curiosity, and purpose. Throughout this book, students are encouraged to become responsible innovators who understand that technology should always serve humanity.

Purpose of This Book

The purpose of this book is to help students:

- Understand what Artificial General Intelligence (AGI) is and how it differs from today's AI systems.
- Recognize how intelligent technologies are becoming part of everyday life.
- Develop critical thinking and responsible decision-making skills.
- Learn how to work alongside AI rather than depend on it.
- Build confidence in discussing emerging technologies.
- Explore future careers influenced by intelligent systems.
- Practice ethical technology use and responsible digital citizenship.
- Prepare for a future where human intelligence and artificial intelligence work together.

Rather than teaching students to fear AI or blindly trust it, this book teaches balanced understanding, responsible use, and thoughtful leadership.

How This Book Is Organized

This textbook contains **16 instructional chapters**, making it ideal for use as a **one-semester course**.

Suggested Semester Schedule

- **Week 1:** Chapter 1
- **Week 2:** Chapter 2
- **Week 3:** Chapter 3
- **Week 4:** Chapter 4
- **Week 5:** Chapter 5
- **Week 6:** Chapter 6
- **Week 7:** Chapter 7
- **Week 8:** Chapter 8
- **Week 9:** Chapter 9
- **Week 10:** Chapter 10
- **Week 11:** Chapter 11
- **Week 12:** Chapter 12
- **Week 13:** Chapter 13
- **Week 14:** Chapter 14
- **Week 15:** Chapter 15
- **Week 16:** Chapter 16, final review, discussion, and assessment

Each chapter is designed to provide approximately one week of instruction, discussion, classroom activities, and independent learning.

Chapter Structure

Every chapter follows a consistent instructional format that supports both classroom teaching and independent learning.

Each chapter includes:

- Two instructional reading sections (Part 1 and Part 2)
- Chapter Summary
- Student Reflection Questions
- Personal Reflection Activity
- Chapter Worksheet
- Chapter Quiz
- Answer Key

This consistent structure helps students build confidence while allowing teachers to maintain a predictable instructional routine throughout the semester.

Instructional Goals

Throughout this course, students will:

- Explain major AGI concepts using their own words.
- Apply critical thinking when evaluating AI-generated information.
- Demonstrate ethical reasoning when discussing intelligent technologies.
- Identify both the opportunities and challenges created by AI.
- Connect classroom learning to real-world situations.
- Communicate ideas clearly through discussion and writing.
- Build confidence using AI as a learning partner while maintaining independent thinking.

Teaching Strategies

Students learn best when they actively participate. Teachers are encouraged to:

- Facilitate classroom discussions.
- Encourage respectful debate.
- Connect lessons to current events.
- Invite students to analyze real-world AI examples.
- Promote teamwork and collaborative problem-solving.
- Encourage students to explain concepts using their own words.
- Reinforce that asking thoughtful questions is an essential part of learning.

Because AI is constantly evolving, students should be reminded that learning how to think is more valuable than memorizing isolated facts.

Assessment Opportunities

This book provides multiple ways to evaluate student learning.

Teachers may assess students through:

- Classroom participation
- Reflection responses
- Written assignments
- Worksheets
- Chapter quizzes
- Small-group discussions
- Student presentations
- Research projects
- Final semester projects

These varied assessment methods allow students with different learning styles to demonstrate understanding.

Cross-Curricular Connections

The concepts in this book naturally support instruction across multiple subject areas, including:

- Computer Science
- Digital Literacy
- Technology Education
- English Language Arts
- Social Studies
- Civics
- Business Education
- Career Technical Education (CTE)
- STEM Programs
- Media Literacy
- Ethics

Teachers may integrate these lessons into interdisciplinary projects that connect AI with science, history, communication, economics, and civic responsibility.

Supporting Responsible AI Use

One of the central themes of this book is responsible technology use.

Students should understand that:

- AI is a powerful learning tool—not a replacement for thinking.
- Human judgment remains essential.
- Information should always be verified.
- Personal privacy should be protected.
- Academic honesty matters.
- Ethical decisions guide responsible innovation.
- Technology should improve people's lives.

These ideas appear throughout the book to help students become thoughtful digital citizens.

Preparing Students for Tomorrow

Many of today's students will enter careers that do not yet exist. Regardless of their profession, they will likely work alongside intelligent technologies. This book prepares students not only to understand those technologies but also to develop the uniquely human abilities that intelligent machines cannot replace, including:

- Creativity
- Curiosity
- Communication
- Collaboration
- Integrity
- Compassion
- Leadership
- Adaptability
- Critical Thinking
- Ethical Decision-Making

These skills will continue to be valuable throughout their lives, regardless of how technology evolves.

A Message to Educators

Education has always prepared students for the future. Today, that future includes intelligent technologies that are transforming nearly every aspect of society. While artificial intelligence will continue to evolve, the mission of education remains unchanged: to develop knowledgeable, ethical, creative, and responsible individuals who improve their communities and contribute positively to the world.

As educators, you play a vital role in helping students understand not only what AI can do, but also what people must continue to do—lead with wisdom, think critically, act ethically, and use technology in ways that strengthen humanity.

The students sitting in today's classrooms will become tomorrow's engineers, scientists, healthcare professionals, teachers, entrepreneurs, policymakers, artists, and innovators. By helping them understand Artificial General Intelligence today, you are preparing them to shape a future where human intelligence and artificial intelligence work together for the benefit of all.

Thank you for investing in the next generation of thoughtful learners and responsible leaders.

IntelliGloss AI Education Series

Module 2: Artificial General Intelligence (AGI)

"Building the knowledge, character, and confidence students need to thrive in an intelligent world."

— Susie Hala